T0314299

SAFE HAVENS FOR HATE

Safe Havens for Hate

THE CHALLENGE OF MODERATING ONLINE EXTREMISM

TAMAR MITTS

PRINCETON UNIVERSITY PRESS

PRINCETON & OXFORD

Published by Princeton University Press
41 William Street, Princeton, New Jersey 08540
99 Banbury Road, Oxford OX2 6JX

press.princeton.edu

All Rights Reserved

Library of Congress Cataloging-in-Publication Data

Names: Mitts, Tamar, 1984– author.
Title: Safe havens for hate: the challenge of moderating online
    extremism / Tamar Mitts.
Description: Princeton: Princeton University Press, 2025 | Includes
    bibliographical references and index.
Identifiers: LCCN 2024019998 (print) | LCCN 2024019999 (ebook) |
    ISBN 9780691258522 (hardback) | ISBN 9780691258546 (ebook)
Subjects: LCSH: Online hate speech—Prevention. | Online social networks. |
    BISAC: POLITICAL SCIENCE / Terrorism | COMPUTERS /
    Internet / Social Media
Classification: LCC HM851 .M56 2025 (print) | LCC HM851 (ebook) |
    DDC 303.3/76—dc23/eng/20241008
LC record available at https://lccn.loc.gov/2024019998
LC ebook record available at https://lccn.loc.gov/2024019999

British Library Cataloging-in-Publication Data is available

Editorial: Bridget Flannery-McCoy and Alena Chekanov
Production Editorial: Theresa Liu
Jacket/Cover Design: Karl Spurzem
Production: Erin Suydam
Publicity: Maria Whelan and Kathryn Stevens
Copyeditor: Cynthia Buck

Jacket image: nipithstudio / Shutterstock

This book has been composed in Arno

Printed in the United States of America

10 9 8 7 6 5 4 3 2 1

In memory of my dear father,
the most loving person I have ever known

CONTENTS

ACKNOWLEDGMENTS

WRITING A BOOK IS LIKE GROWING A TREE. The seeds for this book were planted almost twenty years ago, when I was sitting with my father in a coffee shop, pondering the deep changes our societies are facing in the age of the internet and with the emergence of social media. At the time, I didn't have the knowledge, training, or skills to write such a book, so the tree needed time to grow. In the years that followed, I had the privilege to learn from amazing scholars and mentors and become part of a vibrant community of researchers—many of whom had a hand in the successful completion of this book by providing guidance, feedback, and support.

I first would like to thank my colleagues at Columbia University. I thank Keren Yarhi-Milo for her mentorship and encouragement throughout the process. From the first day we met, Keren amazed me with her sharp feedback and guidance on the book-writing process. She was also instrumental in creating opportunities for me to pursue this project in depth, for which I am grateful. I also thank my longtime mentors, Jack Snyder and Page Fortna, who guided my thinking on this project from its very early stages. Working with Jack on questions related to media freedom and the regulation of speech helped sharpen my thinking on the dynamics of content moderation in the digital information environment. Page's clever insights into the behavior of nonstate actors during conflict and her constant encouragement to "define my concepts" were foundational in helping me build the theoretical framework for this book. I also thank Dick Betts, Stephen Biddle, Allison Carnegie, and Jay Healey for their feedback on the initial chapters of the book and for their insights when I had just started writing. Vicky Murillo, Sarah Daly, and Erica Lonergan offered helpful guidance on the book publication process.

I am deeply grateful to the Saltzman Institute of War and Peace Studies and the Data Science Institute for their support for the project. In particular, I thank Ingrid Gerstmann and Alba Taveras for their help with arranging workshops and hiring research assistants and for providing such a wonderful space to pursue this project at Columbia. I also thank Hazel May and her team at the School of International and Public Affairs for making it possible for me to take time off from teaching to write this book.

I was lucky to have the opportunity to work with top-notch research assistants when collecting data and gathering evidence for the empirical chapters of the book. I thank Nusrat Farooq, who helped me lead the data collection effort on militant and hate groups' usage of social media and in developing a codebook and research protocols for the project. The time Nusrat spent on the project and her dedication to it were invaluable, and for that I'm filled with gratitude. I also thank Maggie Baker, Vrinda Handa, Arielle Herman, and Katya Kantor for their help digging through hundreds of accounts on various social media platforms to find information on where extremist actors push out their content to target audiences.

I am grateful for the incredible work of Olivia Grinberg and Nittai Huberman, who helped me gather information on regulatory initiatives by national governments; their research provided important background on which I built when writing the third chapter of the book. I thank Inbar Pe'er, Courtney Manning, Juliet Paiva, and Virginia Lo for their meticulous work gathering data on the content moderation policies of over sixty social media companies. Kiki Tuttle and Lola Seibert did a terrific job of collecting, validating, and cleaning data on the activity of extremist organizations in less-moderated social media spaces and Elliott Tran was invaluable in helping collect historical data on platform policies from the Internet Archive.

Beyond Columbia, I was lucky to get feedback from many scholars whose work I admire. I thank Richard Nielsen, Jennifer Pan, Margaret Roberts, Jacob Shapiro, Alexandra Siegel, and Thomas Zeitzoff for coming to my book conference and providing detailed comments on various chapters. Incorporating their insights significantly improved the book. For their terrific comments and questions, I also thank the participants in MIT's Security Studies Seminar, Johns Hopkins University's Faculty Seminar, Brown University's Security Studies Seminar, the Big Data for Development and Governance Conference at the University of Pennsylvania, and the Political Economy and Behavior Speaker Series at the Hebrew University of Jerusalem.

The fifth chapter of the book started as a working paper on "deplatforming" (social media platforms' suspension of accounts). The generous feedback I received on this paper from many colleagues made me realize that it uncovers important patterns of online behavior that directly speak to the theory I advance in the book. I would like to thank participants in the workshops where

I presented this paper for their insightful comments. These include the University of Oxford's International Relations Colloquium, Monash University's SoDa Lab Webinar Series, Columbia University's Political Methodology Colloquium, Humboldt University's Politics Lectures Series, the Politics and Computational Social Science Annual Conference, Korea University's Soodang Distinguished Speaker Colloquium, the Comparative Politics Annual Conference at Washington University in St. Louis, the Empirical Studies of Conflict Annual Meeting, the National Bureau of Economic Research's Summer Institute on the Economics of National Security, the workshop on international politics at the University of Chicago, the Political Science Department seminar at Tel Aviv University, the faculty seminar at the Lauder School of Government, Diplomacy, and Strategy at Reichman University, the political science workshop at Aarhus University, and Meta's Computational Social Science Seminar.

I thank Bridget Flannery-McCoy and her team at Princeton University Press for their support throughout the process. I particularly appreciate Bridget's guidance through the book publication process, which was invaluable to me as a first-time book author. I thank the anonymous reviewers for their terrific feedback on the manuscript and their suggestions for improving the book in its final stages.

Finally, I would like to thank my wonderful family for their endless encouragement in this journey of writing a book. First and foremost, I am deeply grateful to my husband Josh for being my pillar of support in every part of this project. His unconditional love and kindness kept me going even at times when I did not see how this book would become a reality. I thank him for reading multiple versions of the manuscript, offering sharp analytical feedback, and being a sounding board and a brainstorming partner, even when he was slammed with the demands of his own work. He is a huge part of this project, and the book would not have been possible without him.

I also thank my kids, Emily and Liam, for their endless curiosity about "Mommy's book on the internet." I appreciated the little notes of encouragement they posted on the walls of my office and their important questions about this research. I hope that this book will contribute to efforts to make online spaces safer for children and the next generation. I am grateful for my mother Kati and my sisters Hadas and Shaked for their love and support, and for celebrating with me every time I completed a new chapter. Describing my research to them helped me learn how to communicate my academic insights to a more general audience.

Last but not least, I thank my father, Yehuda. The book is, in so many ways, the outcome of my long and wonderful conversations with him about social and political life in a dynamically changing world. His insights on the role of the internet in society and the impact of geopolitics and globalization on social processes around the world, as well as his interpretation of current events from a historical perspective, contributed immensely to my thinking for this book. I loved sharing my work-in-progress with him and getting his feedback on various chapters of the book. Unfortunately, he was diagnosed with cancer while I was still writing the book and passed away before I finished. But his ideas and insights are deeply embedded in the pages of this book and will long outlive him, just like a tree. To express my gratitude for my father's love and support, I dedicate this book to him.

SAFE HAVENS FOR HATE

1

Introduction

ON FEBRUARY 3, 2015, the Islamic State (IS), a violent extremist organization based in the Middle East, posted a video on YouTube that showed the killing of a Jordanian pilot the group held hostage. The video depicted brutal acts of violence carried out against the hostage and called for the murder of anyone who did not agree with the group's mission.[1] Within a short amount of time, the video went viral. It was shared in tens of thousands of posts on Twitter by Islamic State sympathizers,[2] received millions of interactions on Facebook,[3] and was reposted and discussed in other online media.[4] The video was just one of many other videos showing brutalities that the organization posted on the internet. Thousands of other messages glorifying violence were shared by the group on various online platforms in an effort to attract support around the world.

Harmful content on social media, like the Islamic State's video described here, has become an urgent challenge for societies in the digital age. The stories seem to never end. From hate-filled campaigns that can lead to violence and even genocide[5] to extremism and polarization fueled by misinformation and manipulated media generated by artificial intelligence,[6] to problematic content that targets children or can inspire self-harm,[7] safety problems on online platforms have become a pressing concern.

As disturbing episodes linked to harmful content multiplied around the world, public calls for immediate action from social media companies started to intensify. Some threatened to boycott social media, calling on technology companies to do more to address harassment and abuse on their sites.[8] Others, such as large advertisers, withdrew their paid ads to protest platforms' insufficient handling of misinformation and hate speech.[9] And those who became victims of violence that was believed to be inspired by content posted online demanded legal action against companies that did not sufficiently combat incitement on their platforms.[10]

The most intense pressure came from governments. Between 2018 and 2022, forty-seven national governments enacted legislation or were in the process of passing legislation to regulate harmful content on social media. The regulations sought to address a range of social ills for which digital media platforms were believed to be responsible, and they reflected governments' view that leaving content moderation solely in the hands of private companies was insufficient to combat harmful content online.

For example, after the livestreaming on Facebook of the terrorist attack in Christchurch in March 2019, the prime minister of New Zealand said that "we cannot simply sit back and accept that [social media] platforms just exist and that what is said on them is not the responsibility of the place where they are published."[11] The prime minister of Australia agreed, adding that "big social media companies have a responsibility to take every possible action to ensure their technology products are not exploited by murderous terrorists."[12] Indeed, when crafting the Digital Services Act—the European Union's ambitious legislation to combat harmful content online—one regulator warned that "the time of big online platforms behaving like they are 'too big to care' is coming to an end."[13]

To put pressure on social media companies to do more, governments started requiring a range of actions. They asked companies to publish transparency reports detailing their content moderation actions and to set up measures to protect against misuse. They also required platforms to engage in risk assessments and audits to ensure that they were not exploited to promote offline harm. Governments further dramatically increased their requests for removal of specific pieces of content that they considered harmful, in hopes that tighter policing of speech would lead to a safer internet.[14]

But an interesting aspect of the public's attention and the regulatory pressure placed on technology companies was the almost exclusive focus on large social media platforms. Technology companies like Meta, Twitter, and YouTube faced strong public pressure, while smaller sites such as Telegram, Gab, and Rumble were subject to much less oversight. There are various reasons for this differential treatment of platforms, including efforts to lower the barrier to small social media companies to enter the digital media market and the view that smaller platforms are inconsequential.[15] Regardless of the reason, the result was a diverse, uneven moderation landscape in which social media platforms that were considered "big" or impactful moderated content at increasingly higher rates, while smaller platforms did not.

For example, in the past several years, Meta, which faced the highest public pressure among all technology companies, has developed over twenty categories for harmful content and removed over 64 billion posts promoting misinformation, hate, and extremism from its services.[16] TikTok, which also started experiencing pressure from regulators and the public, has increased its moderation substantially since 2020, taking down over 1.2 billion videos that violated its new policies.[17] But other technology companies that have not been at the center of the public's attention, such as Gab, Rumble, and Telegram, had much less robust content moderation standards and did not remove harmful content to the same extent.

How effective is content moderation at combating online harms in such diverse environments? We currently have little knowledge on the effects of content moderation when different technology companies adopt different standards to restrict harmful content on their sites. Most scholarly work on the regulation of social media either focuses on the legal aspects without examining the consequences of regulatory provisions or examines platforms' content moderation from a "within-platform perspective"—that is, by evaluating the effectiveness of moderation only among platforms that engage in it. As a result, we have a limited understanding of the effects of content moderation in the broader online ecosystem. What happens when one social media platform adheres to regulations and moderates harmful content and another does not? How do producers of harmful content adapt to moderation across platforms with different moderation policies? And what happens when social media companies collaborate to align their moderation standards?

I answer these questions by focusing on one of the most central areas in social media regulation: online extremism. Nowhere have public pressure and regulatory efforts been more prominent than the moderation of extremist and terrorist activity on digital media platforms. "Dangerous organizations"—militant or hate-based groups, extremist organizations, and other violent movements—have become one of the main targets of online regulation and content moderation. But despite mass content takedowns, account suspensions, and other sanctions that these organizations have been subject to, they continue to flourish online, advancing their cause, recruiting supporters, and inspiring violence. The new policies targeting harmful content on social media have thus not stopped extremist organizations from operating online. Why?

Moderating Harmful Content in
a Diverse Online Environment

In this book, I provide a deep dive into content moderation on social media platforms to study how extremist organizations that produce harmful content online react to moderation. I define content moderation as the "organized practice of screening user-generated content (UGC) posted to Internet sites, social media, and other online outlets, in order to determine the appropriateness of the content for a given site, locality, or jurisdiction."[18] I argue that divergence between platforms' content policies allows these actors to become resistant to online regulation. Focusing on the strategic interaction between technology companies and national governments, I explain how different moderation standards emerge in the online information ecosystem. I then offer a theory that explains how different moderation standards across platforms create virtual safe havens in which extremist actors can organize, launch campaigns, and mobilize supporters. Drawing on data on the online activity of over a hundred militant and hate organizations, archives of banned terrorist propaganda, and platform moderation policies, I explain how digital resilience is shaped by the degree of variation in the way technology platforms police speech online.

Understanding how extremist actors adapt to moderation sheds light on important challenges at the frontier of mitigating online harms. Divergent standards in content moderation are a feature of our increasingly decentralized online information ecosystem, yet their effects on the ability to moderate harms are rarely considered in debates over social media regulation. Policymakers often rush to suppress or take down offensive content online, while failing to consider the consequences of these approaches in the broader digital environment. By explaining the ways in which variation in content moderation across social media platforms can be exploited by militant and hate organizations, the book provides an important account for why extremism continues to be a problem for our digitally connected societies.

Why Does Extremism Thrive Online?

A key question driving governments seeking to regulate internet platforms is determining how extremist actors are able to exploit social media for malicious purposes. The oft-cited answer is that social media companies are "not doing enough" to moderate harmful content—which naturally leads to policy solutions requiring more moderation. In this book, I show that this answer is incomplete, because it ignores the broader online ecosystem in which social media platforms are embedded. By taking a more comprehensive, cross-platform perspective to answer this question, I illustrate the important role played by the *structure* of the online information environment and the way platforms relate to each other in shaping extremist organizations' online campaigns.

Specifically, I show that militant and hate organizations' online success centers on their ability to operate across many platforms in parallel—a phenomenon not well captured by current legislation. Most regulations of social media platforms operate under the assumption that inducing technology companies to take stronger action against extremist organizations will decrease their ability to exploit the internet. As a result, the main metric of success employed by governments and the public is a decline in harmful content on regulated platforms. What the new regulations tend to overlook is that these actors operate in tandem in multiple online spaces, many of which are unregulated.

My theory explains how dangerous organizations build resilience to content moderation by focusing in particular on a multi-platform environment. The context of my theory is an information ecosystem characterized by variation in the levels of platform moderation in which some online spaces have tight moderation of harmful content, while others do not. I show that much of the complexity in extremist group behavior on social media can be captured by two important dimensions in platform characteristics: (1) the level of moderation—how lenient or restrictive platforms are in their content moderation practices; and (2) impact—the size of the audience on the platform. This approach yields systematic and falsifiable predictions as to the mechanisms that facilitate dangerous organizations' resilience on social media.

The mechanism that most people point to when considering extremist groups' adaptation to content moderation is *migration* to alternative platforms. Faced with bans on moderated platforms, extremist actors can shift their online presence to social media spaces that have more lenient content policies. There are many examples of migration of this sort, including the Islamic State's move to Telegram after Twitter and Facebook banned the group from their platforms and the relocation of far-right groups to "alternative platforms" after experiencing crackdowns on mainstream social media sites. The ability to migrate to other platforms allows extremist organizations to maintain their presence online, but it comes with a cost. Since platforms that moderate less tend to have smaller user bases, extremist actors who migrate to less-moderated online spaces risk becoming "irrelevant" by losing the audience they once had on larger platforms.

To remain influential in a regulated online context, extremist organizations have an incentive to continue reaching out to broader audiences, even on moderated platforms. I show that they do that by shifting *messaging* strategies based on platform moderation rules. When there is variation in the policies that determine what is allowed (and not allowed) on different platforms, extremist actors can modify the way in which they disseminate their messages across platforms. This tactic is particularly useful as content moderation becomes more automated, since it is often easier to "trick" artificial intelligence systems with borderline content that is not clearly violating platform policies. Thus, for example, these actors advance their message by sharing 'mild' content that does not trigger moderation algorithms on regulated platforms, while at the same time disseminating more extreme material in less-moderated spaces. Inconsistency in content moderation policies across platforms allows dangerous organizations to maintain a significant level of audience reach despite increased regulation.

The third mechanism for adapting to content moderation is *mobilization*— the ability to draw audiences to support the group's cause. When dangerous organizations maintain a presence on several platforms in parallel, they are not only able to evade moderation and increase the probability that their content will flow to target audiences, but they can also engage potential recruits in a more effective way. It turns out that experiencing moderation on social media—for example, by having one's posts deleted or account suspended— can generate strong reactions among affected users that can propel engagement with extremist content. Followers of the Islamic State who experienced bans on Twitter and Facebook subsequently became much more motivated to seek out the group's online networks on less-moderated platforms.[19] Similarly, sympathizers of the far-right conspiracy theory QAnon, which was one of the narratives inspiring the January 2021 attack on the US Capitol, increased their engagement with QAnon content after their accounts were deleted from mainstream platforms.[20] Targeting users who experience moderation can be very beneficial for extremist organizations, as these audiences might be more susceptible to their narratives.

I offer rich empirical evidence from various sources, including data on extremist groups' online networks, archives of banned terrorist propaganda, and data on technology companies' enforcement actions, to show how cross-platform migration, messaging, and mobilization allow militant and hate organizations to remain resilient to online regulation. I show that even though content moderation can succeed in reducing extremist presence on specific, highly moderated platforms, it often fails to address online harms in the broader internet ecosystem. I present data on the online activity of over a hundred groups that promote extremist ideologies on various social media platforms, and I supplement these data with deep quantitative and qualitative case studies.

It is often difficult to study the consequences of content moderation because information on such interventions is usually not available to the public. In many cases, banned content cannot even be found in the archives of social media platforms because of data archiving laws and other restrictions. For this reason, I rely on several forms of external data collection that allow me to track instances of platform moderation and extremist activity in real time. I use these data sources to answer the following questions: Where do extremist actors migrate after experiencing bans on regulated social media platforms? What content do they post in different online spaces, and does content dissemination vary between moderating and nonmoderating platforms? Do users who experience bans increase their engagement with extremist content on unregulated social media sites? And how do extremist actors target audiences who are aggrieved by moderation? The evidence that I present demonstrates that even though content moderation can be effective in combating harmful content on specific platforms, its ability to prevent harm in the broader digital environment is more limited.

My findings help explain why online extremism—and harmful content more generally—continues to persist on social media. The political process leading governments to exert greater control over online platforms and the public pressure on technology companies to invest in content moderation are not uniform across social media platforms. This inconsistency creates opportunities for actors who produce harmful content to innovate in the online space, which can strengthen, rather than weaken, their online campaigns.

The evidence presented in this book demonstrates that we need to better understand the ways in which content moderation shapes dangerous actors' behavior in the broader digital ecosystem. Although there is a growing body of research on the movement of messages, ideas, and different types of content between social media platforms, we know much less about the nature of cross-platform spillovers in the context of content moderation—and in particular the role of these spillovers in extremist organizations' strategic attempts to overcome regulation.[21] This book shows that the movement of harmful content between platforms is often the outcome of more calculated efforts by these actors to evade moderation while maintaining their impact on moderated platforms. With an ever-expanding set of policies dictating what is not allowed on social media, understanding how extremist actors adapt to new rules can ensure that content moderation is more effective at achieving these important policy goals.

Defining Extremism

Before we continue, it is important to define "extremism," as the concept can have different meanings in different contexts. Scholars have long debated the meaning of extremism and have devoted entire articles or even books to discussion of the concept. Here I describe three broad definitions on which I draw in the book. The first defines "extremism" as a set of ideas, beliefs, or preferences that diverge from the views of the majority of the population.[22] If political preferences can be placed on a spectrum, then extremism would reflect the preferences on the far end. For example, organizations that promote fundamentalist religious beliefs that are not endorsed by the majority of a religious population would be considered extremist under this definition.[23] Similarly, groups that promote the transformation of a political system in a way that disrupts the popular status quo would be defined as extremist.[24]

The second definition focuses on intergroup relations. According to this definition, extremism is viewed as the belief that survival depends on taking a hostile action against others.[25] Organizations that promote hostility, such as verbal attacks, hate speech, or harassment, or even physical discrimination and violence against other groups are defined as extremist. Although extremism can emerge in many types of social contexts, the most common cases relate to groups that define themselves on the basis of religious, nationalist, racial/ethnic, or class-based identities.[26]

The third definition views extremism as synonymous with violence. Groups or individuals that promote physical harm against people or property, such as indiscriminate violence or terrorism, are defined as extremist. The large literature on preventing or countering violent extremism (PCVE) often views extremism as closely tied to violence and physical harm. Thus, "violent extremism" and "extremism" under this definition are seen as the same thing.[27]

In this book I draw on all three definitions when studying activity on social media. I examine groups and movements that promote fringe ideas that are not popular among the majority in their society but that do not directly endorse violence against civilians. But I also study organizations that openly use indiscriminate violence to achieve their goals. By taking this approach, I put together in one bucket many different types of organizations that are often not studied at the same time. The reason for adopting a broad definition of extremism is that these different organizations, despite espousing different ideologies and tactics, face similar constraints when using social media. The theoretical framework in my book applies to many different organizations that fall under various definitions of extremism.

In addition, variants of these definitions are used by social media companies at various points in time. As I show later in the book, different definitions of extremism even become part of the story when they result in diverging policies to address the activity of dangerous organizations across platforms.

Defining Harmful Content

In a similar manner, the book focuses on policy efforts to combat harmful content on social media. But what is "harmful content"? Who decides what information is "good" and what is "bad"? This is a controversial question that results in different answers, depending on who we ask. For example, in polarized societies—where there is great animosity between two opposing sides of the political aisle—each camp may consider the other's ideology, worldview, or policy positions harmful. In a recent poll studying polarization in the United States, over 55 percent of the respondents believed that the other side's policy positions were subverting American democracy, and about 20 percent supported freezing the social media accounts of journalists who identified with the opposing party.[28] In another study examining public attitudes toward content moderation, researchers found a large difference in the views of Republicans and Democrats on whether news articles promoting misinformation should be removed from social media.[29]

The belief that online content is harmful if it does not support one's political goals is also found in other contexts. For example, in civil war and intrastate conflict, online content produced by nonstate actors is often considered terrorist propaganda by the governments fighting them, but some parts of the population that these organizations seek to represent view this content as resistance to a repressive regime. Disagreement over what constitutes harmful content is also found in debates over vaccine safety, where pro- and anti-vax activists see each other's online campaigns as harmful content.[30] Similar dynamics exist in disagreements over political advertisements in the context of democratic elections, where opposing sides consider the others' campaigns misinformation.[31]

Here I avoid making normative judgments about what is "good" or "bad" content by focusing on information that national governments and technology companies have themselves deemed to be harmful in regulations and content moderation rules. My theoretical framework is thus agnostic on the exact definition of harmful content, allowing different stakeholders to define it according to their political views. Approaching this question in a liberal way allows me to directly examine a core aspect of my theory: heterogeneity in the ways that technology platforms define online harms. It also enables examination of policy evolution where the definition of harmful content changes over time.

For example, the QAnon conspiracy theory was not considered harmful by technology companies when it started spreading from fringe internet forums into mainstream social media. Platforms such as Facebook, Twitter, and You-Tube did not include conspiracy theories in their definition of harmful content until QAnon communities grew significantly on their sites (see chapter 6). But at the same time that these platforms defined the QAnon ideology as harmful, other platforms, such as Gab, took a different position, maintaining that there was "nothing wrong" with the QAnon philosophy.[32] Embracing the varying definitions of harmful content allows me to study how QAnon supporters advanced the conspiracy's message on different platforms, thus testing important empirical implications of my theoretical framework.

Sometimes, however, there is broad consensus on certain types of harmful content. For example, many agree that content that promotes violence and terrorism is harmful.[33] In this book, I focus on extremist organizations—actors that, in many cases, promote violence to achieve political goals. Thus, the harmful content that I analyze often consists of messages shared on social media (in textual, visual, or audio format) that can cause injury, suffering, distress, or trauma outside of the platforms on which they are disseminated. This includes content that can inspire or instruct people to engage in violence, messages that promote hate and can lead to harassment of people, as well as information that can inspire individuals to harm themselves, such as content promoting suicide.

But even when there is agreement about what is harmful content, there can be disagreements about whether it should be moderated. For example, the leadership of Telegram has long agreed that content promoting violence and terrorism is harmful.[34] Despite this view, it did not put in place policies that officially prohibit such content, citing its belief that user privacy is "more important than our fear of bad things happening, like terrorism."[35] Whether differences in content moderation across platforms stem from disagreement over what is harmful content, from different views about how it should be moderated, or from varying regulatory pressures, the outcome is the same: an uneven online information ecosystem in which some platforms have tight moderation rules and others do not. The discussion in this book thus applies equally to all types of scenarios: by taking variation in content moderation policies as given, it examines how heterogeneity in moderation standards shapes extremist activity online.

Contributions to Existing Literature

This book contributes to several strands of scholarly literature. First, it advances knowledge on the digital battleground where dangerous organizations operate. Over the past decade, the rise of internet platforms has inspired a wave of new scholarship examining how extremist actors use social media. This research has produced valuable insights into the ways in which militant and hate organizations produce propaganda, attract recruits, plan violent attacks, and—importantly—adapt to content moderation.[36] Although this work identifies important patterns in this book's outcomes of interest—for example, migration between platforms or the strategic modification of propaganda messages—it does a poor job of explaining the "independent variable," that is, the factors that give rise to these outcomes. In other words, existing research often treats the online information environment as having a "disorganized content moderation system." But as I show in this book, this system actually has predictable structural properties that are driven by the strategic incentives of technology companies and governments. By offering a framework to understand the properties of this environment and how it shapes the behavior of dangerous organizations, the book adds to knowledge on the causes of extremists' resilience on social media.

For example, it is well known that actors who are banned from one social media platform will try to migrate to another,[37] However, the literature has been underdeveloped on the incentives driving such migration and on where banned actors are most likely to end up. I draw on novel data on the online activity of a large number of militant and hate groups to show that, contrary to conventional wisdom, extremist actors do not migrate to the platforms that moderate the least. Rather, the choice is a trade-off: they are drawn to platforms that reach a broad audience so long as the degree of moderation is tolerable. The book therefore offers new insights into the decisions that drive dangerous organizations' resilience on social media by systematically characterizing the online information environment in which these actors operate.

Relatedly, while we have research on how extremist mobilization takes place on social media, we do not have a good understanding of how content moderation policies drive mobilization *across* platforms.[38] Since the bulk of current research on extremist activity online focuses on a handful of platforms, the broader structure of the information environment and its influence on extremist activity is not systematically studied or theorized. By focusing on a wide range of social media platforms (including less-researched online spaces) and providing a framework that allows systematic characterization of their affordances, the book offers new insights into the consequences of content moderation—insights that allow us to make policy-relevant predictions about when interventions to combat harmful content online are most likely to succeed or fail.

Furthermore, the book sheds light on how changes in the regulatory landscape are likely to shape dangerous actors' online behavior in the future. Chapter 7 and the conclusion discuss policy responses to online extremism in light of the structural factors driving this information ecosystem. I provide novel evidence about what happens to extremist activity online when platforms converge in their policies to combat harmful content. Although the importance of collaboration between platforms to combat extremism is widely acknowledged, there is no systematic empirical research on this issue. The theoretical framework and empirical analysis offered in the book yield specific implications for regulatory safeguards that go well beyond our existing understanding of how extremist groups operate on social media.

Beyond online extremism, the book also adds to the growing body of work on censorship in the digital era. This stream of research—which often centers on digital repression in authoritarian regimes—points to different factors that allow citizens to become resistant to information suppression.[39] But censorship is not limited to authoritarian countries. Democratic governments are increasingly looking for ways to use similar tools to combat content that they consider harmful in their societies as well. This book explains how democratic governments grapple with the tension between censorship and free speech when faced with violence, hate, and extremism on social media platforms.

Finally, the book adds to work on resilience to online censorship—which tends to focus on information *consumption*—by providing a theoretical framework to understand how information *production* changes in the face of growing censorship. As such, the book pushes forward the frontier of knowledge on how actors who face bans on social media continue spreading their message online despite growing restrictions.

Implications for Mitigating Harms in a Digital Society

The theoretical argument and empirical findings that I present in this book shed light on the consequences of online regulation and content moderation and have implications for ongoing research on social media and politics, political violence, and the wider research agenda on online influence operations.

Content Moderation May Not Weaken Extremists

First, this book speaks to the strategies used by militant actors to exploit the internet to advance their cause. Many scholars have been puzzled by the ease with which groups like the Islamic State, Al-Qaeda, and other far-right organizations have used social media to recruit supporters and inspire violence around the world. Some argue that militant groups' creative online campaigns and sleek propaganda allow them to publicize their cause and successfully attract supporters on social media platforms.[40] Others maintain that extremist actors' capacity to effectively target audiences facilitates their success online.[41] Still others point to "offline" drivers of online extremism, highlighting militant and hate groups' ability to draw on grievances from the physical world to inspire audiences to engage with radical virtual communities.[42]

In this book I show that extremist groups have developed new methods to exploit the internet that go beyond propaganda dissemination, audience targeting, and offline grievances. The new information environment, which consists of various platforms that significantly differ in their content moderation standards, allows extremist actors to become resilient to online regulation. By migrating from platforms with strict moderation to those with more lenient policies, adapting messaging to platform rules, and mobilizing supporters on alternative platforms, militant and hate groups are able to continue operating successfully on social media, despite efforts to disrupt their campaigns.

The Broader Online Ecosystem Matters

This book also speaks to the growing body of research on social media and politics, which has made significant strides in understanding how rapid information dissemination in online networks shapes political behavior in the digital age.[43] The vast majority of this research tends to focus on large platforms, such as Twitter, Facebook, and YouTube.[44] But as I show in this book, the important dynamics on smaller platforms can be missed if online behavior is understood solely from the perspective of large social media platforms.

For example, when scholars study topics like online polarization, the spread of misinformation, and foreign and domestic influence operations, depending on whether they examine mainstream platforms, "alternative" platforms, or more private online sites, they may observe very different patterns. Researchers studying misinformation in India, for example, found that the vast majority of content promoting falsehoods was shared in small groups on encrypted messaging applications.[45] Scholars examining the spread of hate speech similarly found different patterns on alternative online networks, as opposed to mainstream platforms.[46] And studies on foreign influence operations identified similar activities on smaller online sites. For example, an investigation of Russia's influence operations targeting audiences in Europe and the United States found that networked accounts detected on Facebook were just the "tip of a much larger iceberg" of a campaign spanning many other, less-studied platforms.[47]

Understanding online behavior in the broader internet ecosystem is particularly important in the context of online extremism, as a growing portion of the activities of militant and hate groups take place on less-moderated sites. Indeed, many recent violent events have been linked to content shared on such platforms, including the terrorist attacks in France, Germany, and Belgium in the mid-2010s (facilitated by information shared on Telegram),[48] the 2018 Pittsburgh synagogue shooting (linked to Gab),[49] and the January 6, 2021, attack on the US Capitol (driven by misinformation related to the 2020 elections that spread on platforms such as MeWe, Gab, and Parler).[50] It therefore becomes increasingly important to expand our understanding of online political behavior by studying less-moderated platforms.

More generally, taking a cross-platform perspective can help explain the behavior of social media companies. For one, platforms may benefit from knowing where they are located in the broader online ecosystem; this information can help them better anticipate activities like sudden migration from other platforms. In addition, examining social media companies' content moderation decisions in light of the broader online ecosystem can help explain why some platforms may choose to situate themselves in a place that captures the right mix of authenticity and impact—to attract extremists and grow their user base.

More Centralized Moderation Can Help, but It Has Costs

Beyond advancing knowledge on online behavior in the broader digital ecosystem, the book also speaks to the benefits and costs of cross-platform cooperation in the context of content moderation. In the face of growing urgency to combat online harms, many have called for greater cooperation between platforms, asking technology companies to work together to collectively prevent malicious content from spreading on the internet.[51] These efforts have propelled forward new initiatives, including New Zealand's Christchurch Call to Action, which over fifty countries have joined, and the Global Internet Forum to Counter Terrorism (GIFCT), which facilitates collaboration between online service providers in the removal of extremist content.

While industry collaboration in combating online harms is often cited as the primary solution to online extremism, I show that centralizing moderation across platforms also has costs. Drawing on a growing body of scholarship on online regulation and platform governance, I show that aligning moderation policies can indeed help technology companies create a "united front" against extremist exploitation. At the same time, however, it can give too much power over online speech to a small number of actors, potentially leading to abuse, as some have cautioned.

For example, centralizing content moderation across platforms can result in "collateral damage"—the mistaken removal of nonharmful content from many online sites in parallel. Since the line between violating and nonviolating content can be blurry at times, platforms sometimes make errors in their moderation decisions. When the moderation policies of technology companies converge, the impact of erroneous content removals can be even harsher, as those whose content is mistakenly deleted from one platform can experience bans on other platforms as well. Using examples of digital campaigns by civil rights organizations seeking to document human rights abuses around the world, I discuss centralized moderation's capacity to limit nonharmful actors' ability to share their messages online and the ethical questions about banning protected speech through such cross-platform collaboration that arise.

The book discusses other caveats to multi-stakeholder coordination in moderation, including "censorship creep"—a problem identified in the literature in which moderation extends beyond its initial set of categories and centralization tools are misused by authoritarian leaders seeking to suppress dissent.[52] Thus, greater alignment in content moderation can facilitate the efficient removal of extremist material from social media platforms, but it comes with a cost to human rights and civil liberties, at least in some settings.

Relevancy to Other Online Campaigns

Finally, even though this book's focus is on militant and hate organizations, its findings are relevant for understanding other actors' adaptations to online regulation. Indeed, building resilience to content moderation is not unique to violent extremist groups. Even state actors seeking to influence domestic politics in their country or interfere in the political processes of other countries increasingly rely on multi-platform operations.

For example, a study by the Atlantic Council's Digital Forensic Research Lab found that a Russian intelligence campaign seeking to interfere in the domestic politics of the United States, Germany, and Ukraine (among other countries) spanned over thirty social media platforms and nine languages.[53] To evade moderation and increase impact, the operation employed "fake" accounts and impersonated user identities—a sophisticated messaging strategy that, as I show in the book, is often a part of more general efforts to overcome moderation.

Similarly, an influence operation by the Nicaraguan government in the run-up to the November 2021 elections employed hundreds of accounts on seven platforms to shape domestic audiences' vote choice. While some platforms, such as Facebook, Twitter, and YouTube, took action against this content, other platforms, like Telegram and TikTok, did not ban the campaign.[54] These examples illustrate the important role played by cross-platform variation in content moderation in the ability of malicious actors to spread their message online. By providing a framework for understanding these actors' adaptations to moderation in the broader internet ecosystem, the book illuminates often-overlooked consequences of online regulation.

Outline of the Book

The next chapter offers a theory that explains how policy divergence in content moderation leads to digital resilience. The theory focuses on the strategic interaction between national governments, technology companies, and dangerous organizations and explains the mechanisms that allow extremist groups to continue advancing their goals online despite rising regulation. Focusing on democratic countries, I argue that governments develop policy interventions compelling content moderation by technology platforms—which is in some tension with liberal values of freedom of expression—when they perceive the risk of online harms crossing a certain threshold. Because this threshold is informed by activity taking place on large and high-impact social media platforms, government regulation tends to focus on this portion of the online information ecosystem. The result is variation in moderation levels across platforms: while larger, highly regulated platforms invest in moderation policies and enforcement, smaller, less-regulated platforms have a freer hand.

I argue that when social media platforms differ in their content moderation policies, militant and hate groups adapt through *migration*—moving from highly moderated platforms to less-moderated ones; *mobilization*—leveraging audience grievances from content bans to inspire support for their cause on less-regulated spaces; and *messaging*—adapting content to the moderation rules of different platforms. The key insight that emerges from my theoretical framework is that variation in content policies between platforms is central to extremist organizations' ability to build resistance to moderation.

In chapter 3, I provide an overview of recent efforts to regulate social media platforms to combat online harms. By tracking the evolution of social media regulation in various countries around the world, I show how governments' push to moderate content is closely related to activity that is perceived as "too harmful" because it is violent, threatening, or disruptive to democratic processes. I further show that regulations, or proposed regulations, tend to focus on "high-impact" platforms, and demonstrate how government pressures incentivize technology companies to invest in moderation. The chapter shows that when extremist material online is at issue, many democratic governments do not hesitate to mandate strong censorship that delves deep into the specifics of how private companies should moderate content.

Chapter 4 is the first of three chapters that provide evidence on the mechanisms that enable dangerous organizations to become resilient to moderation. In this chapter, I focus on cross-platform migration. Building on the theoretical framework in chapter 2, I show that two factors drive extremist groups' migration between platforms: the level of moderation and audience reach. Drawing on original data on the social media activity of over a hundred militant and hate organizations, I demonstrate that when choosing platforms, groups tend to gravitate to online sites that provide the best "mix" of moderation and reach.

The chapter also includes two case studies that trace the migration of militant and hate groups between platforms. First, I use data on the Islamic State's networks on Twitter and Telegram to show that the enforcement of moderation policies that targeted the group in 2016 and 2019 led its members to migrate to less-moderated platforms that served as safe havens for its online campaigns. Second, I describe the migration decisions of the Proud Boys in the wake of their deplatforming from mainstream social media, showing the important role of lenient moderation and audience size in the group's migration decisions. This chapter sheds light on current debates around deplatforming by not only illustrating how migration happens but also explaining where banned actors are most likely to move.

In chapter 5, I discuss dangerous organizations' use of less-moderated platforms for mobilization and recruitment, focusing on the audience from which extremist groups seek to mobilize supporters. I argue that even though less-moderated platforms have smaller audiences, they can be useful for mobilization when the content disseminated by militant and hate groups appeals to their users. I show that individuals' personal experiences with content moderation can make them susceptible to propaganda, especially when propaganda content effectively targets their grievances from moderation. Drawing on novel cross-platform data on social media users' reactions to deplatforming, I show that militant groups leverage frustration from moderation to attract support for their cause. In particular, I focus on the case of the Oath Keepers' mobilization on less-moderated platforms in the wake of the 2020 US elections to demonstrate how frustration from "Big Tech censorship" attracted users to the group's online campaign to "Stop the Steal" and "Defeat the Coup"—a campaign that flourished on less-moderated social media sites in the leadup to the attack on the US Capitol on January 6, 2021.

Although dangerous organizations commonly use less-moderated platforms as targets for migration and mobilization, these actors also often seek ways to reach audiences on larger, more moderated sites. In chapter 6, I explain how militant groups overcome moderation even on highly regulated platforms by changing how they communicate. First, I show that these actors often sacrifice the "authenticity" of their message by toning down violating content in order to gain greater impact. I demonstrate this adaptation process with data on the Taliban's networks on Twitter, which shows how the group strategically shifted its messaging to adapt to the platform's rules banning the glorification of violence. I further show that adaptation to moderation takes place across platforms by presenting a study of the QAnon movement's messaging shifts on Twitter and Gab in response to changes in moderation rules. A second adaptation strategy involves "smuggling in" prohibited messages under the guise of content that appears innocuous. I argue that regulatory pressures to make platforms' content moderation policies transparent and accessible have the unintended consequence of allowing groups to more easily find ways to evade moderation. Drawing on examples from the Islamic State's evasion of moderation on Facebook, I describe how understanding moderation practices allows groups to build resilience, even on large regulated platforms.

In chapter 7, I discuss the role of interplatform cooperation in preventing dangerous organizations' exploitation of social media. Returning to the theoretical framework, I ask the following question: If divergence between platforms' content moderation policies increases extremist actors' resilience to moderation, does convergence weaken their ability to do so? I argue that alignment in moderation across platforms can limit migration and mobilization on smaller platforms and—to some extent—mitigate evasion on larger platforms as well. I examine trends in moderation alignment by drawing on original data that track changes in the content moderation rules of sixty social media platforms. I show that convergence in moderation across platforms is associated with lower levels of exploitation by extremist groups; in particular, convergence motivates a shift away from migration and mobilization on smaller platforms toward greater messaging adaptation on larger sites. The chapter further discusses the trade-offs of centralized moderation—in particular, its negative impact on nonharmful speech, its threats of over-censorship, and its ability to facilitate the creation of "content cartels."[55] As such, the chapter returns to a theme discussed in the beginning of the book: the role of moderation and censorship in democratic societies.

Chapter 8 concludes the book with a discussion of the broader implications for social media regulation in a multi-platform environment. Departing from the book's focus on extremist organizations, I consider the relevance of the patterns presented in the book to other settings, such as mis- or disinformation campaigns and state-sponsored influence operations. I outline directions for future research on the effects of platform moderation and discuss the potential for online regulation to transform our understanding of media and political behavior in the digital age.

2

A Theory of Digital Resilience

Every day, people use Facebook to share their experiences, connect with friends and family, and build communities. . . . Meta recognizes how important it is for Facebook to be a place where people feel empowered to communicate, and we take our role seriously in keeping abuse off the service. That's why we developed standards for what is and isn't allowed on Facebook.

—META, "FACEBOOK COMMUNITY STANDARDS"

Gab exists to promote the free flow of information online. It is our view that the responsible exercise of one's free speech rights is its own reward. . . . Our policy on "hate speech" is to allow all speech which is permitted by the First Amendment.

—GAB AI INC., "WEBSITE TERMS OF SERVICE"

ALL SOCIAL MEDIA PLATFORMS moderate content—but they vary in the way they do so.[1] While some platforms, like Facebook, engage at times in extensive efforts to moderate harmful content, other platforms, like Gab, moderate content to a much lower extent. What drives technology companies to limit harmful content on their platforms? Why do some companies invest more in content moderation than others? And what are the consequences of different moderation standards for the growth of extremism on social media?

In this chapter, I explain how policy divergence in content moderation leads to the digital resilience of militant and hate organizations. The theory focuses on the strategic interaction between national governments, technology companies, and dangerous organizations and explains the mechanisms that allow extremist groups to continue advancing their goals online despite rising regulation. Focusing on democratic countries, I argue that governments enact policies compelling content moderation by technology platforms—which is in some tension with liberal values of freedom of expression—when they perceive the risk of online harms as too high. Because this perception is informed by activity taking place on large, high-impact social media platforms, government regulation tends to focus on this portion of the online information ecosystem. The result is variation in moderation levels across platforms: while larger, highly regulated platforms invest in moderation policies and enforcement, smaller, less-regulated platforms have a freer hand.

I show that when social media companies differ in their content policies, extremist organizations are able to overcome moderation. In particular, I explain the three strategies used by these groups to adapt to moderation: *migration*—moving from highly moderated platforms to those that moderate less; *mobilization*—leveraging audience grievances from content bans to inspire support for their cause on less-regulated spaces; and *messaging*—adapting content to the moderation rules of different platforms. The key insight that emerges from my theoretical framework is that variation in content policies between platforms is central to militant and hate actors' ability to build resistance to moderation. The nature of online harms, the technologies of content moderation, and the actors responsible for regulation are likely to vary over time. However, my theoretical framework is general enough to account for a wide range of online environments with varying levels of regulation.

Strategic Behavior in a World of Online Regulation

I begin by introducing the actors in question—extremist organizations, technology companies, and national governments—and describing their goals, preferences, and constraints. I then present a simple framework that explains how moderation can effectively restrict harmful content in a world where there is only one moderation threshold—that is, when all platforms are governed by similar content policies. Next, I explain how the expectations formed in a single-threshold environment do not hold in a multi-threshold context by showing that diversity in moderation levels across platforms changes extremist actors' behavior. I then discuss the mechanisms that allow dangerous organizations to build resilience to moderation when platforms have divergent policies to moderate harmful content. Finally, I show how the static, cross-platform focus of my theoretical framework can also apply dynamically over time.

Extremist Organizations

The main goal of militant and hate organizations—nonstate actors that promote ideologies considered harmful by national governments—is to propagate their message on social media in order to publicize their cause, attract supporters, and recruit new members. Because of the large stage that online platforms offer, these actors generally prefer to maintain a presence on social media and are willing to invest resources to do so. Content—such as text, images, and videos—is the "product" that extremist groups seek to "sell" on online platforms. Content exists on a spectrum that ranges from benign to extreme: benign content includes posts that convey nonharmful messages as defined by governments and technology companies (more on that later), and extreme content consists of posts that violate platform rules. Two factors determine the benefit to these groups from disseminating content on social media: the *authenticity* of the message—how close the message is to the group's core ideology—and its *impact*—how many people view the message, the speed at which it is shared online, and the extent to which it attracts supporters.

Technology Companies

Technology companies own platforms that facilitate the dissemination of user-generated content on the internet. As private companies, their main goal is to generate profit, which they do by adapting their platforms' features to the preferences of their stakeholders—whether they are users, investors, advertisers, or regulators. In general, companies prefer not to intervene in the content shared by users on their platforms, as such interventions may aggravate users and drive down profits. Sometimes, however, stakeholders prefer intervention—for example, when extremist content disseminated on the platform inspires real-world violence, or when misinformation interferes with election processes in democratic countries. To respond to these stakeholder demands and combat harmful content, companies design policies that determine what is allowed and not allowed on their platforms. This results in a content moderation threshold above which violating content is removed.

THE CONTENT MODERATION THRESHOLD

To simplify the analysis in this chapter and the rest of the book, I treat content moderation as a one-dimensional variable, even though technology companies' policies have many different categories for violating content (see chapter 4 for details). The reason for using a single dimension to examine levels of moderation is that it provides conceptual clarity on the variation between technology companies' overall approach to restricting harmful content. Since my analysis focuses on differences between platforms, collapsing the multidimensional policy space into one dimension helps to clarify the mechanisms used by extremist actors to adapt to content moderation in a diverse online environment. Thus, when analyzing content moderation policies, I summarize them into one variable that can take low or high values. Low values indicate restrictive thresholds, and high values reflect lenient policies.[2]

National Governments

Among the stakeholders that shape technology platforms' moderation policies, national governments are arguably the most important ones. One of the main goals of government actors is to maintain political stability in their countries—for example, by preventing social unrest or violence. In democratic societies, governments also strive to promote liberal values, such as media freedom and open debates in the "marketplace of ideas."[3] Thus, governments in democratic countries prefer to not intervene in private technology companies' content policies. However, as social media platforms become increasingly influential, and when content shared on these platforms can be clearly linked to offline harms, democratic governments are willing to trade off freedom of expression to promote greater safety. They do so by advancing legislation that makes technology companies legally responsible for the content shared on their platforms and demanding changes to moderation policies to address content that they define as illegal or harmful.

Since governments seek to prevent the spread of harmful content that affects wide swaths of the population in their country, they tend to focus on large, mainstream, and high-impact platforms. Thus, technology companies with large user bases are most strongly targeted by legislation, facing fines, sanctions, and other punishments if they do not abide by regulations. At the same time, technology companies that own platforms with smaller user bases are held to a lower standard and therefore do less to restrict harmful content on their sites. The result is variation in content moderation policies across platforms.

Figure 2.1 shows what this variation looks like when examining the social media ecosystem as a whole. The x-axis represents platform size, with higher values reflecting platforms with larger user bases. The y-axis represents the moderation threshold, where higher values indicate more lenient moderation—that is, more content is allowed on the site. Because of their focus on harmful

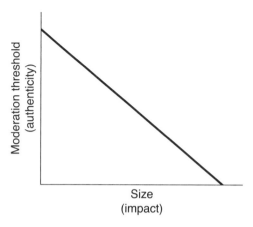

FIGURE 2.1. The Relationship between Moderation Threshold and Size
Note: Platforms with larger user bases have lower moderation thresholds—that is, they impose more restrictions on the content that can be posted on their sites. Platforms with smaller user bases tend to have higher thresholds. This relationship also reflects the trade-off between authenticity and impact that dangerous organizations face when using social media.

content on large platforms, governments tend to regulate platforms on the right side of the figure, while paying less attention to social media sites on the left.

This variation in content moderation shapes the behavior of dangerous organizations. On the one hand, militant and hate actors would like to use high-threshold platforms, as these sites allow posting more freely and maximizing the authenticity of propaganda messages. On the other, platforms with high moderation thresholds also have the smallest audience, limiting impact and reach. The opposite is also true: large social media platforms, where messages can have the highest impact, have the most restrictive moderation policies (often as a result of public pressure and government regulation). This tension reflects a trade-off that drives militant and hate actors' strategies for adapting to content moderation across platforms.

Information Flows in a Moderated Online Environment

To understand how extremist organizations build resilience to moderation in this diverse information environment, it is crucial to consider how information flows in a social media ecosystem with varying moderation policies. Here I focus on the surface web—the part of the internet that is largely accessible to the public—and not on the "dark web," a decentralized network of websites that are harder for the average internet user to access. To be sure, militant and hate actors operate on both the surface web and the dark web.[4] My theory focuses on publicly accessible websites and online applications, as these are the spaces where groups invest the most resources to attract supporters and where regulators focus their efforts.

We can think about information flows on social media as beginning with content producers, moving through platforms, and reaching target audiences. Platforms—or "intermediaries," as they are commonly called[5]—decide whether to let information flow freely on their sites or limit the types of content that can reach the audience. If there are no content moderation policies, all information moves from the producers to the audience. If moderation is present, then only part of the content that producers create reaches the audience. In the context of online extremist content, the goal of moderation is to limit what dangerous organizations can share on the platform so that the audience will not be exposed to their messages.

Figure 2.2 presents different ways in which information flows in a moderated information environment. In panel A, information moves from producers to the audience in a world where there is a single-moderation threshold—that is, where all platforms are governed by the same content policies. In this case, only part of the information that producers create passes through the platform and reaches the audience, as indicated by the thinner lines flowing from the platforms to the audience. Thus, in a context where there is a single-moderation threshold, lowering the moderation bar directly affects the information that the audience sees.

Panel B shows a different scenario. Here, where different platforms have different moderation thresholds, a low moderation bar on one platform (for example, platform A) does not limit harmful content from reaching the audience because information can flow through other channels (such as platforms B and C). This can be seen in the thicker lines marking greater movement of content from the producers to the audience, even in the face of low thresholds on some platforms. This inconsistency in moderation policies, which allows easily available platforms with lenient moderation thresholds to be present, can inadvertently increase extremist groups' resilience to online regulation.

Of course, the ability of harmful content producers to reach the audience in panel B relies on the fact that some platforms have lenient moderation rules (high moderation thresholds). If the variation in content moderation were

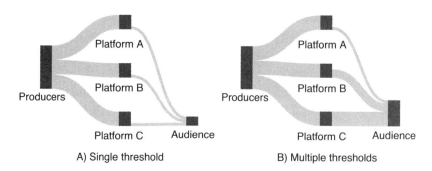

FIGURE 2.2. Information Flows in a Moderated Information Environment
Note: In a single-threshold context (panel A), moderation can effectively limit harmful content from reaching the audience. When there is divergence in moderation thresholds and some platforms have lenient moderation thresholds (panel B), more harmful content can flow to the audience.

more limited, such that all platforms had different but restrictive policies, then less harmful content would move from producers to the audience.

In the next sections, I explain how extremist organizations adapt to content moderation in both the single-threshold and multi-threshold scenarios and outline the mechanisms that enable these actors to advance their goals online by leveraging variation in moderation between platforms.

A Single-Moderation Threshold

Let's begin by considering a simple context in which only one moderation threshold governs all platforms. This is just a simplified conceptual framework, of course—a single-moderation threshold does not actually exist in reality, as social media platforms differ in their content policies. I use this simplified example as a baseline framework on which I will build complexity throughout the chapter.

Assume that an extremist group is interested in attracting supporters and plans to post content on online platforms. Since the group's payoff from using social media is driven by the authenticity and impact of its message, it will generally prefer to post content that is closest to its core ideology as long as the message is able to reach the intended audience. With a single-moderation threshold, the group faces the same restrictions on all platforms. It therefore invests its resources in the platforms on which it can have the highest impact. In general, social media platforms prefer not to intervene in the content shared by their users unless their stakeholders demand that such action be taken.

At the outset, the group may or may not know the content moderation threshold. We can think about the threshold as a simple variable with low or high values. A low value reflects a scenario in which almost all pieces of content fall above the threshold and are therefore removed, and a high value represents a situation in which anything is allowed on the platform—no content falls above the threshold. Since the location of the moderation threshold is not always publicly known, the group forms an expectation about the threshold and posts the "most authentic" content it can—right up to its estimate concerning the platforms' moderation bar.[6]

If there is consistent enforcement—that is, if technology companies always remove content that violates their rules—then the group's content will be taken down when it crosses the threshold and will remain online when it does not. (In a later section, I discuss what might happen when there is no consistent enforcement.) After several rounds of trial and error, the group will learn the level of content that it can post on social media without having it removed. Thus, we would expect the group to post content that is right up to, but not above, the true moderation threshold.

Changing Moderation Policies

What happens when the moderation threshold changes? Thus far, we have assumed that platforms' thresholds are fixed, but as I show in the following chapters, technology companies often change their moderation rules. Because platform policies are driven by stakeholder preferences, moderation thresholds will vary when stakeholders' preferences change. Take the case of a high moderation threshold resulting in excessive amounts of harmful content on the platform. Too much "bad" content can scare away users and investors alike, leading to a decrease in the company's profits. If an excessive amount of harmful content inspires violence, then governments may also step in and demand a change in the moderation policies.

This is what happened after the terrorist attack in Christchurch, New Zealand. On March 15, 2019, a white supremacist stormed two mosques during Friday prayers and murdered and injured almost a hundred people. To publicize his terrorist act, the gunman livestreamed his shooting on Facebook Live, a new feature that the platform launched in 2015. Even though the company had a policy in place to ban graphic violence, its automated moderation systems were not sufficiently developed to rapidly detect violence in the livestreamed content. As a result, the footage stayed online for almost half an hour before it was reported and taken down. By that time, however, the content had been viewed thousands of times on the platform and millions of copies were disseminated to other platforms.[7]

The horrifying outcome of the Christchurch attack led many to demand greater action from social media companies to moderate extremist content. Governments began to call for more regulation, highlighting the insufficiency of platforms' self-moderation. In the United States, for example, Congressman Bennie Thompson sent a letter to Facebook, Twitter, and YouTube a few days after the attack, urging them to take stronger action against violent extremism. "Your companies must prioritize responding to these toxic and violent ideologies with resources and attention. If you are unwilling to do so, Congress must consider policies to ensure that terrorist content is not distributed on your platforms," he wrote.[8] Even greater pressure came from the government of New Zealand, which, under the leadership of Prime Minister Jacinda Ardern, launched the Christchurch Call to Action in collaboration with President Emmanuel Macron of France. The initiative sought to put pressure on companies to "eliminate terrorist and violent extremist content online" by inviting governments and platforms to commit to working together to mitigate the problem.[9] Over fifty countries and fourteen online service providers signed the Christchurch pledge.

In response to these pressures, many companies began updating their content moderation policies. Facebook, in particular, sought to improve its moderation capacities, citing the increased "international media pressure" and "regulatory and legal risks [for] Facebook" as reasons for the need to improve moderation. To lower its moderation threshold (that is, make moderation more restrictive), the platform invested in efforts to improve real-time detection of harmful content in livestreamed content, changed its policies to prevent "risky actors" from using Facebook Live, and made several modifications to its reporting system to make it easier for users to report violating content.[10] Other companies followed suit.

How does a changed moderation threshold affect dangerous organizations' content on social media? When platforms lower their moderation threshold, a group begins experiencing new content removals. This leads the group's online media activists to update their expectation about the location of the threshold and to post content that is just below the revised moderation bar. (If the group is risk-averse, it might adjust by posting content that meets an even lower bar to avoid crossing the threshold by mistake.) As platforms continue to add more rules to their moderation policies, the group adapts its messaging by posting content right below the new threshold. In a single-threshold context, the outcome is that less harmful content flows from the group to the audience.

This simple framework is useful for understanding how extremist actors strategically adapt their messaging to platforms' content moderation policies. Since the benefit from using social media is a function of both message authenticity and impact, militant and hate organizations generally benefit from posting *something* on a moderated platform, even if the content is not in its "most authentic" form. Because the size of the audience on social media can be so large, given the choice between posting a sanitized version of its content on a platform with a huge user base or not posting at all, these groups often prefer to post. Thus, in a single-threshold context, changing moderation policies directly affects the content that extremist groups can disseminate online.

The expectation that more moderation will reduce the level of harmful content is at the core of current regulatory efforts. Much of the new legislation reflects a single-threshold paradigm, assuming that inducing a social media platform to take stronger actions against extremist groups will lead to a decrease in their ability to exploit the internet. As a result, the main metric of success is a reduced level of harmful content on the regulated platforms. For example, Germany's Network Enforcement Act (also called NetzDG) requires platforms with at least two million users registered in Germany to remove, within twenty-four hours, any content that is deemed illegal within the country's jurisdiction. To ensure that platforms abide by the rules, the regulation requires platforms to publish transparency reports reflecting their successful removal of prohibited content.[11] The United Kingdom's Online Safety Act is premised on a similar notion: it demands that online service providers "swiftly" remove harmful content and publish reports detailing what they have done to make their platforms safer.[12] Many other countries have taken a similar approach to moderation—one whose main outcome of interest is a within-platform, single-threshold measure of harmful content removal (see chapter 3 for more details).[13]

What the new regulations overlook is that most of the adaptation of extremist groups to content moderation does not happen in the context of a single threshold, but takes place across many platforms that are governed by diverse moderation standards. In the next section, I expand the single-threshold framework to explain what happens when groups operate in a context with diverse content moderation policies.

How Extremists Build Digital Resilience When Platform Policies Diverge

Several factors make a multi-platform environment particularly attractive to militant and hate actors. First, because platforms have different user bases, groups can target audiences across social media sites in a more nuanced way. Second, platforms vary in the features they provide: some serve as "beacons," disseminating content rapidly to a large number of people, while others archive large volumes of content. Still others specialize in secure communications.[14] Operating in a multi-platform environment allows groups to leverage various platform features to maximize the impact of their online campaigns. Finally, and most importantly, in a multi-platform environment, levels of content moderation vary: while some online sites tightly moderate dangerous organizations' content, others do not. This heterogeneous environment provides opportunities for building resilience to moderation.

To consider how content moderation shapes the behavior of militants and hate actors in an environment with diverse moderation policies, let's return to our single-threshold framework and add the complexity of multiple thresholds. As before, we examine the behavior of an extremist group that seeks to maximize message authenticity and impact on a target audience. But instead of having just one threshold governing moderation, platforms have different content policies. How will the group advance its goals in this diverse setting?

If we consider the structure of the online information ecosystem, where larger platforms have low moderation thresholds and smaller platforms have higher thresholds (see figure 2.1), we can see that divergence in moderation can facilitate several mechanisms of adaptation. I argue that three mechanisms in particular allow groups to build digital resilience to content moderation. I discuss each of these in turn.

Migration

The mechanism that most people point to when considering militant groups' and hate groups' adaptation to content moderation is migration to alternative platforms. When banned on social media sites with high levels of moderation, extremist actors have the option of shifting their online presence to other sites with looser moderation rules. The strategy of migrating to alternative platforms is central to the online operations of militant and hate actors because it allows them to continue advancing their message on the internet in the face of tightening regulations. It comes as no surprise, then, that content moderation has led many groups to migrate across platforms. For example, after being suspended from Facebook, YouTube, and Twitter, the Islamic State and Al-Qaeda began migrating to sites like Telegram and a host of other small platforms that do not actively moderate.[15] Similarly, when mainstream platforms began to crack down on hate speech and the conspiracy theories promoted by far-right groups, many of these groups moved to promote their ideologies on other platforms, such as Gab, BitChute, Telegram, and Parler.[16]

However, moving to platforms with less moderation is not always the optimal strategy for militant and hate groups. Since platforms that moderate content also tend to have the largest user bases, content disseminated in less-moderated spaces finds much smaller audiences and garners significantly less publicity. Consider, for example, the case of Britain First, a UK-based hate group. When Facebook banned the group in 2018, it lost the lion's share of its audience when it migrated to Gab and Telegram. Before it was suspended, the group had over 1.8 million followers on Facebook; after the ban it was able to attract only about 0.6 percent of its audience on these alternative platforms.[17] Operating on unmoderated small platforms distances groups from the main area of political contestation, potentially reducing their audiences and impact.

So what are the best options for militant groups looking to migrate to new platforms in the face of content moderation? Recall that the benefit that groups derive from posting on social media is a function of the authenticity of their message (how close it is to the group's core ideology) and the impact of that message (as reflected, for example, in the size of their audience). If the impact is the same on all platforms, then groups will always prefer to use a platform with a higher (more generous) moderation threshold. Similarly, if the moderation threshold is equal on all platforms, then militant and hate actors will seek to maximize impact by targeting platforms with more users. Of course, since audience size and moderation thresholds vary between platforms, groups prefer social media sites that provide the best "mix" of these two dimensions.

Figure 2.3 illustrates the trade-off that extremist groups face between their ability to post "authentic" content on social media and the prospect of impacting a large audience. In the figure, the x-axis reflects the platform size (the number of active users), and the y-axis reflects the moderation threshold.

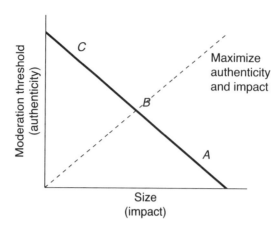

FIGURE 2.3. Migrating between Platforms with Varying Moderation Thresholds and Size
Note: Platform C has a higher moderation threshold, which allows dangerous actors to post the "most authentic" content, but it also has a much smaller audience and therefore a lower impact. Platform A has the largest audience, but it also has the lowest moderation threshold. Because of this trade-off, militant actors prefer to migrate to platforms, like platform B, that equally maximize authenticity and impact.

Because there is a negative relationship between the size of the platform and its moderation threshold, groups face a trade-off that some have called the "online extremists' dilemma": on the one hand, operating on large social media platforms enhances audience reach and groups' ability to attract supporters. On the other hand, it increases the risk that their messages will be deleted, and their accounts suspended, because of the stronger moderation policies of these platforms. Similarly, while limiting their presence to platforms with high thresholds increases the "operational security" of these actors' online campaigns, this also greatly reduces their outreach and overall impact.[18]

For these reasons, groups prefer to operate in online spaces that maximize their audience reach while minimizing the impact of content moderation. This is illustrated in figure 2.3. Even though platform C has a higher threshold, which allows groups to post more authentic content, it also has a much smaller audience and therefore a lower impact. Similarly, platform A has the largest audience but also the lowest threshold, which severely limits the content that groups can post there. Because of these dynamics, extremist actors prefer to operate on platforms like platform B, which equally maximize authenticity and impact. Such platforms have less moderation than online spaces whose size and impact make them subject to strong government regulation. At the same time, they are big enough to allow groups to reach larger audiences than is possible with fringe platforms that are not regulated at all. Thus, militant and hate groups encountering moderation bans will choose to migrate to platforms with higher thresholds as long as they can maintain a reasonable level of audience reach.

What happens when moderation thresholds change over time? If platforms that traditionally have a high threshold decide to lower their moderation bar, then groups will simply migrate to new platforms that better enable maximizing content authenticity and audience reach. As a result, migration is a dynamic mechanism that varies when platform policies change. (See a later section for a discussion of these dynamic processes.)

Mobilization

Another mechanism that allows militant and hate groups to overcome moderation is mobilization. When extremist actors maintain a presence on several platforms in parallel, not only can they evade bans and increase the probability that their content will flow to target audiences, but they can also engage potential recruits more effectively. Recall that extremist organizations' payoff from using social media is driven by their ability to post content that closely reflects their ideology ("authenticity") and their ability to influence the audience ("impact"). Until now, I have primarily referred to the size of the audience when discussing impact, assuming that on platforms with large user bases impact will be higher. However, impact is not limited to audience size—it can also be driven by other factors, such as the susceptibility of the audience to extremist groups' messaging.

Consider a situation where two platforms vary in the types of audiences that use their services. On one platform, the audience does not find militant groups' narratives interesting or appealing, while on the other, these groups' messages resonate deeply. If militant and hate actors can identify the platforms on which even a small audience will find their content appealing, they have an incentive to concentrate their online efforts on those platforms, where they are more likely to have an impact.

What makes users on a social media platform susceptible to extremist groups' campaigns? Although there is not much research on this question in the context of content moderation, a large body of literature on the drivers of radicalization (both online and offline) points to various factors. These include social, economic, or political grievances that make individuals receptive to extremist narratives and a sense of exclusion and social isolation that leads them to search for a sense of community and belonging.[19] Experiences of rejection have been shown to be particularly impactful in driving individuals into militant and hate groups' online circles, especially when the ideologies promoted in these communities resonate with a sense of isolation.[20]

The evidence indicates that experiencing content moderation on social media platforms (for example, by having one's posts deleted or account suspended) can similarly generate grievances that propel engagement with extremist content. Followers of the Islamic State who were banned on Twitter and Facebook became much more motivated to seek out the group's online networks on less-moderated platforms after their suspension.[21] Similarly, sympathizers of the far-right conspiracy theory QAnon, which was one of the narratives that inspired the January 2021 attack on the US Capitol, increased their engagement with QAnon content after their accounts were deleted from mainstream platforms.[22]

Thus, being targeted by content moderation can motivate individuals to engage with the banned material elsewhere. This may stem from feelings of rejection and seeking comfort among like-minded communities or from a sense of injustice over perceived bias in content moderation. In the US context, for example, some have argued that Big Tech has a "pro-liberal bias" that leads companies to take down content by users and groups associated with the political right but not content posted by those on the left.[23] As I show in chapter 5, this type of grievance has inspired individuals who were suspended from mainstream platforms to mobilize in support of far-right groups on other platforms. Another way in which content moderation can mobilize social media users relates to content monetization. When individuals (especially those with large followings) get banned from social media, their ability to profit from their online activities can be dramatically reduced. This sort of "blocked ambition" can lead to anti-system ideas and actions that extremist groups can draw on when mobilizing support in less-moderated spaces.[24]

The mobilizing effect of content moderation was also observed by Margaret Roberts, who studied how social media users in China reacted to censorship. Analyzing the online behavior of users whose content was censored, she found that they were more likely to mobilize against the government and to seek out banned information than were those who had not been censored.[25] Although the contexts are very different, the mechanisms driving the behavior of Chinese users after being censored online are similar to those that mobilize banned users in more democratic countries. For militant and hate actors seeking to increase the impact of their online campaigns, targeting users who experience moderation can be very beneficial, as these users might be more susceptible to their narratives.

Where are we most likely to see mobilization taking place? Since mobilization requires the ability to post high levels of "authentic" content, extremist groups focus their mobilization efforts on social media platforms that have higher moderation thresholds.

Messaging

The third mechanism that enables groups to build resilience to moderation is a shift in messaging strategies. Unlike migration and mobilization, which focus on higher-threshold platforms with smaller audiences, messaging is a mechanism that extremist actors use to overcome moderation even on large platforms with more restrictive content policies. Since large social media sites are those that also moderate the most, militant actors who wish to operate on these platforms need to change how they communicate.

I argue that extremist groups use three main tactics to change their messaging so that they can get around moderation in a multi-threshold environment: *content adaptation*, *message distribution*, and *threshold evasion*. Content adaptation is a group's alteration in its messages to fit platforms' moderation policies. This type of adaptation is similar to groups' behavior in a single-threshold context, but adapting content across several platforms with varying moderation policies can be more difficult to do. Message distribution is a group's dissemination of its content across a wide range of online spaces in order to increase the survivability of that message. Finally, threshold evasion is seeking to maintain a presence even on highly moderated platforms by posting messages that mimic content that falls below the moderation thresholds, even though those messages actually violate platform rules.

CONTENT ADAPTATION

As explained earlier, technology companies design content moderation rules to prevent harmful messages from reaching their users. Since different companies face different pressures from stakeholders, the process that determines the policies varies by company and results in varying moderation rules across platforms. Facebook, for example, has many different categories for violating

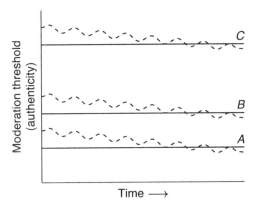

FIGURE 2.4. Adaptation to Moderation Thresholds across Platforms
Note: The figure shows how extremist actors adapt their content to the moderation thresholds of different platforms. The solid lines represent the thresholds, and the dashed lines illustrate groups' content adaptation.

content, such as "violence and incitement," "dangerous individuals and organizations," and "hate speech." TikTok, on the other hand, has only some of these categories, while Telegram has even fewer of them. Extremist groups that wish to use these platforms need to adapt their content to each platform's moderation rules in order to avoid bans.

Figure 2.4 illustrates how militant and hate actors adapt their messaging to the moderation thresholds of different platforms. In the figure, platform C has the highest threshold, which allows groups to post almost any type of content, and platforms B and A have lower thresholds, which limit the kinds of messages that can be shared. In order to adapt, groups learn the location of each threshold and optimize their messages to fit platform policies. This is shown in the dashed lines surrounding each threshold in figure 2.4, which depicts the process of trial and error through which groups optimize their content in light of platform rules.[26] Because technology companies vary in their policies, harmful content flows from extremist groups to audiences at different rates on different platforms, resulting in an overall higher audience exposure to their content in the broader online ecosystem.

Adapting content dissemination to platform moderation rules has another advantage for militant and hate actors: it helps them optimize their messaging according to audience preferences. As explained earlier, technology companies' moderation policies are driven by the preferences of their stakeholders, including the users of their platforms. A low moderation threshold for certain types of content is likely to reflect the preferences of the majority of a social media platform's users: adapting content to these platforms' moderation policies therefore makes the content more appealing to the audience. Groups wishing to attract supporters on moderated platforms therefore benefit from tailoring their messages to the tastes of the users.

In earlier work on the Islamic State's propaganda campaigns, I showed that individuals who engaged with the group's content on Twitter tended to dislike extreme content depicting violence and brutality. These users were much more susceptible to positive, milder messages.[27] At the same time, hard-core supporters of the Islamic State who were more attracted to extreme content tended to operate on smaller, less-moderated platforms.[28] Militant groups that are aware of these dynamics can exploit variations in moderation levels to make their content more attractive to audiences on different platforms. Thus, by targeting audiences on various social media sites through content adaptation, militant and hate groups are able not only to evade moderation but also to promote their messages to audiences in a broader set of online spaces. Chapter 6 provides additional evidence on how groups adapt content to platform rules to appeal to a broader audience by creating "sanitized" versions of their messaging on platforms with lower (that is, more restrictive) thresholds. Since groups can tailor their messages to platforms' moderation rules, the amount of harmful content they disseminate is not reduced; instead, it simply shifts between platforms based on their moderation policies.

MESSAGE DISTRIBUTION

Another way in which groups evade moderation is by distributing their messages on a wide range of social media sites. Unlike content adaptation—sending different types of content to different platforms based on their moderation policies—message distribution is sharing the *same message* on many platforms in parallel. The benefit of message distribution is akin to a fisherman spreading a wide net to catch as many fish as possible in the face of uncertainty about where the fish are located. Since extremist groups do not always know which platforms will take down their content, they have an incentive to spread their messages on a wide range of platforms, in the hope that at least some of them will reach their target audience.

Illustrating how this works is the case of Al-Shabaab, a jihadist group affiliated with Al-Qaeda. Every year the group has been posting a special message for the end of Ramadan on YouTube. In 2017, YouTube changed its policies and lowered the content moderation threshold, resulting in the removal of Al-Shabaab's messages from the platform. To adapt to this change, Al-Shabaab began spreading its message on a wider range of social media sites. On June 26, 2017, Al-Shabaab's official media wing posted 129 unique URLs with the group's end-of-Ramadan message. In 2018, it posted its message through 431 unique web links.[29] Although the majority of these links were eventually taken down, some have remained online, allowing the group to reach audiences despite platforms' moderation efforts.

Indeed, militant and hate groups have increasingly used parallel sharing of content on many platforms in their use of the internet. A report by the Global Internet Forum to Counter Terrorism (GIFCT), an organization that facilitates information sharing between platforms, showed that between 2019 and 2021 the number of harmful items uploaded to several platforms at the same time by extremist groups rose by about 60 percent. Each of these items was shared in an average of seventy-one unique links.[30] Similarly, Tech Against Terrorism identified over eighteen thousand web links containing terrorist content in 2021.[31] Distributing propaganda across several social media sites in parallel, while leveraging the variation in the rate of moderation across platforms, provides another channel through which dangerous organizations are able to become resilient to moderation.

THRESHOLD EVASION

Content adaptation and message distribution target a wide range of platforms across the moderation spectrum. But as explained here, militant actors receive the highest payoff from spreading their messages on the most restrictive platforms—those that also have the largest audiences. Thus, a third tactic for building resilience to moderation is threshold evasion, which can be done, for example, by "smuggling in" violating content alongside messages that seem innocuous. The goal of threshold evasion is to disassociate the content shared on highly moderated platforms from groups' official propaganda. In other words, militant and hate actors can spread content that closely aligns with their ideology even on platforms that restrict their content as long as they keep the messaging vague and unofficial.

One overlooked consequence of technology companies' increased transparency on moderation is that it can strengthen dangerous organizations' evasion efforts. Government regulation of social media platforms often demands greater transparency on how moderation is done. This compels platforms to not only publicize their moderation policies but also provide details on their approach to removing harmful content. This information is very valuable for actors seeking to overcome moderation. In a review study on citizen resilience to online censorship in authoritarian countries, Roberts shows that an important condition for censorship evasion is knowledge that censorship is happening.[32] Although very different purposes often underlie evasion in authoritarian contexts than is the case with moderation evasion in more democratic settings, the same logic drives both: actors who seek to overcome censorship are best equipped to do so when they know how censorship is done.

To see how this can happen, assume that technology companies detect harmful content on their sites by combing social media posts for signals of violating content. These signals can be words, phrases, or visual cues such as certain objects in images and videos. For example, words such as "kill," "attack," and "enemy," especially when combined with an image showing violence, can be useful signals for content that violates platform policies against the glorification of violence. If militant actors who seek to evade moderation can avoid using these signals when spreading propaganda, they increase the survivability of their messages even on platforms that remove such content.

In chapter 6, I provide some examples of this kind of threshold evasion. Focusing on the Islamic State's evasion of moderation on Facebook, I show how the group used broken text to prevent matches with certain keywords that are used as signals for harmful content, employed Photoshop to hide its logos, and embedded its official propaganda in video clips that appeared as news coming out of innocuous sources such as the BBC. (See chapter 6 for more details.) Thus, perhaps counterintuitively, greater transparency on content moderation can inadvertently strengthen militant actors' efforts to evade it.

Disseminating what looks like "regular" content on platforms with low moderation thresholds has another benefit. As a result of the large volume of information shared on social media every day, a growing portion of moderation takes place via automated algorithms. These AI-based models are trained to rapidly detect and take down content that violates platform policies, but their ability to separate violating from nonviolating messages depends on the degree of dissimilarity between these two types of content. In other words, while it is quite simple for machine learning algorithms to differentiate between brutal violence and other types of content, it is much more difficult to determine whether a message that shares news or is critical of a policy issue violates the moderation rules, since such messages often look very similar to content that is allowed on the platform. By sharing messages that appear similar to nonviolating content, militant actors can unofficially promote their ideology online, even on highly moderated sites.

But threshold evasion is not restricted to the way content appears on platforms that engage in high levels of moderation. Dangerous organizations can also rely on networks of supporters to spread propaganda on moderated sites. Supporter networks that are not formally affiliated with militant organizations can aid the online efforts of those groups by indirectly sharing their propaganda. The Taliban, for example, used networks of thousands of individuals to spread its messages on Twitter, YouTube, and Facebook.[33] Similarly, supporters of the QAnon conspiracy spread the movement's message on mainstream online sites using coded, seemingly innocuous language.[34] Since supporter networks are not formally affiliated with militant and hate groups, they are not subject to platform bans unless they share rule-violating content. Extremist actors can thus evade moderation by inspiring individuals in their follower networks to share content that advances their ideology but is not officially linked to the group.

A related method to overcome moderation is for a different *actor* to post the same *content*. While many moderation policies are based on the content itself, a growing number of platforms also moderate content based on actor identity. This means that platforms look not only at *what* is being posted on their sites but also at *who* is posting it. The justification for actor-based policies is that certain entities should not have a presence on social media at all because of the harmful ideology that they promote. Facebook, for example, created an extensive list of dangerous organizations that are banned from its platform regardless of the content that they post online. Other platforms draw on lists of designated terrorist organizations, such as those developed by the United States and the European Union. In contrast to content-based moderation, actor-based moderation results in platforms taking down "mild" content posted by banned actors—messages that would have remained unmoderated had they been posted by other entities.

To evade actor-based moderation, militant and hate groups can engage with audiences under alternative identities. Posing as other actors allows groups to continue disseminating content while remaining below the moderation threshold. Even though the content that they disseminate cannot be officially branded as theirs, it can nonetheless advance their ideology indirectly. Far-right groups, for example, have been posing as youth organizations to inspire young audiences on moderating platforms to disseminate content that aligns with their ideology. To promote their narratives and avoid bans, they have also created accounts in which they act as journalists (selectively) sharing news that supports their worldviews.[35] The Islamic State's social media operatives have been using similar tactics by identifying as independent news agencies promoting information that strengthens the group's public image.[36]

The ability to shift messaging strategies in a multiplatform environment is an important mechanism that allows groups to continue engaging audiences despite content moderation. Adapting messaging to platforms' thresholds, distributing content in many online spaces at the same time, and mimicking nonviolating content allows groups to build resilience to moderation even on highly regulated platforms, and in ways that current approaches do not usually consider.

Cycles of Content Moderation and Extremist Activity Online

The theoretical framework that I presented in this chapter focused on cross-platform differences in content moderation—treating the time dimension as mostly static (with the exception of figure 2.4, which shows adaption to thresholds over time). However, as I show later in the book, the moderation of harmful content can vary over time within the same platform. Such variation can take place when technology companies change their content policies in response to stakeholder pressure, or when they change the resources that they dedicate to enforcing these policies. How does variation in content moderation within the same platform shape the online behavior of extremist organizations? In this section, I explain the cyclical nature of content moderation and its tendency to induce corresponding cycles of extremist adaptation that follow the same logic of the theory I outlined earlier.

Content Moderation as a Cycle

Technology companies are not naturally incentivized to address harmful content on their platforms without stakeholder pressure, since content moderation is costly and does not often generate profit.[37] Technology companies prefer to not invest in moderating harmful content unless failing to do so will incur even higher costs. This means that companies' attention to content moderation varies with the level of pressure put on them by stakeholders—pressure that changes over time.

This variation often looks like a cycle, where companies' investment in content moderation rises and falls in a repeated pattern. At the first stage of the cycle, there is often (but not always) a scandal due to insufficient moderation; for example, a terrorist attack is linked to content shared on the platform, or there is evidence that the platform is being used to spread misinformation, or it becomes publicly known that the platform is manipulated to influence elections. This leads stakeholders to push the company to address the scandal: advertisers may pull back on their ads, shareholders might threaten to sell their shares or to vote out management, and governments may impose fines and demand greater moderation. The company responds to this pressure by shifting its resources and attention to the trust and safety teams that lead its content moderation efforts, a move that leads to the growth of these teams within the organization.[38] With additional personnel, resources, and attention, the company successfully suppresses the harmful content.

As the scandal subsides, stakeholder interest in the issue drops. They no longer push the company to engage in content moderation as they did when the scandal was discovered. With less pressure from stakeholders, the company shifts back to its normal operations—focusing on activities that generate profit and giving less attention to trust and safety. Over time, the company's lower investment in moderation enables harmful content to slip back onto the platform. When there is another scandal, the cycle repeats, and the company again begins investing in moderating harmful content.

Corresponding Cycles of Extremist Adaptation

How does the cyclical nature of content moderation shape extremist activity on social media? Recall that militant and hate organizations' online behavior is driven by two considerations: their ability to post "authentic" content that aligns with their core ideology, and their capacity to reach a wide audience. When technology companies' investment in content moderation moves between high and low levels, extremist organizations' payoff from using these platforms varies as well. For simplicity, I'll explain the change in their online activity by focusing on one group's behavior on one platform.

When a social media platform does not invest many resources in restricting harmful content, an extremist group can use it to easily disseminate propaganda to its audiences. Sometimes the group's messaging campaign will inspire real-world harm, such as a violent attack, which will reveal the company's low investment in content moderation and lead to a scandal.

As the platform begins spending resources on content moderation, the group experiences limits on its ability to post content. It may face suspension of its networks of accounts, censorship of the activities that it promotes online, and deletion of the content that it posts on the platform. To survive the restricted phase of the content moderation cycle, the group will engage in the adaptation mechanisms described earlier: migrating to less-moderated platforms to continue its online operations, looking for ways to mobilize support on more lenient platforms, and adapting its messaging strategies to evade moderation.

Over time, as attention to the group's activity on the platform subsides, the group will face fewer restrictions on the content it can post. Thus, it will slowly shift resources back to the platform and start to generate more content and spread its messages more freely. If the platform's continues to pay little attention to content moderation, eventually another scandal will erupt and the cycle will repeat.

Thus, variation in content moderation—across platforms as well as over time—creates a complex online information environment that extremist organizations seek to arbitrage. What I have shown here at a conceptual level (and will illustrate empirically later in this book) is that even though these actors' online activity varies within platforms over time, their adaptation strategies are never limited to a single platform. Extremist organizations' online resilience rests on their ability to operate on different platforms to maximize the authenticity and impact of their messaging campaigns. The choices that they make regarding which platforms to use depend on the structure of the online information environment at different points in time.

Conclusion

So what do these dynamics tell us about the ability of content moderation to prevent online harms? The core idea that emerges from my theoretical framework is that variation in moderation policies across platforms is central to militant and hate groups' adaptation to online regulation. Unlike a single-threshold context, where there is only one standard by which platforms moderate content, a multi-threshold environment allows groups to build digital resilience in the broader online ecosystem. That is, when platforms have different policies for moderating harmful content, dangerous organizations are able to migrate between platforms more easily, mobilize supporters in less-moderated spaces, and adapt their messaging to platforms' moderation thresholds.

From a policymaking standpoint, even though a single-threshold frame-work can be a promising mitigation strategy in theory, it is often unrealistic, as it requires buy-in from a large number of stakeholders. In particular, since government regulators often target large, high-impact platforms, the modera-tion of harmful content on social media ends up being highly uneven: larger platforms facing regulatory pressures invest in content moderation, while smaller, less-regulated platforms are moderated more leniently. This chapter has shown that divergence in content moderation across platforms can em-power the same actors whose activity these policies are trying to combat.

More broadly, this chapter explains why online extremism has remained a problem for our digitally connected societies. Although efforts such as the Christchurch Call to Action led to more cooperation in content moderation across various online platforms (see chapter 7 for a detailed discussion), this trend has started to clash with the growing decentralization of the online eco-system. When social media platforms first emerged in the mid-2000s, only a handful of online spaces offered militant and hate groups the opportunity to reach an audience. In the years since, the number of platforms has increased exponentially. Today nothing prevents those who are unhappy with content moderation to establish new platforms with looser policies, especially as the infrastructure for building online apps continues to improve. As a result, mi-gration, messaging, and mobilization will remain important mechanisms underlying the resilience of militant and hate groups, as well as other danger-ous actors, in the face of future regulation.

3

Regulating Social Media Platforms

WHEN SOCIAL MEDIA BECAME POPULAR during the first decade of the 2000s, many democratic governments viewed it as a technology of liberation.[1] The common view was that the internet could become the new "public square" where anyone could freely express their opinion, engage in debates on various issues of the day, and participate in the marketplace of ideas.[2] Indeed, the ability to express one's opinion on digital media was in sharp contrast to the censorship and restrictions posed on media outlets in nondemocratic countries. Liberal democracies, led by the United States, thus sought to provide legislative protections to internet companies that would allow them to continue offering a free space for public discourse.

However, as online platforms continued to grow in size and reach, many democratic governments started questioning the hands-off approach. In particular, when harassment and hate speech became endemic on social media, terrorist propaganda started inspiring violence around the world, and misinformation began interfering with elections in different countries, democratic governments started pushing for more regulation to ensure that social media platforms promoted the social good—not the bad—and raising several central questions in the process. To what extent should technology companies be held accountable for the content circulating on their sites? What actions should they take to prevent misuse? And can governments mandate what information should be allowed on the internet?

Over the past decade, there have been major changes to the regulatory landscape governing social media platforms around the world. While some countries continued to advocate for the hands-off approach that gave technology companies the freedom to moderate as they wished, others pushed for tighter control over what content could be allowed and what should be removed. In this chapter, I describe different approaches that democracies have taken to regulate harmful content on social media, starting with the United States, which emphasizes platform self-moderation, and continuing with the more hands-on approach taken by European countries before moving to a discussion of social media regulation from a global perspective. I show that when it comes to extremist material online, many democratic governments do not hesitate to mandate strong censorship that goes deep into the specifics of how private companies should moderate content.

National governments are arguably one of the most powerful stakeholders that influence technology companies' content moderation policies. By codifying into law what platforms ought to do with the content shared on their site, governments have an important role in shaping the online information environment. For example, governments decide what type of content is illegal in their countries—decisions that become rules by which any platform seeking to operate in their jurisdiction must abide. Governments can also impose restrictions on legal content that they consider harmful by mandating censorship or other actions against that sort of information. The rules and restrictions that governments place on platforms are becoming increasingly broad, as I show in this chapter.

One particular pattern in the emerging regulation of many governments matters greatly for the digital resilience of extremist organizations. When creating legislation to regulate social media, many governments tend to focus on large, high-impact platforms and to let smaller platforms go largely unchecked. There are various reasons for this differential treatment of platforms, ranging from efforts to lower the barrier to entry into the digital media market to the view that smaller social media sites are inconsequential and therefore do not need to be regulated. The outcome is an uneven moderation landscape in which social media platforms with large user bases have many moderation policies, while smaller platforms do not. This variation in moderation rules, I argue, is what empowers extremist organizations to build resilience to content moderation.

In the following sections, I describe the approach that different democratic governments have taken to regulate harmful content on social media.

The US Approach: Minimize Regulation

American regulation of media and communication technologies can be traced back to the early 1900s with the expansion of radio, telephone, and broadcast communications across the United States. To ensure that these technologies could be made available to all citizens, the US government enacted the Communications Act of 1934, which sought to put under "a single regulatory body" all types of communication that existed at the time.[3] As part of this legislation, the US government established the Federal Communications Commission (FCC) as the body responsible for enforcement.[4]

The FCC was involved in various regulatory actions over the years as it gave broadcasting licenses to radio and TV providers and initiated the breakup of several communication monopolies. But most relevant to our discussion is the FCC's fairness doctrine of 1949, which sought to influence the content of broadcast media. The fairness doctrine had two major components: it required radio and television broadcasters to dedicate airtime to discussion of controversial issues that were important for the public to know about, and it demanded that they do so in a way that allowed for different viewpoints to be aired.[5] The idea was to give American citizens the opportunity to be informed about all sides of the debate on controversial political issues.

But as communication technologies continued to expand, support for the fairness doctrine declined. Some cited its use as a political tool to suppress free speech.[6] Others saw it as unnecessary in a world with many different channels through which people could express their opinions.[7] In 1987, as part of a large deregulatory move by the US government, the FCC abolished the fairness doctrine, calling it an "intrusion by government" that "restricts the journalistic freedom of broadcasters."[8] By putting an end to the fairness doctrine, the FCC sought to give electronic communication technologies the same First Amendment guarantees that were previously given to print media.[9] In the following years, the US government's push for minimal regulation continued through amendments to the Communications Act—in particular, the Telecommunications Act of 1996, which I discuss next.

Limiting the Regulation of the Internet

To understand the American approach to regulating social media, it is important to understand how US legislators generally viewed the regulation of the internet and their approach to addressing harmful content online in particular. When Congress passed the Telecommunications Act of 1996, it believed that in order to allow people to freely connect on the internet, share ideas, and innovate, the government had to protect the services that provided spaces for online speech. This led to the addition of Section 230 to the 1996 Act, which, as many argue, "created the modern internet."[10]

What made internet-based communication different from other forms of media was its sheer size. With rapidly growing connectivity, it became clear to American regulators that companies that provided platforms for online communication would not be able to review every piece of content posted on their sites. "There is no way that any of those [online service providers] . . . can take the responsibility to edit out information that is going to be coming in to them from all manner of sources. . . . We are talking about something that is far larger than our daily newspaper. We are talking about something that is going to be thousands of pages of information every day," said Representative Bob Goodlatte in a congressional hearing about the proposed law.[11]

To facilitate the growth of the internet while guarding against harmful content, the US government sought to incentivize private companies to moderate content on their own. American regulators opposed government involvement in the moderation of harmful content, for both ideological and practical reasons. "We do not wish to have content regulation by the Federal Government of what is on the Internet," said Christopher Cox, one of the authors of Section 230. "The fact of the matter is that the Internet operates worldwide, and not even a Federal Internet censorship army would give our Government the power to keep offensive material out," added his colleague, Ron Wyden, when Congress was about to vote on the new regulation.[12]

To incentivize internet companies to offer their services and self-moderate harmful content, the US government included two important provisions in Section 230 that facilitated the evolution of platform-led content moderation as we know it today. The first stated that providers of "interactive computer services"—which included social media companies—could not be held responsible for content posted by others on their site. In other words, if someone posted (legal) content that was deemed offensive by others, the platform hosting the content was not the party to blame. The idea behind this rule was the view that online service providers were not publishers that edited the content posted on their sites; they simply provided a platform for others to publish. Thus, US regulators decided that if content posted on these companies' platforms was considered offensive, the original poster should be held liable.

The second provision sought to encourage internet companies to take the initiative to moderate harmful content on their own. According to this rule, if platforms wished to create moderation policies, they were free to do so without being sued for their content removal decisions. The goal was to incentivize the private sector to create new solutions to remove or block harmful content online without being worried about lawsuits. "Ironically, the existing legal system provides a massive disincentive for the people who might best help us control the Internet to do so," said Cox.[13] "We want to encourage [technology companies] to do everything possible . . . [to remove] offensive material for their customers."[14]

Section 230 and the Telecommunications Act facilitated rapid growth in internet use in the following three decades. In 1995, a year before the act passed, there were about 40 million internet users worldwide.[15] In 2023, this number rose to 5.18 billion, including 4.8 billion social media users.[16] The freedom that the law gave internet companies to host user-generated content led to the largest growth in digital media and communication technologies that the world has ever seen.

Technology Companies' Self-Moderation of Harmful Content

But with size comes responsibility. As social media platforms continued to grow, they also became hosts to large amounts of harmful, extremist, and violent content. Thus, technology companies, especially large platforms like Facebook, Twitter, and YouTube, began experiencing pressure from regulators to increase their self-moderation of harmful content. For example, after the terrorist attacks in Paris and in San Bernadino, California—which were perpetrated by individuals inspired by Islamic State propaganda—top security officials from the Obama administration met with these companies' representatives to discuss how they could do a better job of preventing violent organizations from using the internet for radicalization and recruitment.[17] The idea was not to tell companies how to moderate content, but to ask them to help "make it harder for terrorists to use technology."[18]

Platforms like Facebook and Twitter were initially reluctant to take action against extremist material online, even though they knew it existed on their platforms and some even argue that they allowed and encouraged it.[19] But they began to shift their approach after it became widely known that violent organizations were exploiting their services to promote real-world harm.[20]

Thus, they designed new rules that banned violent and extremist actors from operating on their sites and developed sophisticated moderation systems to remove their content. Facebook, for example, significantly expanded its counterterrorism team, developed extensive policies to combat the activities of dangerous organizations, and began experimenting with new AI-based tools to moderate extremist and violent material.[21] In a blog post published in June 2017 on the company's website, Monika Bickert, the head of global policy management at Facebook, and Brian Fishman, who at the time was the company's counterterrorism policy manager, stated:

> We agree with those who say that social media should not be a place where terrorists have a voice. . . . There's no place on Facebook for terrorism. We remove terrorists and posts that support terrorism whenever we become aware of them. When we receive reports of potential terrorism posts, we review those reports urgently and with scrutiny. . . . We are currently focusing our most cutting edge techniques to combat terrorist content about ISIS, Al Qaeda and their affiliates, and we expect to expand to other terrorist organizations in due course.[22]

The efforts of large technology companies to combat extremist content online were significant. Between 2017 and 2023, over 250 million pieces of content related to dangerous organizations were removed from Facebook and Instagram.[23] Almost six million posts linked to terrorism and violent extremism were removed from Twitter between 2018 and 2021.[24] And over three million videos promoting extremist propaganda were banned from YouTube during the same time period.[25]

But companies did not stop there. As time went on, mainstream social media platforms continued to expand their policies to moderate harmful content, adding new actors, behaviors, and types of content to the list of banned categories. One of the most significant expansions of these companies' policies against hate and extremism took place in 2019 and 2020, after a series of terrorist attacks by individuals supporting white supremacist ideology used their platforms to advertise their violent acts. During this period, many large social media companies moved beyond moderating jihadi extremist organizations to banning white supremacist groups as well. "We've been taking a close look at our approach towards hateful content," said the YouTube team in an update posted on the company's website. "Today, we're taking another step . . . by specifically prohibiting videos alleging that a group is superior in order to justify discrimination, segregation or exclusion."[26] In making similar policy changes, Twitter stated that the company's "primary focus is on addressing the risks of offline harm," and that it would continue to develop its rules "in response to changing behaviors and challenges."[27]

Self-moderation by large technology companies of extremist content became much more expansive than what was legally required by many democratic governments. As Fishman explained, "Perhaps counterintuitively, [Meta, which owns Facebook] has a far more aggressive policy approach toward white supremacist organizations than any western government."[28] Thus, three decades after it was enacted, Section 230 of the Telecommunications Act continued to enable internet companies to take action against harmful content on their sites.

Calls to Reform Section 230

But the hands-off approach to the regulation of social media platforms did not go uncontested. When harmful content continued to circulate on social media—even as technology companies expanded their content moderation policies—political actors from both sides of the aisle began calling to reform, update, or even repeal Section 230.

American legislators' reasons for expanding the regulation of social media varied between the left and the right. Democratic legislators said that more regulation was needed because large technology companies were not doing enough to moderate extremism and misinformation. Calls for regulation increased after the January 6, 2021, attack on the US Capitol, which was organized and publicized in large part on social media platforms.[29] "Congress . . . must prioritize taking swift and bold action on reforming Section 230," said Congresswoman Anna Eshoo a few days after the attack. "These companies have shown they won't do the right thing on their own."[30] Others agreed, saying that in order to prevent harms such as the Capitol attack, Congress needed to make changes to Section 230.[31]

Democratic lawmakers in the United States were also concerned about the ease with which extremist organizations could use social media to plan violence and spread hate speech. In bills proposed in California and New York, legislators sought to require social media companies to create frameworks for people to report hate speech in order to prevent real-world violence. One such bill passed in New York in June 2022 as part of a broader effort to curb gun violence in the state. "The racist domestic terrorist who murdered 10 innocent Black New Yorkers in a Buffalo supermarket was radicalized online in an environment where hate speech is encouraged," said New York state senator Anna Kaplan.[32] Sticking to the hands-off approach, she said: "We are not in any way telling social media what policy to put in. . . . It's about just empowering the users to be able to report hateful content."[33]

Although many bills were proposed by US lawmakers in Congress, no formal action was taken at the federal level.[34] President Biden also called for bipartisan legislation to "hold Big Tech accountable" in an op-ed he published in the *Wall Street Journal* in January 2023. Biden said that Republicans and Democrats needed to come together to reform Section 230 to make sure that large social media platforms were held responsible for the algorithms they used to spread harmful content online.[35]

On the right side of the political spectrum, however, the reasoning was very different. Republican legislators who called for social media regulation believed that technology companies moderated too much content and that their policies were biased against conservative viewpoints. During his time as president, Donald Trump sought to repeal Section 230 through various bills and executive orders that would limit companies' legal protections if they did not moderate content neutrally.[36] Other Republican lawmakers pushed for similar legislation, calling large technology platforms "the single biggest threat to free speech and democracy."[37] They sought to advance laws that would allow American citizens to sue companies for censoring political speech.[38]

At the state level, the most notable regulations came in bills that were passed by Republican legislators in Florida and Texas in 2021; they prohibited social media companies from deplatforming political candidates and removing posts based on their expressed views. Regulators argued that social media companies should not be protected under Section 230 but instead should be viewed as "common carriers," since they provided communication services to the general public.[39] Thus, these state laws held, social media platforms, just like telephone and cellular companies, could not discriminate in their moderation on the basis of content.[40] Both laws were contested in American courts by technology companies and, at the time of writing, had yet to be implemented.

American Regulators' Focus on Large Platforms

Despite calls to update or reform Section 230, the law has remained an important pillar protecting technology companies' right to decide how to manage content on their own. Although American lawmakers did not directly tell social media companies how to moderate content, they nonetheless put informal pressure on them to take a more serious stance against harmful material online. Indeed, as individuals who worked on the trust and safety teams of social media platforms admit, government pressure was what motivated their companies to invest resources in moderating harmful content, and what made their efforts more comprehensive than they would have been otherwise.[41]

Interestingly, however, the US government's focus has almost always been on the very large mainstream platforms. Even as early as the 2010s, when it became clear that technology companies needed to do more to combat misinformation and extremism, the focus of legislators was on the largest platforms—Facebook, Instagram, Twitter, and YouTube.[42] For example, when US lawmakers started calling for more social media regulation, they almost always talked about "Big Tech." In congressional hearings about online harms, such as "Disinformation Nation: Social Media's Role in Promoting Extremism and Misinformation, or the "Hearing on Social Media Influence in the 2016 United States Elections," only executives of large companies were invited.[43] Even the bills recently passed in Florida and Texas to regulate social media explicitly targeted large platforms with many millions of monthly active users.[44]

The US government's focus on platforms with large user bases facilitated the creation of an uneven moderation landscape of harmful content in the broader online ecosystem: while large mainstream platforms were often pressured by lawmakers to do more moderation, smaller platforms were not. In the next section, I show that a similar focus on large platforms can be found in recent regulations by European countries, which, unlike the United States, took a more restrictive approach to the regulation of online content.

The European Hands-On Approach to Social Media Regulation

Content regulation in Europe has several historical starting points. More recent technological developments surrounding the internet have increased calls for a more stringent approach, but in fact the story largely begins in the 1930s with Nazi Germany. As Anu Bradford explains in her recent book on European regulation: "The EU's stand against hate speech is best understood in light of its history of racist and xenophobic violence, including most predominantly the incitement of hatred by the Nazis against the Jews leading up to World War II."[45] This historical underpinning contributed to a very different approach to the regulation of social media in many European countries, which stressed in their legislation that freedom of expression must be balanced against the need to curtail speech that incites hatred, violence, and intolerance.[46]

Germany's Network Enforcement Act

The Network Enforcement Act (NetzDG), which passed in the German parliament in 2017, stands out as one of the more stringent regulations targeting social media companies in recent years.[47] The law was the first of its kind, not only because it significantly increased technology companies' liability for hosting harmful content, but also because it specified, in great detail, how platforms should moderate content.[48]

Even before NetzDG, Germany already had strict laws on what it considered to be acceptable speech. In the late 1950s, German lawmakers passed several regulations that made it illegal to distribute content inciting hate on the basis of nationality, religion, or ethnicity. The laws were, in large part, a response to the country's experience with Nazism and authoritarianism, which had flourished in previous decades partly because of the free circulation of incendiary propaganda and racist content in the country.[49] Over time, evolving modes of communication—in particular, the rise of social media—led German lawmakers to question whether the country's existing hate speech regulations were sufficient to combat online harms.[50]

The most notable increase in hateful rhetoric in Germany took place in 2015, after nearly 1.4 million migrants arrived in the country as a result of the Syrian civil war. While Chancellor Angela Merkel's decision to open Germany's borders was initially met with public support, resentment over migration resulted in a dramatic increase in hate speech.[51] Various social media platforms were soon flooded with the xenophobic voices of citizens who believed that German politicians had let too many foreigners into the country.[52] Far-right extremist organizations began to flourish in this environment and became more active in organizing anti-immigration protests throughout the country and used social media to inspire violence against refugees.[53] Between 2015 and 2017, over three thousand anti-refugee hate incidents were reported in Germany.[54]

The growth in hate speech and intolerance, particularly on social media, greatly concerned German lawmakers, who looked for ways to induce technology companies to take a more serious stance against hateful and racist content. Their dissatisfaction with companies' moderation practices stemmed from the finding that companies did not adequately respond to reports of harmful speech on their platforms. Germany's justice minister wrote to Facebook's public policy director in the summer of 2015 to say that German citizens who used Facebook were "complaining increasingly that [Facebook] is not effectively stopping racist 'posts' and comments despite their pointing out concrete examples."[55] The company said that it took his letter seriously, and in a statement its spokesperson emphasized that "there is no room for racism on Facebook" and that the company's representatives would meet with the justice minister to make sure that Facebook users were protected from abuse.[56]

A few months after this exchange, the German government launched an initiative for "dealing with illegal hate speech on the Internet" that included a task force to help combat harmful content on social media.[57] The task force included members of the German government and representatives from civil society organizations as well as Facebook, YouTube, and Twitter.[58] Through the task force, German lawmakers sought to incentivize companies to self-moderate harmful content by creating mechanisms and a set of commitments to ensure "sustainable and effective handling" of harmful content online.[59]

In December 2015, the task force published a paper, "Together against Hate Messages," which consisted of several concrete commitments that the three companies had voluntarily made to remove hateful content. These included an agreement to respect German law about what constituted illegal content, remove messages reported to them within twenty-four hours, and improve their mechanisms for user reporting of harmful content.[60]

Several months after the publication of the task force paper, the German government initiated an audit study of companies' compliance with their commitments. The results were not great. In a September 2016 press release, German lawmakers said that the three companies were not doing enough to combat harmful content reported to them by users. Among six hundred reports of harmful content, Facebook deleted or blocked about 46 percent, YouTube about 10 percent, and Twitter only 1 percent.[61] "The spread of hate crime is becoming an ever-greater threat to the democratic culture of debate online," said Germany's justice minister. "No company should allow its services to be misused to spread criminal hatred, racism, anti-Semitism, or Islamist terrorist fantasies. . . . The biggest problem is that the platforms do not take user complaints seriously."[62]

With voluntary mechanisms doing little to curb the spread of harmful content online, the German government began drafting the Network Enforcement Act in March 2017. German government officials used the findings from the audit study to justify more hands-on legislative action, with Germany's justice minister affirming that the big stick of the law was the only way to fight the scourge of harmful content on social media.[63]

According to the Network Enforcement Act, technology companies were required to remove or block "content that is manifestly unlawful within 24 hours of receiving the complaint."[64] For content that was not "manifestly unlawful" but still "unlawful," platforms were required to remove or block access within seven days.[65] If the companies failed to comply with these obligations, they could be fined up to fifty million euros.[66] The regulation also included a reporting obligation for social media companies that received more than one hundred complaints per year: they were required to publish half-yearly German-language reports that cataloged and detailed their handling of complaints.[67]

German regulators used the German Criminal Code's preexisting definitions of offenses to define "unlawful content," which included the dissemination of the propaganda material of "unconstitutional organizations," preparation of violence, and incitement of hate.[68] However, beyond referencing the Criminal Code, the regulation did not define any other offenses and made no distinction between "manifestly unlawful" and "unlawful" material. Some have argued that this ambiguity provided platforms with significant discretionary power, since "one would need to know and practice (national) criminal law and consider the context of the generated content" to sufficiently evaluate complaints.[69]

While the NetzDG was easily passed in the German parliament, it has been considered very controversial, particularly among those who worry that it violates freedom of speech. "Governments and the public have valid concerns about the proliferation of illegal or abusive content online," said the director of Human Rights Watch in Germany. "But the new German law is fundamentally flawed. . . . [It] turns private companies into overzealous censors to avoid steep fines, leaving users with no judicial oversight or right to appeal."[70] Beyond concerns about over-censorship, others argued that the law was not very "user friendly"—that is, it did not make it easy for people to report harmful content.[71] Others argued that the regulation was misaligned with other European countries because it took a "solo" approach—that is, Germany-only—rather than "seeking a European solution."[72]

Despite these concerns, German lawmakers viewed the regulation as necessary to combat online harms in Germany. As the justice minister explained in a statement, regulators viewed the law not as "a limitation, but a prerequisite for freedom of expression."[73] The government's view was that tighter control over technology companies' content moderation practices would ensure that German citizens could express their opinion freely "without being insulted or threatened."[74]

FOCUS ON MAINSTREAM PLATFORMS

But the NetzDG did not apply to all online platforms. Just like their American counterparts, Germany's regulators focused primarily on large social media companies. Since platforms were exempt from the NetzDG's obligations if they had less than two million registered users in Germany, the regulation mainly applied to Facebook, Twitter, and YouTube.

In response to the new regulation, these companies took steps to enhance their content moderation standards, including creating new mechanisms to report harmful content and hiring more moderators with particular understanding of Germany. YouTube published a statement in December 2017 that it would significantly expand both its content moderation team and its tools to automatically detect harmful content on its platform. "In the last year, we took actions to protect our community against violent or extremist content, testing new systems to combat emerging and evolving threats," said Susan Wojcicki, the company's CEO. "Our goal is to stay one step ahead of bad actors, making it harder for policy-violating content to surface or remain on YouTube."[75]

Facebook similarly expanded its content moderation teams in Germany, opening new centers and hiring more moderators to monitor content that might violate the NetzDG. Particular attention was given to hateful content targeting refugees. According to Facebook employees who moderated content in Germany, the "change was made so that hate speech against refugees could be reviewed and deleted."[76] In 2018, Twitter explained in its first transparency report addressing the new regulation how it was handling complaints "regarding specific allegedly unlawful content in Germany" and said that it had mobilized more than 50 employees to handle complaints related to the Network Enforcement Act. In a subsequent report in June 2021, the company said that it had expanded this team to over 150 employees.[77]

Thus, the Network Enforcement Act's regulatory pressure on these platforms led them to invest more in content moderation. To avoid large fines, Facebook, Twitter, and YouTube made efforts to remove harmful content that they might have not made without the German regulation.

Social Media Regulation in Other European Countries

Germany's Network Enforcement Act had a significant influence on other European countries, which sought to enact similar laws to exert influence on technology companies' content moderation policies. Austria, for example, passed a new law in January 2021 to combat harmful content on social media. The Austrian Communication Platforms Act (KoPl-G) mimicked, almost word for word, the German regulation. Just like the NetzDG, the KoPl-G targeted large platforms (those with over one hundred thousand users in Austria) and required that harmful content be taken down within twenty-four hours of notification.[78] The French government was also inspired by the German regulation, and a similar approach was taken by the European Union in its emerging Digital Services Act.

FRANCE'S AVIA LAW

In May 2020, France passed a new regulation called the Avia Law to combat harmful content on the internet. Whereas the NetzDG in Germany emerged largely out of a need to tackle anti-immigration speech, the legislative impetus for the Avia Law in France was far more personal: National Assembly member Laetitia Avia—the principal sponsor and namesake of the law—argued for its exigency based on her own experiences of being harassed online. In proposing the regulation, Avia made an argument that would later be key to the resulting legislation: "We cannot tolerate on the internet what we won't tolerate in the street."[79] (This rationale would later be used by the European Commission president to justify the European Union's Digital Services Act: the DSA "gives practical effect to the principle that what is illegal offline, should be illegal online."[80])

Even before the new law was enacted, France already had several regulations targeting harmful content on social media. In November 2014, for instance, France passed a counterterrorism bill that gave the Central Office for the Fight Against Crime Related to Information and Communication Technology the administrative authority to ask "editors and hosts to remove content that incites or apologizes for terrorism."[81] In November 2015, after the Islamic State's attacks in Paris killed 130 people and injured close to 500 others, the French government declared a state of emergency that gave the interior minister the power to block websites, including social media platforms, in order to prevent the dissemination of content that "glorifies or incites acts of terrorism."[82]

The Avia Law thus emerged in a context where the French government was already taking a "hands-on" approach to content moderation. The original version of the law, which was adopted on May 13, 2020, resembled the German regulation in many ways. It stated that online platforms had to "render inaccessible," within twenty-four hours of notification, any content that violated France's laws against hate speech, sexual violence, or harassment, among other crimes.[83] The law also required that terrorist content be removed within one hour of notification. If platforms failed to take these actions, they could face fines of up to twenty million euros.[84]

In addition, just like their German counterparts, France's regulators targeted large social media platforms. According to the regulation, only sites that surpassed a certain metric of monthly usership within France would be subject to its provisions. The precise number, though set to be determined at a later date, was likely to have been "somewhere between 2 and 5 million French users per month."[85]

The majority of the law's provisions, however, were never fully realized. On May 18, 2020, just five days after its adoption, senators from the party Les Républicains submitted a prepromulgation challenge of the law to France's Constitutional Council.[86] On June 18, the council released its verdict: striking down many of the law's provisions, it ultimately ruled that the regulation "brought an attack on the freedom of expression and communication which is not appropriate, necessary and proportionate to the aim pursued."[87] In other words, the council agreed with the bill's opponents that the aspects of the law requiring platforms to remove content on very short notice were unconstitutional and harmful to freedom of expression.[88]

Despite the council's ruling, France's debate around online content regulation did not lose momentum. On October 16, 2020, a French schoolteacher was decapitated by an eighteen-year-old Chechen refugee in what President Emmanuel Macron called an "Islamist terrorist attack."[89] Although the attack certainly represented France's struggle to adequately respond to militant Islamism on a broader level, French anti-terrorism prosecutors also identified a "direct causal link" between the killing and a social media campaign.[90] MP Laetitia Avia highlighted this relationship, saying in an interview: "The one who is responsible for this attack is the terrorist, it's not the platforms who are responsible. However, they played a part and we cannot deny the part they played."[91]

Having just had her own legislative solution almost entirely struck down by the Constitutional Council, Avia further expressed her hope that legislation at the EU level would be ambitious and impose stronger regulations on platforms, reasoning that "we need to make sure that every European country has laws that apply there."[92] Věra Jourová, the European Commission vice president, echoed this sentiment: "Hate knows no borders. We need to respond to it together, in a European way."[93]

THE EUROPEAN UNION'S APPROACH TO SOCIAL MEDIA REGULATION

Although France's unsuccessful attempt at passing content moderation legislation may have inspired calls for action at the European Union level, it is important to note that the EU's regulatory framework was already quite robust and had considerable momentum by the summer of 2020. On May 31, 2016, for instance, the European Commission and the largest technology companies— Facebook, Twitter, YouTube, and Microsoft—released a collaborative Code of Conduct on illegal online hate speech in an effort to "respond to the challenge of ensuring that online platforms do not offer opportunities for illegal online hate speech to spread virally."[94] The agreement, though not legislatively binding, required companies to address requests for removal of harmful content in less than twenty-four hours, as well as increase their users' awareness of their content moderation guidelines.[95]

Two years later, on September 12, 2018, the European Commission presented a proposal for a regulation on preventing the dissemination of terrorist content online. The proposal, which would ultimately evolve into the EU's most recent Terrorism Regulation (TERREG), included a "one-hour rule" that required platforms to address government removal requests within one hour of notification. They were also obligated to take proactive steps to ensure that their platforms were not misused by terrorist groups seeking to disseminate content on their sites and also to create mechanisms for strengthening platforms' cooperation with European state governments, among other provisions.[96]

The proposal was critiqued by human rights organizations, which were concerned about its vague definition of terrorism and its potential to harm freedom of expression.[97] Thus, the EU Parliament and the Constitutional Council included certain exceptions for journalistic, artistic, and educational information and agreed to align the definition of terrorist content with the EU Directive on combating terrorism.[98]

The final version of the TERREG, which entered into force on June 6, 2021, gave European Union member states authority to issue removal requests to technology companies that would apply in all EU jurisdictions, and it required companies to remove reported content within one hour of a removal order. The regulation went even further by requiring social media platforms to include in their terms of service "provisions to address the misuse of [their] services for the dissemination to the public of terrorist content."[99] This opened the door for European governments to influence platforms' moderation policies in a more direct way.

When crafting these provisions, EU legislators had in mind the March 15, 2019, attack in Christchurch, New Zealand. That attack, which resulted in the death of fifty-one individuals and the injury of forty others, was livestreamed by the perpetrator on Facebook.[100] For example, Margaritis Schinas, the vice president of the European Commission's program "Promoting Our European Way of Life," explained that "with these landmark new rules, [the EU is] cracking down on the proliferation of terrorist content online and making the EU's Security Union a reality" in an effort to ensure that "attacks like the one in Christchurch cannot be used to pollute screens and minds."[101]

The TERREG, however, was just a precursor to a much larger and more ambitious piece of content regulation in Europe: the Digital Services Act (DSA). Whereas the TERREG specifically targeted content relating to terrorism, the DSA package (which included both the DSA and the Digital Markets Act) had broader aims. These included creating a "safer digital space" in Europe and creating opportunities for innovation and growth among businesses operating in Europe and beyond.[102] In the words of the European Commission president, the goal was to ensure that the online information environment in Europe "remains a safe space, safeguarding freedom of expression and opportunities for digital businesses."[103]

An important aspect of the DSA, which started applying to all regulated entities in February 2024, was the way in which its rules distinguished between platform sizes. European regulators' view was that "very large online platforms" (VLOPs) should be more responsible for harmful content than smaller platforms, because of the greater risk they posed with their broader reach across society.[104] "With the DSA, the time of big online platforms behaving like they are 'too big to care' is coming to an end," said Thierry Breton, the EU commissioner for internal market. "The DSA is setting clear, harmonised obligations for platforms—proportionate to size, impact and risk," he added.[105]

While very large platforms were subject to many obligations—including requirements related to content moderation practices, user reporting, and risk management mitigation plans—smaller platforms had fewer obligations under the DSA (see table 3.1). The regulation defined very large platforms as those with more than 45 million monthly active users in the European Union. Facebook, Instagram, LinkedIn, Pinterest, Snapchat, TikTok, Twitter, YouTube, and several others were all considered VLOPs.[106]

The EU's focus on very large platforms was not driven solely by the view that these platforms posed greater risk. It was also a product of the second aim of the DSA Package to promote the activity of small digital businesses in Europe. As explained by Henna Virkkunen, rapporteur for the opinion of the Committee on Industry, Research, and Energy:

It is important for European businesses, especially for our SMEs [small and micro-enterprises], that we ensure a level playing field and fair competition and make sure that European values and legislation are respected in the online world . . . we must ensure that the smallest enterprises are not faced with excessively heavy administrative burdens. Therefore, . . . we also introduced various exemptions for small and micro-enterprises.[107]

The EU's reasoning for differentiating its rules on the basis of platform size related to the view that smaller companies would not be able to thrive if burdened with heavy regulatory obligations, while larger social media platforms—which were already perceived as posing greater risks—were able to bear such burdens.[108]

Table 3.1 shows how the DSA's rules varied with platform size. Although some regulations applied to all online platforms—such as the requirement to include information on content moderation policies in the terms of service (article 12) and provide annual transparency reports detailing content moderation actions (article 13)—the vast majority of the provisions applied only to larger platforms, including the requirement to put in place measures to protect against misuse (article 20) and the obligation to engage in risk assessments to evaluate the risks of content moderation systems (article 26). Thus, like other regulations in Europe, the Digital Services Act exempted small social media companies from most requirements to moderate harmful content. Regulators paid less attention to smaller platforms' content moderation activities because they had more limited resources and were viewed as posing a lower risk.

And indeed, government pressure on large technology companies seems to have been effective at prompting more content moderation. As the example of the NetzDG in Germany shows, regulation motivated large platforms to invest resources in the moderation of harmful content. However, since governments' pressure focused mainly on the larger companies, the result was an uneven moderation landscape in the broader online ecosystem. As I show in the following chapters, this variation in content moderation across platforms of different sizes has become an important facilitator of the digital resilience of extremist and violent actors, who were able to take advantage of different content moderation policies across platforms to build resistance to moderation.

Social Media Regulation in a Global Perspective

The American and European approaches to the regulation of harmful content on social media varied greatly, but they did have many similarities in the way they focused on large platforms. What do regulatory trends look like when we considering a broader range of countries? Analyzing social media regulation globally can be tricky, as different countries define harmful content in different ways. For example, some governments may decide that content that can inspire real-world violent activity constitutes an online harm, while others may

TABLE 3.1: The Digital Services Act's Provisions, by Platform Size

	All Providers of Intermediary Services	Providers of Hosting Services, Including Online Platforms	Medium to Large Online Platforms	Very Large Online Platforms
Article 10: Points of contact	■	■	■	■
Article 11: Legal representatives	■	■	■	■
Article 12: Terms and conditions	■	■	■	■
Article 13: Transparency reporting	■	■	■	■
Article 14: Notice and action mechanisms		■	■	■
Article 15: Statement of reasons		■	■	■
Article 17: Internal complaint-handling system			■	■
Article 18: Out-of-court dispute settlement			■	■
Article 19: Trusted flaggers			■	■
Article 20: Measures and protection against misuse			■	■
Article 21: Notification of suspicions of criminal offenses			■	■
Article 22: Traceability of traders			■	■
Article 23: Transparency reporting			■	■
Article 24: Online advertising transparency			■	■
Article 26: Risk assessment				■
Article 27: Mitigation of risks				■
Article 28: Independent audit				■
Article 29: Recommender systems				■
Article 30: Additional online advertising transparency				■
Article 31: Data access and scrutiny				■
Article 32: Compliance officers				■
Article 33: Transparency reporting (VLOPs)				■

Source: Husovec 2023; European Commission 2020.

Note: I assembled this table from a review of each of these articles of the DSA. Gray shading indicates that a provision applies to a platform. Medium-to-large online platforms include companies with more than fifty employees or turnover below ten million euros. Very large online platforms include those with more than forty-five million monthly active users in the European Union.

define harm as anything that threatens the social order or the stability of the (undemocratic) regime. The definition of harms is thus closely tied to other aspects of a country, including its regime type, levels of media freedom, and openness to the internet more generally. Furthermore, governments' desire for regulation may be related to a perception that platforms based in other countries—such as US companies—are "invading" their country and governing speech without their influence. Thus, regulation may reflect an effort by these governments to reassert power over their own jurisdictions.

In this section, I examine governments' regulation of social media platforms by taking their definition of harmful content as given. My goal is to document how many countries seek to exert influence on social media platforms' content moderation through regulation, and to gauge the extent to which their laws discriminate on the basis of platform size in applying the rules.

To do this, I created a country-level dataset that documented legislation by national governments that imposed rules on what technology companies ought to do to remove harmful or illegal content—as defined by the government. To ensure that the cases are comparable, I focused only on regulations that seek to induce technology companies to moderate content on their own platform. That is, I excluded regulations that expand the government's authority to block content, shut down websites, or restrict the internet more generally and focused instead on those aiming at put pressure on platforms to self-moderate harmful content. (See the appendix for more details on the countries and regulations included in the dataset.)

For countries that passed legislation to regulate social media, I also examined whether the regulations had provisions that differentiated between platforms on the basis of their size. These often looked like thresholds based on the number of active users in the country's jurisdiction, the size of the company in terms of the number of its employees, or its overall revenue. My goal was to see whether the patterns that I found in the regulation of social media companies by European countries—which exempted smaller platforms from many of their legislation's requirements—extended to other parts of the world.

I gathered the data by conducting country-specific research on social media regulation and consulting Freedom House and Human Rights Watch reports that documented restrictions on the media as well as other reports on social media regulation, such as the Online Regulation Series by Tech Against Terrorism.[109] To examine how regulation varied depending on country-level

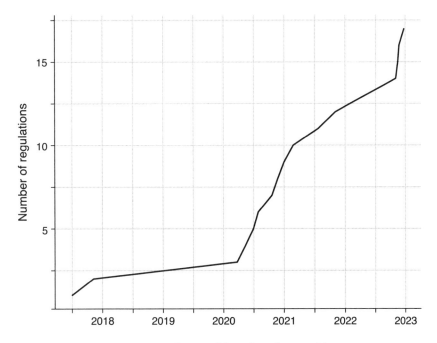

FIGURE 3.1. Government Regulation of Social Media over Time
Note: The figure shows the cumulative number of government regulations that impose rules on social media platforms' self-moderation of harmful content.

characteristics, such as regime type and media freedom more generally, I also used cross-national data from the Varieties of Democracy (V-Dem) project to measure these variables.[110]

Overall, I found that 47 countries had legislation, or were in the process of passing legislation, to regulate harmful content on social media. These included laws such as the NetzDG in Germany, the Avia Law in France, or the European Union's DSA (which applied in 27 EU Member States), as well as many other laws such as Australia's 2021 Online Safety Bill, New Zealand's 2021 Films, Videos and Publications Classification Amendment Bill, and Singapore's Online Safety Act of 2022. Figure 3.1 shows the trend in the number of regulations over time. After Germany passed the Network Enforcement Act in June 2017, many other countries followed with their own regulations. This trend increased since 2020, and the number of regulations is likely to grow given ongoing legislation by other countries.

I further examined whether the existing regulations differentiated their rules on the basis of platform size. Figure 3.2 shows the number of countries

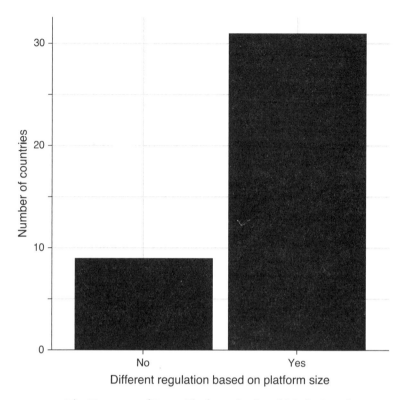

FIGURE 3.2. The Targeting of Large Platforms by Social Media Regulation
Note: The figure shows the number of countries whose regulation of social media differentiates between large and small platforms.

that placed similar responsibilities on all platforms, regardless of the number of their users, as well as those that had regulations exempting smaller platforms from most of their laws' obligations. I find that many countries put more regulatory burdens on platforms with larger user bases, while giving more leeway to smaller sites. For example, the United Kingdom's Online Safety Act, which passed in October 2023, determines that regulated social media services are those that have "a significant number of United Kingdom users."[111] India's 2021 Intermediary Guidelines and Digital Media Ethics Code differentiates between "social media intermediaries" and "significant social media intermediaries" with more than five million users in India; the latter are subject to additional obligations.[112] These patterns mirror my findings from the previous sections that social media regulation by national governments tends to focus mostly on the largest online sites.

Since my focus is on regulations that seek to induce technology companies to self-moderate harmful content (as opposed to increasing governments' power over the media), my coding is likely to capture legislation in more democratic countries. That is, while authoritarian regimes have increased their control over the media—including social media—through laws and regulations that restrict media freedom, democratic governments seeking to restrict harmful content online have opted for regulations that, at least on paper, aim to protect freedom of expression.[113]

I examined the distribution of regulations by regime type by counting the number of countries that passed social media regulations for each of four types of governments, using the Varieties of Democracy's "Regimes of the World" variable. This measure classifies countries into one of four regime types, based on the "competitiveness of access to power" and other liberal principles.[114]

Table 3.2 shows variation by regime type in regulations aiming to pressure technology companies to self-moderate harmful content. As mentioned earlier, the variable "Regulates social media platforms" (in the rows) excludes legislation that gives national governments more power to control the internet or the media more generally. In other words, it does not include rules that authorize governments to block websites or shut down the internet and focuses instead on regulations that seek to induce social media platforms to moderate harmful content on their own (see appendix for details). I find that the majority of the new legislation is concentrated in electoral and liberal democracies, with some regulation of social media, as defined earlier, occurring in nondemocratic countries. The latter include Ethiopia's Hate Speech and Disinformation Prevention and Suppression Proclamation, which calls for social media platforms to remove content promoting hate speech within twenty-four hours.[115] Also included is Pakistan's Citizens Protection (Against Online Harm) Rules, which require platforms to take down or prevent the dissemination of extremist content deemed harmful by the government.[116]

I find similar patterns when examining variation in social media regulation by the level of a country's freedom of expression: 77 percent of the countries with social media regulation are those that respect press and media freedom, allow their citizens to freely talk about politics in the public sphere, and ensure academic and cultural expression.[117] This illustrates the growing desire by democratic governments to put more restrictions on internet platforms— changes that reflect lawmakers' view that these companies need to take more proactive action to combat harmful content on the internet.

TABLE 3.2: Social Media Regulation, by Regime Type

		Closed Autocracy	Electoral Autocracy	Electoral Democracy	Liberal Democracy
Regulates social media platforms	No	28	44	43	12
	Yes	3	8	11	18

Conclusion

This chapter illustrates the important role that national governments play in influencing content moderation decisions by social media platforms. Although governments are not the only stakeholder that companies consider when designing their content moderation policies, they are certainly a central one. Throughout the chapter, I illustrated the process that leads lawmakers to regulate social media platforms and showed the important effect of government pressure on platforms' investment in moderation.

I also showed how governments tend to focus in particular on large social media sites, and I explained how this uneven pressure facilitates an information environment in which large platforms adopt significantly more restrictive content moderation policies than do smaller platforms, which are subject to less regulation. In the next chapter, I analyze the content moderation policies of over sixty social media platforms to show that the size of the platform is indeed a strong predictor of more restrictive content moderation. I further show that variation in content policies among platforms of different sizes has an unintended consequence when it comes to online extremism: it enables militant and hate organizations to build resilience to content moderation in the broader online ecosystem.

4

Adapting to Moderation through Migration

We have to make sure we connect over several platforms so if one goes down, we have the next to move to.

—ISLAMIC STATE MEMBER, QUOTED IN AMARNATH AMARASINGAM, SHIRAZ MAHER, AND CHARLIE WINTER, "HOW TELEGRAM DISRUPTION IMPACTS JIHADIST PLATFORM MIGRATION," JANUARY 8, 2021, 27

[We're] *way* ahead of the game and have already been using other means of mediums for recruitment. [Deplatforming] will not stop us one bit.

—PROUD BOYS MEMBER, QUOTED IN JULIA CARRIE WONG, "TWITTER SUSPENDS PROUD BOYS ON EVE OF DEADLY UNITE THE RIGHT RALLY ANNIVERSARY," *GUARDIAN*, AUGUST 10, 2018

WHEN SOCIAL MEDIA PLATFORMS place bans on militant organizations— removing their content, suspending their accounts, and blocking their efforts to spread propaganda—these actors need to identify alternative spaces from which to reach audiences on the internet. Divergence in content moderation across platforms creates fruitful opportunities for migration. A large body of research in both policy and academia has pointed to the problem of the "whack-a-mole"—when social media accounts affiliated with extremist organizations are taken down, they often reappear on other sites.[1] But a closer look shows that migration between platforms is not arbitrary. The migration decisions of banned organizations are driven by their strategic efforts to build digital resilience. Thus, actors who face moderation gravitate to platforms of a particular kind: those that have less restrictive moderation policies, but that also reach a sufficiently large audience.

In this chapter, I empirically demonstrate how social media platforms' level of moderation and audience reach drive militant groups' migration between platforms. Drawing on original data on the online activity of over a hundred militant and hate organizations, I show that when choosing platforms, these groups gravitate to sites that provide the best mix of moderation and reach. I complement this analysis with case studies that, in tracing the migration of the Islamic State and the Proud Boys between platforms, illustrate the important role of both lenient moderation and audience size to groups' migration decisions. I consider together in one chapter different organizations that espouse a range of ideologies and tactics—such as the Islamic State and the Proud Boys—because they face similar constraints when using social media. By showing that migration is not as arbitrary as the term "whack-a-mole" suggests but rather systematic and predictable, this chapter contributes to current debates on deplatforming, adding important evidence not only on how migration happens but also on where banned actors are most likely to move.

The Trade-off between Authenticity and Impact

As explained in the previous chapter, government regulation of social media platforms tends to focus on a particular portion of the online information ecosystem. Because governments more often focus on platforms where online harms can have the highest impact, they place the strongest regulatory pressures on technology companies whose social media sites have the largest user bases. As a result, larger platforms have incentives to invest more in the moderation of harmful content than do smaller platforms. For extremist organizations, this means that on large social media sites, though the impact of propaganda can be highest, there are also more restrictions on content. At the same time, on smaller platforms content can be posted more freely, but the impact is lower.

I empirically examine the trade-off between authenticity and impact by studying the relationship between platforms' content moderation thresholds and the size of their user bases. I collected data on the moderation policies of sixty-seven platforms by closely reading their terms of service and community guidelines documentation. I include in the analysis both large mainstream sites, like Facebook, Twitter, and YouTube, and smaller and less-known platforms, such as TamTam, ZeroNet, and WTVideo. In addition to platforms that host user-generated content, I also include file-sharing platforms that have been used by extremist organizations over the years, such as the Internet Archive.[2]

In general, almost all social media companies describe their content policies in their terms of service—a legal contract that all users of the platform agree to before creating an account. In recent years, some companies have also created additional documentation describing their content policies that is easier for the average user to understand. Facebook, for example, has a document called "Community Standards" that explains in lay language what is allowed on the platform. Twitter has the "Twitter Rules," while YouTube has the "Community Guidelines." Other platforms provide this kind of information in similar documents.

From these content policies, I created a variable that I call the "moderation threshold." This variable summarizes nine different categories of content moderation that social media companies use to restrict harmful content on their sites. I collapse the multidimensional policy space into one dimension in order to make the cross-platform analysis clearer. As described in chapter 2, I use a single dimension, as it provides conceptual clarity on the variation between technology companies' overall approach to restricting harmful content.

I focus on policies that are most relevant to militant and hate groups' online activity by examining the rules that relate to the categories listed in table 4.1. The first category consists of the ban on 'dangerous actors'—groups or individuals that are known to be linked to violence, such as terrorists, hate groups, and criminal organizations. Platforms that have these policies remove accounts affiliated with banned organizations, as well as any content that they post online. For example, after the Proud Boys were added to Facebook's dangerous organizations list, all the messages that they posted—regardless of the content—were removed from the platform. In addition to actor-based moderation, some platforms also ban content promoting violent events or ideologies (categories 2 and 3 in table 4.1). This consists of the removal of posts that praise terrorist attacks and their perpetrators as well as content that endorses ideologies promoting hate. A related category is the ban on content that glorifies violence (category 4); the vast majority of platforms in my dataset remove graphic content that is disseminated for malicious reasons.

The next two categories—threats and incitement (category 5) and harassment and bullying (category 6)—refer to the removal of content that can inspire harm, either offline or online. Under these sets of policies, social media posts that threaten or call for violence, or that maliciously target individuals

TABLE 4.1: Content Moderation Policies to Restrict Harmful Activity on Social Media

Category	Definition
1. Dangerous actors	Groups or individuals who inspire or perpetrate real-world harm are banned. Any content that they post online is removed.
2. Violent events	Content that supports or praises violent events, such as terrorist attacks, hate crimes, or the perpetrators of these events, is removed.
3. Hateful ideologies	Content that supports or praises ideologies that promote hate (for example, Nazism, white supremacy, white nationalism) is removed.
4. Glorification of violence	Content that celebrates the physical suffering of people and graphic content that is disseminated for malicious reasons rather than to raise awareness is removed.
5. Threats and incitement	Content that incites, threatens, or calls for violence is removed.
6. Harassment and bullying	Content targeting individuals or groups in a malicious way is removed.
7. Hate speech	Content that attacks people or a group of people based on protected characteristics, such as race, ethnicity, gender, sexual orientation, or immigration status, is removed.
8. Misinformation	Content that can promote offline harms, including violence and interference with political processes, such as elections, is removed.
9. Platform manipulation	The use of fake identities to manipulate audiences on the platform or evade moderation bans is prohibited.

online, are removed. Many platforms also have strict policies against hate speech (category 7). These policies, which have become common in recent years, refer to the removal of content that attacks people based on protected characteristics such as race, ethnicity, gender, and sexual orientation, among other attributes.

The last two categories in table 4.1 relate to platform manipulation. Policies against misinformation remove posts that can inspire offline harm through the manipulation of information (category 8). Recent examples include the takedowns of thousands of YouTube channels claiming that the results of the 2020 US elections were fraudulent and the removal of pages on Facebook and Instagram that were linked to a coordinated activity by the Muslim Brotherhood in Egypt.[3] Policies that restrict inauthentic behavior seek to prevent social media users from creating fake identities to manipulate audiences or evade moderation bans (category 9). Since many militant and hate groups have been engaging in these types of manipulation on social media, I include these policies in my analysis as well.

To create the moderation threshold variable, I simply counted the number of categories that were included in the policies of each platform. This approach works in this context because the policies used by social media platforms to combat harmful content are very similar. Thus, having more of them—choosing more rules from the "menu" of possible rules—implies a stricter platform. In my theoretical framework, higher thresholds reflect more permissive policies. Thus, to align the measure with the theoretical concept, I inverted the scale of the moderation threshold such that higher (lower) values reflect less (more) moderation and rescaled it to range between zero and one.

In addition to content moderation, I also measured the size of each platform. Platform size can be measured in various ways, such as monthly active users, web traffic, or the rank of platform apps. Although these measures are not a perfect indicator of audience size, they are commonly used as proxies for social media platforms' user bases. Facebook is by far the largest platform in my dataset, with 2.9 billion monthly active users as of the summer of 2022. YouTube and Instagram are the next largest, with about 2 billion users each. Twitter, TikTok, and Telegram also have very large user bases, ranging from 300 million to 900 million monthly active users. In contrast, Gab and Parler are much smaller, each with about 4 million users (all figures are as of 2022).

I examine the relationship between moderation and size by plotting these two variables against each other in figure 4.1. The x-axis reflects web traffic to each of the sixty-seven platforms in my dataset, and the y-axis represents the moderation threshold, which summarizes platforms' content policies along the nine categories described here. Higher values of the moderation threshold reflect more lenient policies—that is, more content is allowed on the platform. The figure shows that there is a strong negative correlation between the size of the platform and the moderation threshold: larger platforms have stricter policies (lower thresholds), and smaller platforms have more permissive policies (higher thresholds). For example, Facebook, Instagram, Twitter, and YouTube (all located at the bottom-right corner of figure 4.1) have the largest audiences, and they also have the most restrictive moderation policies. On the other hand, platforms at the top-left of the figure, such as Friendica, ZeroNet, and Peer-Tube, have much more lenient content policies but also smaller audiences.

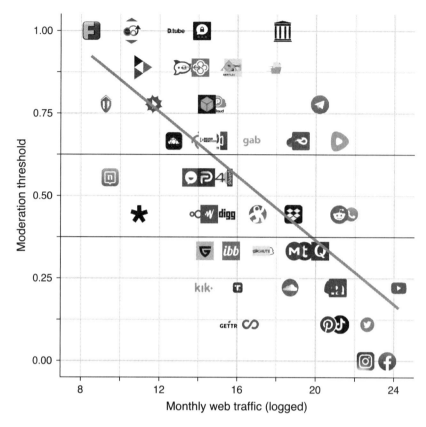

FIGURE 4.1. The Relationship between Platform Size and Moderation
Note: The figure shows the relationship between social media platforms' content moderation thresholds and their size. Larger platforms have lower thresholds (stricter moderation policies), and smaller platforms have higher thresholds (more permissive content policies).

In this information environment, to which platforms do groups gravitate? In the next section, I present evidence on the social media presence of over a hundred militant and hate organizations to examine the parts of the online information ecosystem where these actors tend to migrate when facing bans on moderating platforms.

Where Do Extremist Organizations Migrate?

To examine where groups move when they experience bans on social media, we need information on their online presence on a range of platforms. The vast majority of current research on the use of social media by militant and hate organizations focuses on a small number of groups and a limited set of plat-forms. Because of this focus on a relatively few (mostly mainstream) social media sites, we lack understanding of these organizations' activity in the broader online ecosystem. In particular, we do not have sufficient information to study groups' migration decisions in a digital environment characterized by variation in content moderation.

To examine whether groups gravitate to social media platforms that allow maximizing content authenticity and audience impact, I collected data on the public presence of over a hundred militant and hate groups on twelve social media sites. I tracked their presence on mainstream platforms such as Face-book, Twitter, and YouTube, midsize platforms such as Reddit and Telegram, and smaller platforms such as Discord, Gab and Parler.[4] I gathered information on accounts that were officially and unofficially linked to militant and hate groups on these sites by closely studying their social media handles, while noting whether their accounts had been suspended by the platforms.

In order not to select on the dependent variable (groups' social media pres-ence), I began this research by using external, independent lists of militant organizations and hate groups. This allowed me to examine these organizations' presence on online platforms without relying on a set of actors that are already known to use social media. For militant organizations, I used the Mapping Militant Project (MMP), a dataset collected by Stanford's Center for Interna-tional Security and Cooperation that provides information on over a hundred violent nonstate actors from around the world. The dataset includes compre-hensive case studies of militant organizations that were collected from second-ary sources and open-source publications; it also provides information on the over-time evolution of these groups and their organizational structure, as well as their ideology, goals, and activities.[5] Since I was interested in the *online* ac-tivity of these groups, I focused on organizations that were active in 2020 by removing from my list groups that were disbanded by the time of the data collection. This left me with fifty-nine groups—the vast majority of which operate in the Middle East and South Asia and adhere to Islamist ideologies (an artifact of the MMP's regional focus).

I also used data from the Southern Poverty Law Center's Extremist Files database, which consists of a list of hundreds of hate groups active in the United States.[6] Since there are many groups on SPLC's list, some of which are local chapters of larger organizations, I focus on fifty-five groups that have a presence in at least two US states. These organizations adhere to various ex-tremist ideologies, ranging from white nationalism and neo-Nazism to Black nationalism and other types of hate. Owing to SPLC's focus on US-based hate

TABLE 4.2: Militant and Hate Groups' Regional Focus, Ideology, and Years of Activity

Militant Groups
(*Source*: Mapping Militants Project)

Region	%	Ideology	%	Years Active	#
South Asia	36.7	Islamist	73.3	Minimum	5
Middle East	30.0	Nationalist/separatist	18.3	First quarter	14.5
East Asia	11.7	Far left	5.0	Mean	24.3
Africa	5.0	Criminal, drug trafficking	1.7	Third quarter	31.3
Latin America	5.0	Sunni-Sufi	1.7	Maximum	75
Multi-region	5.0				
North Africa	5.0				
East Europe	1.7				

Hate Groups
(*Source*: Southern Poverty Law Center)

Region	%	Ideology	%	Years active	#
United States	96.4	White supremacist/ nationalist	30.9	Minimum	3
Europe	3.6	Black supremacist/ nationalist	25.5	First quarter	7
		Neo-Nazi	18.2	Mean	22.4
		Anti-LGBTQ	10.9	Third quarter	29.5
		Racist skinhead	10.9	Maximum	92
		Anti-immigrant	1.8		
		Anti-Muslim	1.8		

groups, the vast majority of the groups in this dataset are located in the United States. Compared to militant groups listed in the MMP, hate groups in the United States are on average a little "younger." Table 4.2 presents a summary of these organizations' regional focus, years of activity, and ideology.

Militant and Hate Groups' Presence on Social Media

My next step was to collect data on these groups' presence on a range of social media platforms. To avoid direct interaction with them, I collected the data by passively observing their activity on the platforms under a pseudonymous account. Given the massive amounts of information on social media, as well as these organizations' active efforts to evade moderation, identifying their online presence was often not simple. I worked with a team of research assistants to develop a protocol for systematically collecting data on these groups' presence on social media by considering the local context in which they operated, their ideology and grievances, and their online strategies to evade moderation.

For each of the 114 groups in the dataset, we began by reading background information about their history and ideology, as well as news stories about their recent activities. This gave us an understanding of what potential sympathizers might search for when looking for these groups online and thus clues about how to find their accounts on social media. For organizations that operate in countries where English is not the main language, we conducted additional searches using terms in the local languages, as well as the idioms used to refer to these groups locally. In addition to text-based searches, we also used image searches to identify locations on the web where groups' logos and other branding materials tended to appear.[7]

Some groups had a social media presence that appeared as an official handle with their formal logo; in other instances, their online presence was centered on their leader's account (see figure 4.2). We coded the accounts of groups that formally belonged to the group or their leader as officially present on the platform. But these organizations' presence on social media was not limited to official accounts. Many of them had affiliated sympathizer accounts that helped publicize their activities on the platform. Thus, we collected information on both official and unofficial accounts associated with these groups on the twelve platforms that we were tracking. The content pushed online by sympathizers often gave clues about groups' presence on other platforms, mainly through out-links pointing to their content elsewhere. Finally, since we collected the data during a time when many platforms actively removed militant and hate groups from their sites, we also tracked whether the accounts that we found were banned from the platform or whether they were still active online.

Overall, I found that the vast majority of the groups—about 87 percent—used social media platforms to advance their cause. Among the organizations listed in the Mapping Militants Project, about 80 percent were active online, and over 94 percent of the groups in SPLC's Extremist Files database had active social media accounts. I also found that many groups used several platforms in parallel—most had accounts on about five or six of the twelve platforms, a pattern that looks similar for both militant organizations and hate groups. Twitter, Facebook, YouTube, and Telegram were the most popular among the groups in my dataset, while Parler, Gab, and Discord were less common.

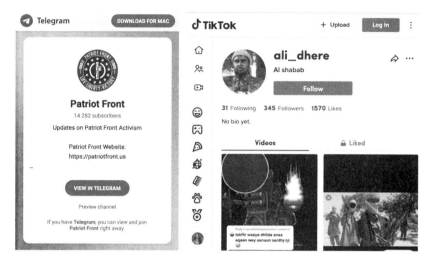

FIGURE 4.2. Examples of Militant and Hate Groups' Accounts on Social Media
Note: The picture shows screenshots of the handles of some militant and hate organizations on social media platforms. Left: The account of the Patriot Front on Telegram. Right: A TikTok account associated with Sheikh Ali Dhere, the official spokesman of Al-Shabaab.

When examining which platforms groups tended to use in tandem, I found that many used mainstream platforms alongside smaller, less-regulated platforms. For example, over the course of the data collection, I found that Hezbollah, a militant organization based in Lebanon, attempted to use Twitter and Facebook, but since its accounts were suspended from these platforms, it also maintained an active presence on Telegram. Similarly, the Atomwaffen Division, a neo-Nazi group with branches in various countries in Europe and the United States, spread its message in parallel on Twitter, YouTube, and Discord before its accounts were removed from these platforms.

I further examined the distribution of official and unofficial accounts and deplatforming on various social media sites in my dataset. I found that the number of platforms on which groups had official accounts was overall higher than the number of platforms on which they had an unofficial presence. That is, the use of unofficial accounts tended to be concentrated on a smaller set of platforms. This might be related to the pattern in account suspension in the data, which indicates that militant and hate group handles that were banned tended to be concentrated on the same set of platforms on which they had unofficial accounts.

Maximizing Authenticity and Impact

To examine whether groups gravitate to platforms that provide the best "mix" of moderation and size, I combined the data on these organizations' use of social media with the information I collected on platforms' user bases and moderation policies. For each group, I created a variable measuring whether it had active (that is, not suspended) accounts on each of the twelve platforms in my study. I then estimated the relationship between groups' online presence and platforms' size and moderation using regression analysis. Since my theory predicts that groups will use platforms that allow them to *jointly* maximize authenticity and impact, I examined how groups' use of social media varied with size and moderation, both separately and when combined. Statistically, this can be done by using an interaction variable that captures cases of platforms that are above the average in their size and moderation thresholds.

Table 4.3 presents my regression results. The first column shows that there is a positive and statistically significant relationship between dangerous organizations' presence on social media and platforms' audience size. Militant and hate groups are almost twice as likely to be present on platforms with an above-average number of monthly active users.[8] The table also shows that there is a positive relationship between the moderation threshold and militant and hate groups' use of social media: platforms that moderate less—those with higher thresholds—have a greater number of active groups.

But groups' official accounts are most highly concentrated on platforms that are above the average on both audience size and moderation threshold (see the coefficient on *Size x Threshold* in column 2 of table 4.3). These are social media sites that allow militant and hate groups to maximize audience while minimizing bans. When comparing these groups' presence on platforms with similar moderation thresholds, such as Gab and Telegram, I find that Telegram, which has a larger user base, has almost three times as many militant and hate group accounts as Gab. Similarly, there are significantly more active accounts on TikTok, whose moderation threshold is similar to Pinterest's. Of course, these platforms vary not only in their size and moderation but also in other features that make them attractive to militant and hate organizations. What this analysis shows is that when looking at groups' platform choice in a diverse online ecosystem, many gravitate to social media sites that provide the best mix of authenticity and impact.

I also looked at how militant and hate organizations' online presence varies with specific moderation policies. Figure 4.3 displays the average number of

TABLE 4.3: The Correlates of Militant and Hate Groups' Presence on Social Media

	Dependent Variable	
	Official Social Media Presence	
	(1)	(2)
Size	0.21***	0.10***
	(0.02)	(0.03)
Threshold	0.15**	−0.06
	(0.06)	(0.07)
Size x Threshold		0.36***
		(0.09)
Observations	1,368	1,368
Number of groups	114	114
Number of platforms	12	12
R^2	0.25	0.27

Note: The table shows the relationship between the presence of militant and hate groups on social media platforms and platforms' size and moderation thresholds. A platform is coded as large if the number of its monthly active users is greater than the median. Estimates from ordinary least squares regressions with group fixed effects. Standard errors clustered at the group level.

$^*p < .10; ^{**}p < .05; ^{***}p < .01$

groups with active accounts on social media platforms that vary in their moderation and size. The gray bars show groups' presence on platforms that include the policies listed in the *x*-axis, and the black bars show the patterns for platforms that do not include these rules. To examine whether moderation interacts with platform size, I break down the data by platforms whose user bases are below average (left-side panel) or above average (right-side panel).

I find that the presence of militant and hate groups on social media tends to be higher on platforms that do not include the moderation policies listed on the *x*-axis—especially for social media sites with larger user bases. Platforms that ban hate speech, harassment and bullying, or hateful ideologies are less likely to see active militant or hate group presence on their sites. I find a somewhat different pattern for policies banning dangerous actors or the glorification of violent events. For example, on smaller platforms, a "dangerous actors" policy is not associated with a lower prevalence of militant and hate group accounts; in fact, they are actually a little higher on smaller platforms that include the policy. But on larger social media sites, where audience reach is higher, there is a significant

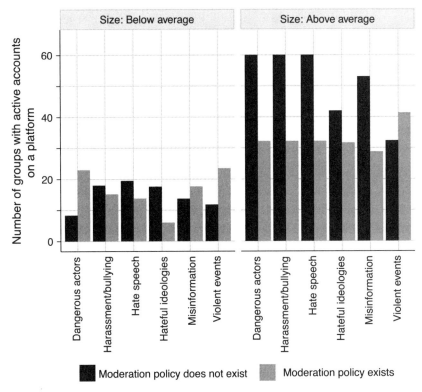

FIGURE 4.3. Militant and Hate Group Accounts by Moderation Policy and Size
Note: The figure shows the number of militant and hate groups with active accounts on social media platforms. The gray bars show the prevalence of groups on platforms that include the policies listed in the *x*-axis, and the black bars show the patterns for platforms that do not include these rules. The left panel shows platforms with smaller-than-average user bases and the right panel shows platforms with larger-than-average user bases.

difference between platforms that have a "dangerous actors" policy and those that do not: militant and hate groups are more than twice as likely to operate on platforms that do not have a policy against dangerous actors but whose size is above average. More generally, the figure highlights that militant and hate organizations gravitate mostly to platforms that have larger user bases and, at the same time, do not restrict hateful, violent, or extremist content.

To check whether this pattern captures something specific to groups that are impacted by content moderation policies—and not just to any organization that seeks to use social media platforms to accomplish its goals—I replicated this analysis by focusing on the online presence of nongovernmental organizations. My theoretical framework suggests that all organizations should prefer bigger platforms with large audiences. However, only actors that produce content that is likely to be acted upon should prefer larger platforms with more lenient moderation policies. In results reported in the appendix, I show that NGOs, which are not subject to bans on social media platforms, do not gravitate toward larger social media platforms with more lenient moderation policies. This is consistent with my theoretical expectations.

Thus, in line with the conventional wisdom, I find that actors who face bans on social media tend to prefer less-moderated spaces. But in contrast to the "whack-a-mole" account, I find that militant and hate groups' migration is not arbitrary: it follows a systematic and predictable pattern that aligns with their strategic goals of maximizing audience impact and content authenticity on social media. In the next sections, I elaborate on these strategic decisions by presenting two case studies that track a group's choice of platforms over time: the Islamic State's migration between platforms after the group experienced moderation bans on Twitter and Telegram in 2016 and 2019, and the migration decisions of the Proud Boys in the wake of their deplatforming from mainstream social media. The case studies show that the groups were attracted to platforms with more lenient content policies but at the same time, grappling with their limited audience, sought ways to maintain reach to the widest possible online crowds. These examples not only illustrate how migration happens but also explain the process that predicts where banned actors are most likely to move.

The Islamic State's Migration between Platforms

The Islamic State (IS) has become one of the most famous militant groups in recent years, partly because of its extensive use of social media. In its heyday, the group used tens of thousands of accounts on mainstream platforms to disseminate propaganda around the world. The group not only attracted mass online support through its social media campaigns but also lured thousands of foreign fighters to join its ranks in Syria, Iraq, and other parts of the world. The Islamic State's successful use of digital media platforms fascinated many, and numerous articles and books have been written about its propaganda campaigns, messaging strategies, and use of the internet for publicity and recruitment.

As the group's success on social media translated into offline harms, governments around the world, some for the first time, publicly called on technology companies to do more to moderate extremist content on their sites. Others pushed online platforms to remove harmful content through less public means. As a result of these pressures, the Islamic State's ability to use social media dramatically changed over the years. How did the group respond to these changes? What platforms did it choose to target? In this section, I trace the group's migration between platforms in the wake of crackdowns by technology companies.

Using Social Media to Reach the Masses

Long before the Islamic State embraced social media, the group's activists used various websites, forums, and messaging boards to spread its content online. On these fringe sites, they published the group's media messages and official statements and engaged with supporters. These activities were complemented by the dissemination of the group's official propaganda through CDs, DVDs, posters, and pamphlets in the physical world.[9] But the Islamic State's propaganda was largely hidden from the general public, as most of its content was accessible only to those who knew where to find it. To the average person, IS propaganda was not visible.

This changed in the early 2010s, when the group began experimenting with social media, posting its messages on platforms such as YouTube, Facebook, and Twitter. On these sites, engagement with Islamic State content skyrocketed. Within a short amount of time after opening its first Twitter account in October 2013, IS already had over twenty-four thousand followers.[10] To boost its audience engagement, the group created various campaigns that utilized social media platforms' unique features. For example, it created an app on Twitter called the "Dawn of Glad Tidings" that allowed it to use the accounts of its followers to disseminate propaganda in a semi-automated way and to reach an even wider audience than it would have reached with only organic engagement.[11] The group also disseminated sleek propaganda videos that appealed to a wide range of individuals in various walks of life. From videos displaying camaraderie between its members to those showing brutal violence, to content calling individuals to join its ranks, the Islamic State's online propaganda began attracting support around the world. "This is a war of ideologies as much as it is a physical war. And just as the physical war must be fought on the battlefield, so too must the ideological war be fought in the media," said a member of the IS social media team, explaining the group's approach to its digital campaigns.[12]

The Islamic State's online propaganda was so effective that by 2015 it had gained over 1.6 million followers on Twitter alone.[13] Many of the group's

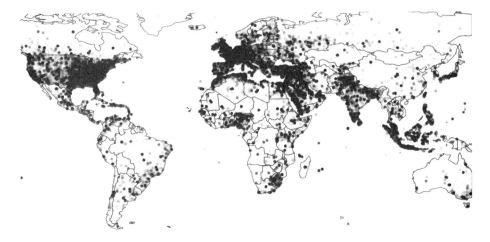

FIGURE 4.4. The Geographic Distribution of Islamic State Followers on Twitter
Note: The figure plots (in black dots) the locations of 1.6 million Twitter users who followed the Islamic State on Twitter between December 2015 and January 2017.

followers were centered in the Middle East, but thousands of others followed the group from Europe, North America, Australia, and various parts of Asia. Figure 4.4 shows the geographic distribution of these followers between December 2015 and January 2017.

By 2016, over thirty thousand foreign fighters had traveled to join the group in Syria and Iraq.[14] Fighters came to IS from all over the world, including the Middle East, Europe, Africa, East Asia, and the United States. While many recruits joined the group via local connections with recruiters, a significant portion of foreign fighters were radicalized online by consuming the group's propaganda on social media.[15] Pro-IS radicalization was not limited to certain social groups or those with national grievances; recruits came from different backgrounds, age groups, education, and income levels.[16] But the Islamic State's propaganda campaigns did more than attract supporters. They also inspired violence that led to the death or injury of thousands of civilians around the world.

Government Calls for Greater Moderation

After several high-profile violent attacks perpetrated by IS and its supporters, many governments began pressuring social media companies to take down the group's content from their platforms. The UK government, for example, published a report calling technology companies to do more to combat the exploitation of their sites by groups like the Islamic State:

> Social media companies are consciously failing to combat the use of their sites to promote terrorism and killings. Networks like Facebook, Twitter and YouTube are the vehicle of choice in spreading propaganda and they have become the recruiting platforms for terrorism. They must accept that the hundreds of millions in revenues generated from billions of people using their products needs to be accompanied by a greater sense of responsibility and ownership for the impact that extremist material on their sites is having. There must be a zero tolerance approach to online extremism, including enticement to join extremist groups or commit attacks of terror and any glorification of such activities.[17]

In France, shortly after the terrorist attack in Paris in November 2015, the French prime minister met with representatives from Apple, Google, Microsoft, Facebook, and Twitter to discuss their approach to combating extremist content on their sites.[18] In the United States, top national security officials sat together with technology platforms' executives to discuss strategies to prevent dangerous organizations' use of the internet for radicalization and recruitment and for planning violent attacks.[19] Similar calls for greater content moderation came from other countries as well.

Technology companies varied in their approach to moderating Islamic State content. Facebook dramatically stepped up its efforts to remove groups like IS from its site. It assembled a team that focused on developing strategies to combat extremist organizations' exploitation of its services, hired thousands of contractors to sift through large volumes of posts to detect harmful content, and expanded its automated systems for content moderation.[20] Google, which owned YouTube, took similar steps, setting up processes that allowed users to flag terrorist content and using targeted advertising to "redirect" potential recruits searching for Islamic State propaganda to content showing counternarratives.[21]

Initially more resistant to moderation, Twitter advanced more lenient policies that aligned with its libertarian views of unfettered free speech.[22] In an interview with CNN in the summer of 2014, one of Twitter's cofounders said, "If you want to create a platform that allows for freedom of expression for hundreds of millions of people around the world, you really have to take the good with the bad." In the fall of that year, Twitter's spokesperson explained that the company did not filter extremist content: "Twitter users around the world send approximately 500 million tweets each day, and we do not monitor them proactively."[23] Even as the Islamic State's messages were rapidly proliferating on the platform, one of the company's officials said that Twitter was not interested in getting into the business of defining what was terrorism and what was not. "One man's terrorist is another man's freedom fighter," he said.[24]

But Twitter's approach to the Islamic State rapidly changed with the rise of government pressures to moderate extremist content after the group intensified its violent attacks. Before Twitter changed its content rules, most of its policies relating to online safety focused on abuse and harassment. The platform did not officially ban terrorist propaganda or other violent extremist materials until later, in 2015. But even before Twitter publicized its new policies banning extremist content, it began cooperating with governments' security agencies by providing information and taking down accounts affiliated with the Islamic State. In an interview regarding Twitter's efforts to combat the Islamic State on its platform, FBI director James Comey said that Twitter was "very good and thoughtful and hardworking at trying to shut down accounts," and that its new efforts were a part of a "temperature change" that led technology companies to take a more active role in combating terrorist misuse of their platforms.[25]

In February 2016, Twitter came out with an official statement explaining how it is combating groups like the Islamic State on its services. "Like most people around the world, we are horrified by the atrocities perpetrated by extremist groups. We condemn the use of Twitter to promote terrorism. . . . As the nature of the terrorist threat has changed, so has our ongoing work in this area." The company said that it removed over 125,000 accounts promoting terrorism, most of which were linked to the Islamic State, in the second half of 2015.[26] In another statement in August 2016, the company announced that it had removed 235,000 additional extremist accounts. It also described its expanded actions to remove IS content from its platform, from increasing the number of content moderators to employing automated tools to remove the group's posts.[27] The new policies and actions that Twitter took against the Islamic State made the platform significantly less hospitable to the group.

The Islamic State's Reaction to Twitter's Policy Changes

After Twitter updated its moderation threshold, IS activists attempted to come back to the platform using Twitter handles with screen names similar to those that were suspended. To rebuild their follower networks, activists sought to reach out to the former followers by publicizing their new handles via "shout-out" accounts that disseminated information on their new handles.[28] This approach to maximizing the group's chances of remaining on a high-impact platform was often counterproductive, however, because Twitter's content moderators could easily identify the new accounts and suspend them again. The result was a recurrent pattern of account deletion and reappearance; some users were persistent enough to accumulate over four hundred reemergent accounts on the platform.[29]

Over time it became clear that Twitter's aggressive takedowns made it impractical to reemerge with an official IS affiliation on the platform. Thus, the group began exploring other platforms on which to operate. Where did the Islamic State choose to migrate in the wake of Twitter's crackdowns?

To investigate the platforms that the group was looking to migrate to, I drew on data on IS Twitter networks that consisted of over 100 million tweets posted by the group's media activists between 2013 and 2017. I used this dataset to detect out-links to other platforms that Islamic State activists shared on Twitter over time—especially after the platform became more aggressive in its moderation of extremist content. The term "out-link" refers to social media posts that include a URL to another website, with the purpose of drawing attention to content shared on that site. Militant groups that seek to migrate to new platforms often use out-links to publicize their presence on new social media platforms and to attract audiences to these spaces.

I tracked the out-links shared by Islamic State activists on Twitter to identify the platforms that the group began publicizing after Twitter's policy change in 2015. Figure 4.5 shows the sites that saw the largest increase in out-links, as well as those that saw a decline. The platforms that IS activists shared fewer out-links to over time were Facebook, YouTube, Pinterest, and Tumblr, among others. These platforms are those that, like Twitter, lowered their moderation thresholds by restricting extremist content on their sites. It is likely that the decline in out-links to these platforms reflects a decrease in the group's activity in these spaces.

But there were quite a few social media platforms that Islamic State activists began referring to more intensively after Twitter's policy change, including instant messaging apps such as Conversations, Matrix, and Discord; peer-to-peer web-hosting applications and file-sharing sites such as ZeroNet and pCloud; and the more popular platforms Snapchat and Telegram. Perhaps not surprisingly, all of these sites had more lenient moderation rules than the platforms that saw a decline in IS out-links. For example, while Facebook,

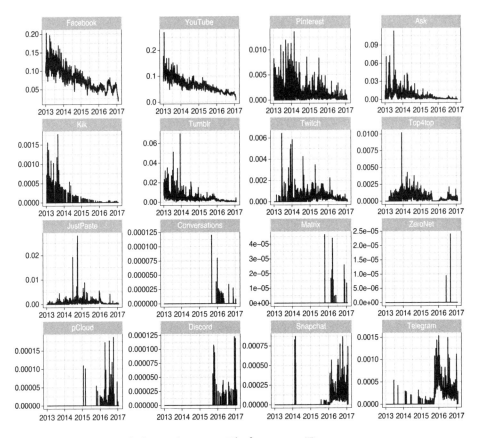

FIGURE 4.5. Out-links to Alternative Platforms over Time
Note: The figure shows the proportion of out-links to alternative social media sites shared by Islamic State media activists over time.

YouTube, and Pinterest expanded their moderation policies to ban content in almost all of the nine categories listed in table 4.1, Telegram, Matrix, and pCloud had only a handful of these policies in their terms of service.

When examining the volume of out-links to these less-moderated sites, I found that the platforms that saw the most referrals were pCloud, Discord, Snapchat, and Telegram. On pCloud, the group began experimenting with new ways of sharing propaganda. IS activists also looked to Discord as an alternative space for organizing, and they shared invitation links to their followers to come join them on that platform instead. "We're trying out @discordapp come check it out," said one activist. "Everyone Join The Discord!" said another. Snapchat saw an even larger volume of out-links as the group's activists turned to that platform to try to build follower networks and attract audiences.

"This platform [Snapchat] is just growing faster than the rest. Get on now. #snapusers," said one of the group's supporters. "Snapchat puts you directly in the heart of the event. Follow and watch new photos and videos!"

These less-moderated spaces, however, turned out to be limited in their ability to attract audiences. In comparison to Twitter and other mainstream platforms, these social media sites did not have the same levels of audience reach. Some of them were better suited for direct communication between a small number of people, and others required specific knowledge of those that accounts shared the group's content. Nevertheless, one of these platforms became particularly attractive for the Islamic State after it opened up a new feature allowing for more widespread content sharing.

Switching Sites: Migration to Telegram

In September 2015, Telegram introduced a new "channels" feature that allowed the dissemination of content to much wider audiences than before. This feature transformed Telegram from a platform that focused mostly on one-to-one communications into a site that allowed messages to be spread to hundreds or even thousands of users at a time.[30] The change has been dramatic for the Islamic State, which was struggling to keep a steady presence on Twitter, on the one hand, while making an impact on smaller and less-regulated platforms, on the other. Telegram's new feature not only increased the size of the audience that the Islamic State could reach online but also allowed the group to operate on a platform that had significantly less moderation. On Telegram, as one of the group's activists said, there were "fewer suspensions, [it is] easier to publish, and reporting is limited."[31]

Indeed, a comparison of Twitter's and Telegram's moderation policies during this period shows that when Twitter introduced rules that banned groups like the Islamic State from operating on its site, Telegram had no such policies. Telegram also strongly resisted collaborating with governments' requests for moderation. "Privacy is ultimately more important than our fear of bad things happening, like terrorism," said Telegram's founder, Pavel Durov, in September 2015. "If you look at ISIS, yes, there's a war going on in the Middle East. . . . We shouldn't feel guilty about it. We're still doing the right thing, protecting our users' privacy."[32] Telegram's lenient moderation policies, as well as its new "channels" feature allowing users to reach a wider audience, made it the platform of choice for the Islamic State starting in late 2015.

The group's migration to Telegram was visible in its Twitter communications at the time. The bottom-right panel in figure 4.5 shows the daily prevalence of out-links to Telegram shared in IS Twitter networks between 2013 and 2017. Referrals to Telegram were very sparse until the platform launched its channels service, which allowed the broadcasting of content to a larger audience. On the day Telegram opened the channels feature, out-links to the platform began proliferating on Twitter: "Telegram introduces Channels, a new tool for broadcasting messages to unlimited audiences," said one of the group's supporters. Since the Islamic State promptly started using the channels feature on the day it was launched, supporters had to update the Telegram application to access the new content. "Tell those who want to subscribe to the channel that they must update Telegram first and then access it from this link," said the group's activists. "For Jihadi videos, pics, PDF books in English that are banned to share in twitter, follow this Telegram channel," another advertised. Many other invitations to Telegram, in other languages, followed in the coming weeks and months.

On Telegram, IS activists used channels to disseminate the group's propaganda—both official channels operated by the Islamic State's central media outlets and many unofficial channels that helped distribute the group's messages among its growing network of supporters on the site. By mid-2016, the volume of messages on Telegram had grown to over thirty thousand messages per week.[33] And according to some estimates, the group operated almost two thousand channels on the platform during this period.[34] The broadcasting features of Telegram's channels allowed the Islamic State to use the platform to coordinate propaganda campaigns on other platforms as well. For example, the group's activists used Telegram to provide text for posts to be shared by sympathizers on other platforms and to organize "raids" using coordinated hashtags to attract audiences from other platforms to find the group on Telegram.[35]

The platform became such an important hub for the Islamic State that some of the group's activists almost completely abandoned Twitter in favor of organizing on Telegram. The site was perceived as both "safer," owing to its encryption services, and softer on moderation. "Many of the brothers [prefer] Telegram," one of the group's activists said, "in view of the small number of deletion operations to which the supporters were exposed on Telegram."[36]

Telegram's Crackdown on Islamic State Channels

The Islamic State's organizing on Telegram changed in 2018, when the platform launched several campaigns to remove IS content from its site. These efforts came after Europol—the European Union's law enforcement agency—curated a list of channels that the group used to promote propaganda on the platform. To help Telegram take down Islamic State content, Europol organized several "Action Days" during which it coordinated the removal of these materials with Telegram's content moderators. In a press release on October 5, 2018, Europol said that it had "performed a qualitative assessment of several hundreds of pieces of suspected terrorist propaganda on Telegram services" and shared them with Telegram representatives in the hope that the company would remove these materials.[37] In 2019, Europol organized another Action Day, after which it applauded Telegram for its "considerable effort to root out the abusers of the platform."[38]

Telegram's takedown of Islamic State channels contrasted with its earlier resistance to collaborating with governments on content moderation. In a statement published in November 2019, the company's representative said that the platform had "found the Referral Action Days productive and useful. We support free speech and peaceful protest, but terrorism and propaganda of violence have no place on Telegram."[39] However, unlike Twitter and other mainstream platforms, Telegram did not change its official moderation policies. Its threshold remained the same as it had been before Europol's removal requests.

How did the Islamic State respond to these crackdowns? I analyzed the out-links used by the group on the platform during this period to identify the spaces that it sought to migrate to. Between April 2018 and June 2020, the Islamic State shared over 232,000 out-links on Telegram to various other platforms (see table 4.4).[40] The platform referred to most often—by far—was Telegram itself. Over 85 percent of the links shared by Islamic State activists were to other Telegram channels operated by the group. This illustrates the high value of the platform for Islamic State members. Other sites that saw a large volume of out-links were JustPaste.it, Rocket.Chat, and Top4top, as well as more mainstream sites like Twitter, Facebook, and even Dropbox—spaces that the Islamic State continued to try to influence.

I examined whether out-link shares reflect a tendency toward sites that maximize content authenticity and audience impact by analyzing the relationship between the number of out-links and target platforms' moderation thresholds and audience size, using a similar regression framework as in the previous section. Since data on monthly active users for some of the platforms were not publicly available, I used a related measure of audience size: web traffic to the platform. Table 4.5 shows where platform out-links tended to concentrate the most. Column 1 shows the patterns for all out-links in the full

TABLE 4.4: Out-links Shared by Islamic State Activists on Telegram, April 2018 to June 2020

Platform	Number of Out-links
Telegram	198,912
JustPaste.it	9,169
Twitter	8,064
Rocket.Chat	5,812
Top4top	4,067
Dropbox	3,403
Facebook	2,447
pCloud	89
nandbox	55
Riot	11

Source: Amarasingam, Maher, and Winter 2021.

TABLE 4.5: The Correlates of Out-Links Sharing from Telegram

	Dependent Variable			
	Number of Out-Links			
	(1) All Out-links, April 2018 to June 2020	(2) All Out-links, Excluding Telegram	(3) Out-links after Europol's Action Days (December 2019 to June 2020)	(4) Out-links after Europol's Action Days, Excluding Telegram
Size	−597.95 (1,341.39)	175.27 (153.85)	−297.98 (339.72)	25.50 (76.12)
Threshold	−106.05 (1,605.60)	413.39** (172.63)	−255.96 (412.66)	39.12 (87.17)
Size x Threshold	**10,585.52*** (1,891.22)**	**1,410.08 (872.26)**	**2,337.07*** (462.43)**	**1,060.57** (358.45)**
Observations	156	129	30	23
R²	0.58	0.26	0.88	0.63

Note: The table shows the relationship between the out-links to social media platforms shared by the Islamic State on Telegram and platforms' size and moderation thresholds. A platform is coded as large if the number of its monthly active users is greater than the median. Estimates from ordinary least squares regressions with date fixed effects.

*p < .10; **p < .05; ***p < .01

time period (April 2018 to June 2020). In column 2, I remove out-links to Telegram from the data. Column 3 shows the patterns only for out-links shared after Europol's Action Days, covering the time period between December 2019 and June 2020, and column 4 shows the same data as column 3 but excludes out-links to Telegram.

The results show that the highest volume of Islamic State out-links from Telegram were to platforms that scored high on both the moderation threshold and size (see third row of the table, *Size x Threshold*). In other words, I find that platforms that saw the most out-links were those that jointly maximized content authenticity and audience reach. These sites saw hundreds (or even thousands) more referrals by Islamic State activists on Telegram.

The Islamic State's movement between social media platforms illustrates the process that drives the migration of militant organizations confronting moderation bans. The case shows that migration between platforms is not arbitrary but driven by strategic incentives to build digital resilience. The group's focus on Twitter between 2013 and 2015 was probably related to the fact that the platform had a relatively higher moderation threshold, compared to peer platforms, while allowing for significant audience reach. After Twitter banned the group, its preference for Telegram over other less-moderated platforms shows the same pattern. Even though the Islamic State did not reach the same level of audience on Telegram as it did on Twitter, Telegram still had a much larger user base than other platforms that the group was experimenting with after the ban.

In the next section, I turn to the case of the Proud Boys to examine whether its migration between platforms was driven by a similar goal of simultaneously maximizing content authenticity and audience impact.

The Proud Boys' Migration Decisions

The Proud Boys, in many ways, is a very different organization from the Islamic State. The group is significantly smaller than IS, it operates primarily in the United States, and it adheres to a very different ideology. And yet the group's reaction to moderation by social media companies was very similar to that of IS. In this section, I describe how the Proud Boys used social media for recruitment, the process that drove technology companies to ban it from their services, and the ways in which it adapted in response. I show that the group's migration between platforms was motivated by similar goals of reaching audiences while minimizing bans.

The Proud Boys was founded in 2016 by Gavin McInnes, a Canadian media personality who, for years before founding the group, promoted his views against left-wing "political correctness" in various mainstream and alternative media outlets. McInnes founded the Proud Boys to provide a voice for (mostly white) men who felt that Western culture was on the decline. In a post he wrote for *Taki* magazine, McInnes officially introduced the group:

> On Sunday, September 11 . . . the NYC chapter of the Proud Boys held its second meet-up at the Tribeca bar Gaslight. Though the exact details are kept secret, the meetings usually consist of drinking, fighting, and reading aloud from Pat Buchanan's *Death of the West*. There were about fifty men at this gathering and no women because women are not allowed. The basic tenet of the group is that they are "Western chauvinists who refuse to apologize for creating the modern world" . . . they long for the days when "girls were girls and men were men." This wasn't controversial even twenty years ago, but being proud of Western culture today is like being a crippled, black, lesbian communist in 1953.[41]

The Proud Boys started organizing around local chapters in various parts of the United States (as well as in Canada, Europe, and Australia).[42] The group's recruitment process had four levels. At the first level, individuals who wished to join the Proud Boys were required to take an oath saying: "I'm a proud Western chauvinist, I refuse to apologize for creating the modern world." At the second level, members had to go through a ritual where they got beaten up while reciting the names of different types of Western cereal. McInnes explained that the rationale for this ritual was to have better "adrenaline control." He said that "defending the West against the people who want to shut it down is like remembering cereals as you're being bombarded with ten fists."[43] The third level of recruitment consisted of showing commitment by getting a tattoo that said, "Proud Boy," while the fourth level was granted to those who got involved in a physical, often violent fight "for the cause."[44]

From its early days, the group actively used social media for recruitment. Proud Boys members used various online sites, including Twitter and YouTube, but their favorite platform was Facebook, whose "groups" feature facilitated effective recruiting of new members. The Proud Boys operated various groups on Facebook that they used for attracting supporters. Some were "vetting groups" in which new members were asked to openly declare their loyalty by taking an oath. For example, in one of the Proud Boys' vetting groups, its members said: "It is here that you will be properly vetted before membership approval into your local chapter. . . . Once you are added here, to be properly vetted you must upload and post a video of yourself reciting our First Degree [the oath]." Hundreds of new members posted videos in these vetting groups in which they pledged their allegiance to the Proud Boys and expressed their excitement about moving up the ranks of the organization.

The Proud Boys used additional Facebook groups for their regional chapters in which they organized events, spread propaganda and memes, and connected with fellow members. To reach new recruits on the platform, they also paid for targeted advertisements that they tailored for various audiences. This enabled the Proud Boys to reach a wider set of new members than would otherwise have been possible. At the end of 2017, the group had over twenty thousand followers on Facebook,[45] and by 2018 membership in various Facebook groups had reached over fifty-five thousand.[46]

Even though the Proud Boys' recruitment process involved engagement in violence, its members were careful not to openly encourage unprovoked attacks on social media. Aware of technology companies' content moderation policies, the group stated that it justified only violence used in self-defense. To clarify the purpose of violence, McInnes wrote in 2017:

> The 4th degree is for someone who has "endured a major conflict related to the cause." In the past I've joked about "kicking the crap out of antifa." This obviously doesn't mean you go to someone's house or even pick a fight with one at a rally. . . . We don't start fights, we finish them.[47]

Despite this rhetoric, many of the organization's members got involved in physical fights in various parts of the United States. One prominent fight was a violent encounter during a rally in Oregon in June 2018 between a Proud Boys member and a member of the far-left organization Antifa. A video of the incident, showing the Proud Boy punching the Antifa member in the head, causing a serious injury, circulated on social media afterwards. The Proud Boys spread the video in their online networks, framing it as an example of left-wing aggression, and praised the Proud Boy who engaged in the violence.[48] The video appealed to many new recruits, and in the month after it went viral membership rose on the Proud Boys' vetting pages on Facebook by almost 70 percent, according to the Southern Poverty Law Center.[49]

Platforms' Changing Policies toward the Proud Boys

The group's rising prominence on social media and the growth in its violence led technology companies to update their moderation policies. Twitter was the first to act: it announced the suspension of several accounts associated with the Proud Boys in August 2018. The company said that the Proud Boys were banned from its services for violating its policy prohibiting violent extremist groups—a rule that the company had added to its terms of service a few years before (see the previous section on the Islamic State's migration between platforms). Some noted that Twitter's ban on the Proud Boys was likely a preemptive action put in place to limit the group from mobilizing online ahead of an event that was planned to mark the anniversary of the 2017 Charlottesville "Unite the Right" rally—a violent demonstration in which members of the group had taken part in the previous year.[50]

Facebook, which was criticized for not moderating the group's content despite its vast activity on the platform, took a similar action in October 2018. The platform's ban came after several members of the Proud Boys were involved in another violent incident, this time in New York. Facebook removed pages and groups associated with the Proud Boys and their leader, Gavin McInnes, and added the group to its list of dangerous actors. In a statement, the company said that it "continues to study trends in organized hate and hate speech" and that it would continue to "take action against hate speech and hate organizations" to keep its community safe.[51]

Migration Decisions

The actions taken by Facebook and Twitter against the Proud Boys disrupted their ability to use these sites for recruitment and compelled them to find alternative spaces to organize. In the first days and weeks following the bans, the group's members agonized over losing followers and looked for various ways to maintain their audience. On Twitter, some created lists of new Proud Boys accounts that they tried to disseminate to their followers to maintain engagement.[52] On Facebook, Proud Boys members who were active in groups that were not yet banned looked for ways to preserve their ability to continue mobilizing supporters on the platform.[53]

Other activists started experimenting with alternative platforms like Parler and Gab, hoping to build a vetting and recruitment structure similar to the one they had maintained on Facebook. Within a day after the Twitter ban, some announced that the group was moving to Gab. "Proud Boys have come to Gab. Welcome them!" said one of the group's members. "F[**] Twitter. I'm here, and I stand with Gavin McInees [sic] and ProudBoysUSA," said another. After the Facebook ban that came two months later, more Proud Boys started using Gab. "Yes. #ProudBoys are slowly migrating to #GAB (legally).

F[**] #Twitter f[**] #Facebook. #follow us and #join today." The group similarly explored Parler—a new platform launched in August 2018—as an alternative site to organize.

But Gab and Parler, despite their more lenient moderation, did not have
the same audience numbers found on Twitter and Facebook. As niche platforms, they did not attract large numbers of users and were limited in their
infrastructure. For example, when Gab experienced technical issues shortly
after the Proud Boys started using it in late 2018, the Proud Boys' ability to
organize on the site encountered friction. Parler similarly experienced problems during these years. "Does anyone still use Parler, or are we shouting into
the ether?" asked one member who tried to use the platform. "??????????
ECHO ECHO??????????? . . . Is this thing still on?" said another.

To find a space that would allow the group to reach more people while still
avoiding bans, the Proud Boys started using Telegram. Not only was
Telegram's user base much larger than Gab's and Parler's, but it also enabled
users to create channels that were similar in structure to those on the Facebook groups that the Proud Boys had used for vetting and recruitment. In
one Telegram channel, the group publicized the channels used by its regional
chapters, calling new members to join the chapter near them. "If you're looking to join and don't see a link to a chapter near you, come back later," said
the administrators of the centralized channel. In another channel, the group's
members said: "We heard there was a large Twitter ban today. . . . We've been
burned too many times by big tech and learned our lessons to not go back on
leftist run platforms."

The group's channels on Telegram soon proliferated. Proud Boys members
from various chapters opened new channels on Telegram and called others to
join them. "Click here and follow the new channel," said a member of a Proud
Boys chapter in Long Island. Another chapter from Miami invited others to
join the group's new space on Telegram, calling them to "help save America
one punch to a commies face at a time." Many other chapters followed.

The growth of the Proud Boys' channels on Telegram dramatically acceler-
ated in September 2020, when Donald Trump nodded at the group during a
presidential debate. "Proud Boys, stand back and stand by . . . somebody's got
to do something about antifa and the left," said Trump during the presidential
election debate.[54] Trump's comment sparked a wave of new recruits to the
Proud Boys on Telegram. After the debate, the group's channels saw a significant growth in membership—some grew by almost 10 percent within the
day following Trump's statement.[55] "Proud Boys will be standing back and

standing by," said the group's chapter in Ohio in its Telegram channel after Trump's statement. Another chapter in Michigan called its members to become "poll challengers" on the day of the election.

Telegram's lenient moderation of the Proud Boys and its relatively larger audience was exactly what the group needed to maintain online resilience. The platform not only allowed the Proud Boys to continue their online recruitment machine without being banned but also enabled the group to reach audiences on a larger scale than had been possible on platforms like Gab and Parler. Soon after migrating to Telegram, many of the group's channels reached hundreds, even thousands, of new subscribers. "Welcome, newcomers, to the darkest part of the web," said the leader of the Proud Boys in a public Telegram message. "You can be banned for spamming and porn. Everything else is fair game."[56] By the summer of 2022, the Proud Boys' channels on Telegram boasted almost forty-nine thousand subscribers—almost 90 percent of the volume of members the group had on Facebook before it was banned. With Telegram's more lenient moderation policies and growing size, the Proud Boys were able to remain active online.

Conclusion

When governments and technology companies seek to limit the activity of militant and hate organizations on digital media platforms, they often evaluate the outcomes of moderation by focusing solely on the banning sites. Under this paradigm, a successful moderation action is usually defined as reduced activity of dangerous actors on the platforms that engage in moderation. What this chapter shows is that focusing on moderating platforms provides only part of the picture: while hateful and violent content may be successfully reduced on sites with stricter moderation policies, it can easily grow in other online spaces that have more lenient policies. By examining the cross-platform activity of a large number of militant and hate organizations, I showed that movement between platforms—and thus spillover of harmful content in the broader online ecosystem—is highly common.

But not all less-moderated spaces experience the same level of militant and hate group activity. The online sites that see the highest in-migration of banned actors are those that maximize both content authenticity and audience impact. Platforms that allow militant and hate organizations to post content freely while at the same time enabling them to reach a large audience are those that militant and hate actors are most likely to choose.

5

Safe Havens for Mobilizing and Recruiting

ALVIN SMALLBERG was an active Twitter user who often posted on Twitter about conservative political issues.[1] Identifying as a Trump supporter, he frequently discussed topics advanced by the Republican Party, and in particular by Donald Trump. In the months leading up to the 2020 elections in the United States, Alvin became agitated by social media platforms' growing moderation of election-related content. "This is censorship police," he said, lamenting the removal of posts discussing the election.[2] "Twitter wouldn't let me post a video [about Trump] . . . and Facebook removed 216 Trump ads," he complained. In early November 2020, Alvin's own account was banned from Twitter for violating the platform's policies. He appealed the suspension, but Twitter did not restore his account.

Frustrated with the ban, Alvin started using Gab, an alternative social media site known for its more lenient moderation. On Gab, he vocally expressed anger over mainstream platforms' content removals, citing examples of what, in his view, constituted unjustified censorship. Over time, Alvin became part of a growing community of users who believed that companies like Facebook, Twitter, and YouTube nefariously banned right-leaning content to influence the election results. "[These companies] abuse their technocratic power to pretend that your truth is lies and their lies are truth," he said. As Alvin spent time on Gab, he became exposed to messages posted by the Oath Keepers, a far-right militant group active in the United States. "They are lying to us in the mainstream media; the public is being lied to," said the group's activists on Gab.[3]

Alvin was impressed with the Oath Keepers' public refusal to recognize Joe Biden as president and their call for action. He felt mobilized to fight back. Alvin started expressing sympathy with the group and their efforts to challenge the election results: "The Oath Keepers, who are called a militia by the left, will refuse to recognize Biden as President. . . . Join Oathkeepers in Demand for Insurrection Act!" As he continued to engage with the group's content on Gab, Alvin became vocally supportive of their efforts to "Stop the Steal" and "Defeat the Coup"—a campaign aimed at delegitimizing the election results by calling on President Trump to use military force to oppose the transfer of presidential power.[4] Alvin joined others in circulating information about a protest that the group planned for January 6, 2021—an event that ended with the violent storming of the U.S. Capitol in Washington, D.C.

Alvin's story is a powerful example of how personal experiences with content moderation can inspire support for extremism on less-moderated platforms. While Alvin had been engaging with hateful content on Twitter, his receptivity to the notion (to which he had been exposed on Gab) that content bans were part of a larger plan to interfere with the election intensified after he experienced moderation himself. Alvin's discussion of censorship on mainstream platforms, his subsequent migration to Gab, and his engagement with content promoting the January 6 attack suggest that deplatforming may have made him particularly receptive to fringe groups' propaganda messages, such as those propagated by the Oath Keepers. This receptivity, in turn, may explain why the Oath Keepers found Gab an attractive platform, notwithstanding its small size—3.7 million monthly active users compared to Twitter's 486 million and Facebook's 2.9 billion.[5]

The theoretical framework in chapter 2 predicted that extremist groups will seek to maximize their reach on social media by choosing platforms with a large audience. Because fringe platforms tend to have smaller user bases, they are commonly viewed as inconsequential when it comes to audience reach. After all, content circulating on these platforms is unlikely to reach a wide audience. Nonetheless, we see extremist organizations increasingly engaging on marginal platforms with smaller user bases. Among the 114 militant and hate groups for which I collected data on their social media presence, 70 had active accounts on smaller platforms. More generally, marginal platforms have seen a sharp increase in web traffic since the heightened content moderation on mainstream platforms in recent years.[6] But the overall number of users on these platforms remains small. Is there a connection between the increasing web traffic to these platforms and the strategic objectives of militant and hate groups on social media?

In this chapter, I show that another factor besides platform size plays a role in the impact of militant groups' social media campaigns: the *susceptibility* of an audience to messaging. Groups' ability to influence audiences on social media is not driven solely by the *quantity* of people who see their messages; it is also closely tied to the *quality* of their campaigns, which is a function of how receptive the audience is to their narratives. Although there are various factors that can drive social media users' attraction to extremists' campaigns, I show that personal experiences with content moderation are particularly important.

For this purpose, I focus in this chapter on the *audience* from which militant and hate organizations seek to recruit supporters. I present a large-scale empirical analysis that draws on cross-platform data on the online activity of thousands of social media users. The analysis shows that Alvin's story is hardly unique: experiences with content moderation aggravate individuals in a way that can make them more receptive to extremists' narratives on less-moderated platforms. Thus, variation in content moderation across platforms not only enables militant and hate groups to establish a presence on less-restrictive spaces, as shown in chapter 4, but also allows particularly susceptible audiences on less-regulated platforms to be targeted. The analysis illustrates the importance of taking an ecosystem-level approach to understanding the effects of content moderation.

How Deplatforming Can Increase Receptivity to Extremism

So far, research on content moderation has not paid close attention to its effects on targeted users. The vast majority of current work examines platform-level effects by looking at the prevalence of harmful content on sites that engage in moderation.[7] This research has shown, for example, that platforms that remove harmful content or ban users who generate such content tend to have better outcomes after the removal. A study conducted on Reddit illustrates this dynamic. In 2015, Reddit enacted a new anti-harassment policy that led to the banning of several sub-Reddits promoting hate speech on the platform. Before the ban, these groups were active at promoting hate speech and attracting crowds to their toxic circles. After the ban, most members of these forums stopped using Reddit, and those who stayed on the platform reduced their engagement with hate speech.[8] Similarly, a study examining the effects of Facebook removal of hate groups found that followers of suspended accounts reduced their production of hate speech on Facebook after the removal.[9] Studies, such as these, that examine "within-platform" effects of content moderation have led many to conclude that moderation is an effective tool to combat extremism on social media. Because platforms that engage in moderation see a decrease in harmful content, this approach is believed to be working.

But looking at this question from a cross-platform perspective tells a different story. Critics of content moderation—in particular, of "deplatforming," the suspension of accounts from social media platforms—argue that even though it reduces undesirable content on mainstream social media, it can nonetheless increase harmful activity on platforms that do not engage in the same level of moderation.[10] For example, a study examining cross-platform activity in the wake of the "Great Deplatforming"—the large wave of account suspensions on mainstream social media that followed the January 6, 2021, attack on the U.S. Capitol—found that it was followed by a large increase in the usage of and spread of toxic content on fringe platforms with more lenient content policies.[11] Thus, examining the effect of content moderation on social media sites that deplatform users provides only part of the picture. To understand the impact of moderation more fully, we need to study what is happening simultaneously on platforms that moderate less. Specifically, we need to analyze the cross-platform effects of content moderation on the audiences from which militant and hate groups seek to recruit supporters.

Current research on the effect of moderation on targeted users is quite sparse. We do not have a good understanding of how experiencing content bans, deplatforming, and other acts of censorship shapes the individuals who are subject to these sanctions. The closest empirical research on this topic has focused on "influencers"—individuals with a large social media following who create content that can be monetized. Studies examining what happens to influencers who are banned from large social media platforms have documented a decline in followership, a reduced ability to monetize content, an increase in anger and frustration, and even a sense of despair and isolation.[12] There has been much less research on the experience of "lay" social media users, who are more likely than influencers to be the target audience for extremist propaganda on less-moderated platforms.

We can expect moderation to affect users in two ways. First, experiencing content moderation may change user behavior in the direction desired by the platform. People who post harmful content and see their messages deleted may change how they communicate to avoid being banned. They may not have known that what they posted was against the rules, or they may wish to self-correct to ensure that they do not contribute to a harmful information environment.

A second possibility is that being subject to content moderation motivates individuals to further seek out the banned information, either on the moderating platform or in less-regulated spaces. Having one's content deleted can lead to anger, frustration, or even a sense of rejection—reactions that can generate behavior in the opposite direction of what is desired by the moderating platforms. For example, experiencing censorship can be seen as unjust, especially if the censored party disagrees about the harmfulness of the content being removed. Social media users may therefore feel motivated to defy the moderators by seeking out and promoting the banned information. This is what Margaret Roberts found in her research on censorship in China. Studying the reactions of social media users who had their posts removed, she found that censorship led users to mobilize against the Chinese government and promote the outlawed content despite the government's ban.[13] This pattern of behavior suggests that content moderation may backfire if it creates grievances that motivate further engagement with the banned information. In democratic countries, we are especially likely to see this sort of backlash, as there are fewer legal repercussions for saying things on the internet.[14]

For militant and hate groups that seek to use social media for recruitment, these moderation-induced grievances are instrumental. One of the primary goals of these groups is to use social media to identify potential supporters who will find their messages appealing, so targeting audiences that experience social media bans can be particularly attractive to them. Identifying these audiences, tying content removals to their propaganda narratives, and framing content moderation as an example of bias against people "like us" can be very useful for luring potential sympathizers who experience moderation themselves.

Content Moderation during the 2020 US Elections

To study how content moderation can affect users across platforms, I focus on actions taken by major social media companies in the run-up to the 2020 US elections and afterward. The 2020 election period posed a unique challenge to technology companies' content moderation policies, as they were determined to avoid a repeat of the 2016 elections, which were marred by misinformation, voter manipulation, and hate speech.[15] To proactively combat these online harms, many prominent social media platforms developed new rules to moderate election-related content and ban messages that questioned the legitimacy of the democratic process.

Facebook, for example, initiated a ban on all political advertisements, removed posts that sought to discourage voters from going to the polls, and added a notification to the top of users' news feed clarifying that no winner would be announced until all votes had been counted. "We have a responsibility to stop abuse and election interference on our platform," said representatives of the company. "That's why we've made significant investments since 2016 to better identify new threats, close vulnerabilities, and reduce the spread of viral misinformation and fake accounts."[16] Twitter and Google took similar measures, banning political ads in the months and weeks leading up to the election, adding warnings to content that shared misinformation, and removing posts that aimed to manipulate voters.[17]

As a result of these measures, users of these platforms experienced greater levels of content moderation during the elections. Some saw changes in their timelines when election-related ads were no longer available; others discovered that posts they shared were removed; some received a warning when they shared content that violated the rules; and others even found their account suspended for a period of time. Here I focus on deplatforming, the permanent removal of accounts, which is perhaps the most severe content moderation measure taken against social media users. Individuals who experience deplatforming cannot come back to the banning platform under the same account, and in some cases they are banned even if they try to open new accounts. Although technology companies generally do not rush to ban users from their platforms, the sensitivity of the 2020 election period and the upheaval that resulted from the January 6, 2021, attack on the Capitol led companies to suspend more users than before—leading many more users of these platforms to become exposed to content moderation.

A Cross-Platform Study on User Experiences with Moderation

How did individuals who were subject to bans react to their suspension? Did they migrate to platforms with more lenient moderation policies? To what content were they exposed in less-regulated spaces? And did moderation make suspended users more receptive to messages posted by extremist groups? To answer these questions, we need information on technology companies' deplatforming activity as well as data on social media users' behavior on platforms with different moderation thresholds. We also need a way to link individual behavior across platforms to understand the relationship between moderation actions on one platform and activity on another.

To gather such information, I focused on two social media sites: Twitter, which had a lower (more restrictive) moderation threshold, and Gab, which had more lenient content policies, especially on issues related to the election. An "alt-right" social media platform established in 2016, Gab has become popular among far-right communities in the United States. Gab promotes itself as "the home of free speech online," and its moderation policies do not restrict content in the same manner that mainstream platforms do.[18] For example, while Twitter had policies banning dangerous organizations, hate speech, and misinformation during the 2020 election period, Gab's policies did not restrict such content. Thus, perhaps not surprisingly, Gab saw a large increase in its user base after the Great Deplatforming that followed the January 6, 2021, attack on the Capitol—growth that the company openly welcomed.[19]

To collect Gab data, my first step was to download all posts that were publicly available on the platform in the months preceding and following the elections.[20] This initial collection allowed me to obtain data on 93,004 Gab users who actively posted content on the platform during this period. My second step was to identify Gab users who had Twitter accounts, which I found by identifying identical "screen names" (the handle that an individual uses on a platform) on both Twitter and Gab.[21] The purpose of matching the accounts of the same individual across the two platforms was to study how moderation shapes users' behavior when they shift their activities to other platforms. If we know that an individual was suspended from Twitter, we can examine how they reacted to their suspension by looking at their behavior on a less-regulated platform, such as Gab. One limitation of this data collection approach is that it focuses on social media users who had accounts on both platforms. Although my analysis allows a study of reactions to content moderation among individuals with accounts on multiple platforms, it may not apply to people who used, for example, only Twitter.

In total, I identified 30,444 Gab users who had active Twitter accounts (33 percent of the Gab users in my sample).[22] A couple of examples of individuals' accounts are shown in figure 5.1. It can be seen that they used similar profile pictures, descriptions, and banners on the two platforms.

The sample of users in my dataset reflects people who probably leaned to the right of the political spectrum in the United States. By having accounts on Gab,

FIGURE 5.1. Examples of Matched Twitter and Gab Accounts
Note: The figure shows examples of the Gab and Twitter accounts of two individuals in my matched dataset. The accounts were matched via screen names.

these individuals had already expressed an interest in engaging with content shared on an alt-right platform. To examine the issues that these users engaged with on both social media sites, I analyzed the texts of their posts using a topic model—a statistical algorithm that identifies themes, or "topics," in documents by analyzing their semantic structure. Specifically, I used a structural topic model, which allows discovery of topics in documents by using not only text but also additional document metadata.[23] I use this model to examine the topics that individuals in my matched sample posted on both Twitter and Gab.[24]

Figure 5.2 shows the prevalence of topics discussed by individuals in my data on both platforms. The topics are listed on the *y*-axis, and the *x*-axis shows the relationship between these topics and the platform. Positive values (black dots) mean that a topic was discussed more frequently in Twitter posts, while

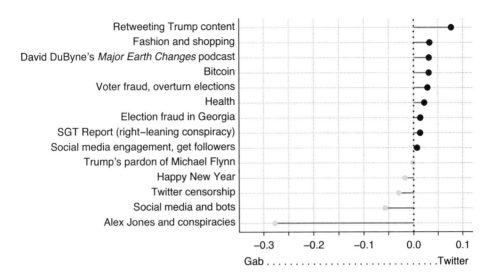

FIGURE 5.2. Topics Discussed by Individuals with Twitter and Gab Accounts
Note: The figure presents the topic prevalence of the social media posts of individuals in my dataset who had active Gab and Twitter accounts, analyzed with a structural topic model. The black circles reflect topics that were more frequently discussed by these individuals on Twitter, and the gray circles reflect topics more frequently discussed by these individuals on Gab.

negative coefficients (gray dots) mean that the topic was more prevalent in Gab posts.[25] Recall that the data reflects content posted by the same users; thus, this analysis allows discovering the topics on which they focused when engaging on each platform.

I find that retweeting Trump's content was the most prevalent topic on Twitter. In the run-up to the 2020 elections, many users shared Trump's posts about bias in left-leaning media and the dangers of mail-in ballots, as well as content seeking to mobilize voters for Trump. In the aftermath of the elections, these users retweeted Trump's posts saying that the elections were rigged and that Trump was the real winner. Many of the individuals in my sample were agitated that Trump did not win, and they posted a large number of messages on Twitter on voter fraud during the elections. For example, one user said that there was "unprecedented election fraud right before our eyes."[26] Another agreed, saying that, "if it looks like a fraud, swims like a fraud, and quacks like a fraud, then it probably is a fraud."[27] Other individuals similarly called for rejecting the election results, and some even said that they "need to start thinking [about] civil war" because "mail in fraud is going to hurt

Trump."[28] Additional topics on Twitter focused on nonpolitical issues. These included posts about fashion and shopping, bitcoin and other cryptocurrencies, and health-related issues.

On Gab, these users discussed a somewhat different set of topics. The topic that was by far the most prevalent on Gab was discussion of various conspiracy theories, which included content promoted by Alex Jones on his website InfoWars, as well as conspiracies related to the QAnon movement. On Gab, these individuals also talked about the use of automated accounts ("bots") and, perhaps not surprisingly, the censorship that they experienced on mainstream platforms like Twitter.

Taken together, the topic model analysis shows that the sample of users in my data consists of individuals on the right of the political spectrum, some of whom engaged with conspiratorial content and many of whom supported Donald Trump in the 2020 elections.

Measuring Deplatforming

My next step was to examine whether these accounts were suspended from Twitter. Although I did not have ex ante knowledge that these accounts would violate Twitter's rules, there was a nonzero probability that suspensions would occur, given the platform's heightened attention to moderating election-related content. For this purpose, I collected real-time data that tracked the status of the accounts of each of the 30,444 individuals every day between September 2020 and February 2021. Twitter did not systematically release information about its deplatforming of specific users, so I checked the account status of each user to see if and when it was suspended. I found that 2,200 of the individuals in my sample were banned during this period.[29] Figure 5.3 shows that accounts were deplatformed almost every day, with two large peaks in the number of suspensions in late September 2020 and early January 2021. These peaks correspond to suspension waves that targeted accounts associated with violent extremist organizations and the January 6 storming of the U.S. Capitol, respectively.[30]

Research Design

To understand how deplatforming shapes behavior on less-regulated platforms—and in particular, whether it makes social media users more receptive to extremist narratives—we might wish to compare the Gab activity of

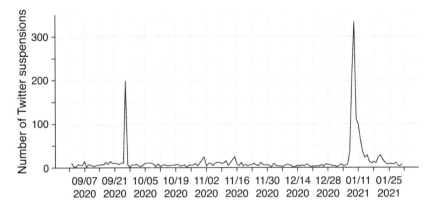

FIGURE 5.3. Twitter Suspensions by Date
Note: The figure shows the daily number of accounts that were suspended from Twitter during the study period. The two large peaks correspond to suspension waves that targeted accounts associated with violent extremist organizations and the January 6, 2021, storming of the US Capitol, respectively.

individuals who were banned from Twitter to the activity of those who were not. But one challenge with such a comparison is that users who were suspended from Twitter may have been more "extreme" in the first place. That is, they may have been more likely to violate the platform's content moderation policies, or they may simply have been interested more generally in different topics than nonsuspended users. From a scientific perspective, if we wished to examine the effect of deplatforming, we would need to conduct an experiment in which we randomly divide Twitter users into two groups and have one group experience suspensions while the other one did not. In theory, if deplatforming was randomly assigned in that way, we would be able to compare the behavior of users in the treatment and control groups on a less-regulated platform like Gab to precisely measure the cross-platform effect of deplatforming. However, this sort of experiment is not ethical to carry out without the agreement of users to participate in the study. Thus, I conducted an observational study by passively observing phenomena that naturally happened in the real world.

Even though Twitter increased its moderation activity during this period, its enforcement of its new moderation policies was not airtight. Some individuals who posted content violating the rules were deplatformed, but many others were not. The moderation system may not have reached them yet, or they may have gone undetected for some other reason. This "imperfect" enforcement of Twitter's rules provides an opportunity to examine the effect of deplatforming. If we can identify pairs of users who behaved similarly on Twitter prior to deplatforming but one was banned while the other was not, we can compare their behavior in the following weeks and months to estimate the impact of deplatforming. This approach is called "matching": we find pairs of individuals who are similar on a range of observable characteristics but differ in their experience of moderation.

To find matched pairs, I used information on the activity of these individuals on Twitter in the month before their suspension, including data on the content they posted on the platform, the engagement they received, and other observable characteristics about their profiles.[31] Of the 2,200 individuals in my data who were banned from Twitter during this period, 836 actively posted content on both platforms in the month preceding their suspension. Focusing here on these suspended users, I identify for each one a matched user who had similar profile characteristics, posted similar content, and received similar engagement in the month before their suspension. This amounts to 1,672 individuals who had active accounts on both Twitter and Gab, where one half were suspended from Twitter, and the other half were not. These individuals posted frequently on topics encompassed by the policies that the platform enforced during this period. But owing to imperfections in enforcement, only some were suspended by Twitter while others were not. This provides an opportunity to examine how a ban from Twitter shaped subsequent behavior on Gab.

Does Deplatforming Make Audiences More Receptive to Extremist Content?

With the matched sample of suspended and nonsuspended users, we can examine how Twitter deplatforming affects behavior on Gab. We are interested in both general usage of Gab and more specific discourse on deplatforming and engagement with extremist content, including messages posted by groups like the Oath Keepers.

Platform Usage Patterns

First, I examine whether individuals who were suspended from Twitter started using Gab more after their ban. If deplatforming pushes people to less-moderated spaces, we should expect to see an increase in the Gab activity of users banned from Twitter, but no such change for individuals who were not banned. To measure Gab activity, I counted the number of messages that each user posted on the platform every day in the two months before and after suspension. (In this setup, I give each nonsuspended user a "placebo" suspension date that is the same as the suspension date of the user matched to them.) The number of messages that social media users post is a useful indicator for the time they spend on a platform. However, posting content reflects only one aspect of people's online activity; it does not capture, for example, the amount of time that they spend scrolling down their timelines or the number of posts that they "like" or read. We can think about the number of daily messages that people post on a platform as capturing a portion of their overall online activity.

Figure 5.4 shows the number of daily posts that individuals in the suspended and nonsuspended groups posted on Gab. The x-axis shows the number of days before and after the suspension date (or the placebo suspension date for the unbanned users), and the y-axis shows the number of posts that each group shared on Gab every day. (See the Appendix for the same results when measuring effects at the user level.) Before the Twitter suspensions, the deplatformed and non-deplatformed groups posted a similar number of messages on Gab—about five hundred to one thousand messages per day on average. After the Twitter bans, however, the deplatformed group increased its number of posts fourfold within two weeks after the ban—a significant increase. We do not observe such a change in activity for the non-deplatformed group. The figure also shows that the Gab activity of the suspended group declined in the two months following their ban from Twitter but remained higher than it had been previously. In the appendix, I show the same patterns when examining the Gab activity of all suspended users—including those who did not enter the matched sample. These patterns suggest that Twitter deplatforming led banned users to shift their activity to less-moderated spaces like Gab.

Frustration with "Big Tech" Censorship

How did deplatformed users feel about their suspension from Twitter? Did they talk about their ban when they switched to Gab? And how did their emotional tone compare to that of users who were not suspended? To answer these questions, I analyzed the content of the messages that individuals shared on Gab. If deplatforming increases frustration and anger, we should see more messages expressing these sentiments among individuals who were banned. Specifically, we should see content expressing anger and frustration become

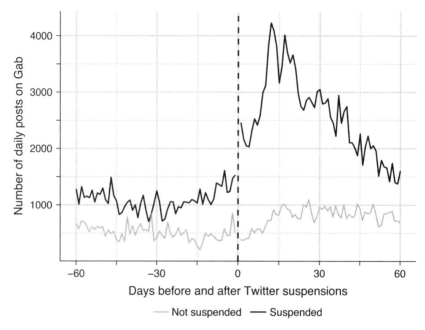

FIGURE 5.4. Gab Activity by Suspension Status
Note: The figure shows the number of daily posts that individuals in the suspended and nonsuspended groups posted on Gab. The *x*-axis shows the number of days before and after the suspension date (or the placebo suspension date for the nonbanned users), and the *y*-axis shows the number of daily posts that each group shared on Gab.

particularly salient in the days following the suspension among deplatformed users, but not among those who were not suspended.

I created two measures of anger and frustration with censorship. First, I used a sentiment dictionary to count the number of words expressing anger that each individual used in their Gab posts. Drawing on an extensive emotion lexicon developed by Saif Mohammad and Peter Turney, I identified words that expressed anger in each Gab message posted by suspended and nonsuspended users.[32] I then counted the number of posts that included anger words in the seven days before and after the suspension to examine whether expressions of anger increased in the posts of individuals who were banned from Twitter.[33] Panel A in figure 5.5 shows that posts expressing anger significantly increased in content shared by deplatformed users on Gab. In the week before Twitter's suspensions, both groups posted a similar number of "angry" posts— about fifteen to twenty messages per day on average. But after the suspensions,

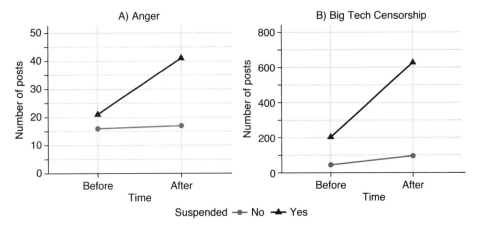

FIGURE 5.5. Expressing Anger over Deplatforming
Note: The figure shows the number of posts expressing anger and frustration with "Big Tech censorship" by users who were suspended from Twitter, in the week before and after they were suspended, and the number of such posts by those who were not suspended. Suspended users were significantly more likely to express anger and frustration from censorship than were nonsuspended users.

deplatformed users' messages expressing anger more than doubled, while nonsuspended users' posts remained largely the same.

I also measured the extent to which individuals expressed frustration with "Big Tech" censorship by counting the number of posts that contained keywords related to the topic.[34] It was common for Gab users to complain about mainstream platforms' content moderation policies—this is, after all, a common reason for using Gab in the first place. I found, however, that expressions of anger about content moderation by mainstream technology companies was substantially higher among individuals who were deplatformed from Twitter (see panel B in figure 5.5). This difference was present in the week before these users were suspended and then was significantly larger in the week following their ban. In the appendix, I show that anger and frustration were particularly strong among individuals who had many followers on Twitter. This suggests that anger from deplatforming may relate to the loss of followers on mainstream platforms.

When examining the specific complaints of these individuals over content moderation, I found a lot of discussion on the perceived injustice of Twitter's moderation policies, specifically, where political content was concerned. Many talked about Twitter's moderation of election-related content as being biased against conservatives, calling out the platform's labeling of posts and removal of content as efforts to meddle with the elections. "Twitter's use of warning labels on President Trump's posts during the election has been pretty ludicrous,"[35] said one individual. "Social media had the BALLS to censor the PRESIDENT of the United States of America and got away with it," said another.[36] Other users framed the moderation of political content as an attack on Trump supporters more generally, calling the increased moderation during the election a "massive coordinated cyber-attack on Trump voters."[37]

In a similar manner, many individuals who were deplatformed said that they believed that supporting Trump was the reason for their suspension. "Twitter suspended me. I guess being a Trump supporter is against the Twitter rules," commented one user.[38] Another agreed, saying that "Twitter just suspended my Twitter account because I'm pro Trump."[39] Other users even called themselves "Internet Refugees" who were "running from Communist media that produces endless hate-filled propaganda" against them, and they described Big Tech's moderation policies as tyrannous toward the right.[40]

There was also a lot of anger over the perceived loss of freedom on mainstream social media more generally. "Freedom of speech is no more. More and more of us are being driven underground," said one banned user.[41] "I was just suspended on Twitter and I don't even know why. No appeal. This is ridiculous. #Censorship #Twitter."[42] In one discussion on mainstream platforms' moderation policies, another deplatformed user argued that mainstream social media sites should not be those deciding what the public should post online. "Freedom of speech does include the right to be wrong, it leaves it up to the listener or in this case reader to decide, do research, thought, or whatever. Who are these people, the correctors, the nann[ies], who think it's their job to correct. . . . The MSM [mainstream media] has already admitted their job is to 'shape public opinion.' That is propaganda, not science or education."[43]

The anger over Twitter's deplatforming often continued into discussions of comradery and "togetherness" among banned users, who connected over their frustration from their suspension. "[Twitter] suspended my account today. They must be totally desperate. . . . Anyway, it's great to be with my patriot friends! Together, we'll go through WHATEVER TRAVAIL IS NECESSARY to preserve our constitutional Republic. Never give up! Never surrender."[44] Others, who noticed the high levels of migration to Gab, welcomed the new users: "FOR ALL THE NEWBIES COMING OVER FROM the swamp known as Twitter . . . this is a great video to watch to help initiate you into Gab. I've been here since September 2016 . . . and it's always been the safe haven for me from the censor-nazis at Twitter."[45] Others commented on their joy at seeing so many new users joining Gab, saying how "funny" it was to watch "all these folks being red pilled and experiencing free speech for the first time in a long while."[46] These connections formed on Gab between banned users, I argue, made the platform an attractive space for hate and militant groups' mobilization.

Engagement with Hateful and Extremist Content

Does anger and frustration from deplatforming make individuals more susceptible to extremist messaging? To answer this question, I examined the extent to which individuals in my matched dataset posted hateful content on Gab and, more directly, their engagement with the messages of extremist groups, like the Oath Keepers, that used spaces with less moderation to mobilize resistance for the election results.

HATE SPEECH AFTER DEPLATFORMING

Since Gab's moderation policies were significantly more lenient than Twitter's during the 2020 elections, it is possible that those who were deplatformed and started using Gab more frequently were also more likely to engage with hateful rhetoric as a result. To examine the effect of Twitter's deplatforming on engagement with hate speech on Gab, I studied the messages that users posted every day. Between September 2020 and February 2021, individuals in my dataset who had Gab and Twitter accounts posted over four million messages on both platforms. To measure hateful content at scale, I used a machine learning model that identified hate speech in the data by learning the words that were often used in messages expressing hate. The goal was to train an algorithm that would detect Gab posts conveying hateful content in the context of the 2020 elections—messages that would likely be banned on Twitter but allowed on less-regulated sites like Gab.

There are many different ways to define hate speech, and the meaning of the concept varies by context. Here I draw on the definition of the *Encyclopedia of Political Communication*, which states that hate speech consists of "comments containing speech aimed to terrorize, express prejudice and contempt toward, humiliate, degrade, abuse, threaten, ridicule, demean, and discriminate based on race, ethnicity, religion, sexual orientation, national origin, or gender."[47] Since I wanted to capture both hateful rhetoric and content in sympathy with Donald Trump's messaging style in the context of the elections—

which often relied on white nationalist sentiment—I focused on two categories in my definition of hateful content.[48] The first consisted of posts expressing prejudice and contempt toward individuals from a nonwhite social group, including "pejoratives and group-based insults" that can appear as "negative labels or narratives about the group's alleged negative behavior."[49] The second included content expressing support for or sympathy with white nationalism in the United States.

To train the algorithm, I created a training set by randomly sampling posts from the data that I downloaded from both platforms, and I worked with a large team of research assistants to annotate this sample as expressing hate speech or not. I then used the labeled data to train a deep learning model to detect hate speech. The appendix provides more details on the model design, training, and performance.

Did engagement with hateful content on Gab increase after individuals were deplatformed from Twitter? I examined this question by counting the number of Gab posts expressing hate speech every day, for both suspended and nonsuspended users in my sample. Figure 5.6 shows time trends in posting hateful content on Gab before and after Twitter's deplatforming. The x-axis shows the difference, in days, between the date of deplatforming and the date on which the suspended and nonsuspended groups posted on Gab, and the y-axis shows the number of posts that included hateful content.

I find that both groups posted similar levels of hate speech on Gab before the suspension—about fifty to seventy-five posts per day on average. These trends shifted dramatically, however, after Twitter's bans. Individuals in the deplatformed group started expressing significantly more hate on Gab after their suspension, while hateful content posted by those in the non-deplatformed group remained unchanged during the same time period. (The appendix shows the same results when conducting the analysis at the user level.) Thus, being suspended from Twitter increased users' posting of toxic content on Gab, either because they were spending more time on a less-moderated platform with higher levels of hateful content or because they felt a sense of "freedom" to post messages without restrictions.

THE OATH KEEPERS' MESSAGING ON GAB

The more interesting question is whether individuals who were banned from Twitter were more likely to engage with content posted by organizations like the Oath Keepers on less-moderated platforms after their ban.

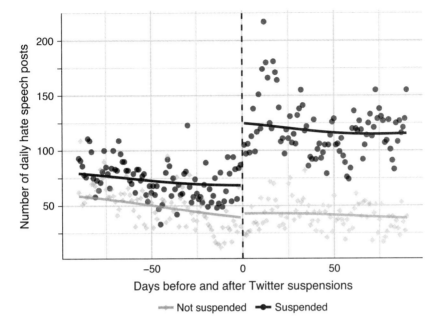

FIGURE 5.6. Posting Hate Speech on Gab
Note: The figure shows time trends in users' posting of hateful content on Gab
before and after being deplatformed by Twitter. The *x*-axis shows the difference,
in days, between the date of deplatforming and the date when the suspended and
nonsuspended groups posted on Gab, and the *y*-axis shows the number of posts
that included hateful content. The suspended group posted significantly more
hate speech on Gab after deplatforming.

Compared to other social media platforms, Gab sits right in the middle: it
has a significantly smaller user base than mainstream platforms like Facebook
or Twitter, but it is still larger than other fringe social media sites (see figure 4.1). Although Gab's content moderation policies are not completely "free"
(for example, it does restrict messages that could lead to an "imminent lawless
action" or other inauthentic behaviors that smaller sites do not restrict), Gab's
rules are much more lenient than large platforms' rules. This makes the platform an attractive space for extremist organizations because it allows them to
maximize both content authenticity and audience impact—factors that matter
for mobilization and recruitment on social media.

The Oath Keepers opened their official account on Gab in October 2018,
but the group was not active on the platform until the fall of 2020, when it was
banned from Twitter and Facebook for violating policies targeting domestic

extremist organizations.[50] On Gab, Oath Keepers' activists posted content seeking to attract new recruits and publicize their activities across the United States. As a group whose membership consisted mostly of current and former members of police forces and the military, the Oath Keepers' messages initially targeted Gab users who had prior experience in these institutions. "America NEEDS for EVERY POLICE OFFICER to uphold their OATH!!! If you are in Law Enforcement you should be an 'Oath Keeper,'" said the group on the platform.[51] Other messages targeted new Gab users: "If you are not already involved check out oathkeepers and join up. welcome to GAB."[52]

The Oath Keepers explained that Twitter's and Facebook's content moderation actions are part of larger efforts by the "radical left" to "cut out communications" for conservative-leaning voices. "This is going to get worse. . . . [The left-wing media] suspend us because they are afraid of our message," said the leader of the Oath Keepers in a video interview that was posted on Gab in September 2020. "They are apparently more afraid of what we are going to do . . . than they are concerned about tracking us."[53]

In the weeks and months following the 2020 elections, the vast majority of the group's messaging on Gab revolved around its members' resistance to Joe Biden's victory, and in particular their call for action to "Stop the Steal" and "Defeat the Coup." The Oath Keepers were adamant that the results of the 2020 elections were fraudulent, and they tried to mobilize resistance to the elections through alternative social media platforms, including Gab. "Trump has already won the 2020 election," they said, "but the Deep State froze the election after the polls closed on Election Day and they're desperately trying to steal this election."[54]

As part of its effort to resist the results, the group sought to mobilize support for a petition asking Trump to invoke the Insurrection Act, which would allow deploying forces to prevent the transfer of presidential power. The group's activists posted many messages on Gab asking users to sign the petition. "JOIN OATHKEEPERS IN DEMAND FOR INSURRECTION ACT—SIGN WH PETITION TODAY!" said one of their posts.[55] "Trump must Declare an insurrection and invoke the Insurrection Act and call up the National Guard into federal service," said another.[56]

To mobilize an even larger number of people, the Oath Keepers decided in November to open the organization to individuals who did not have prior service background. As one activist on Gab explained, "Oathkeepers is organized in all 50 states and have over 30k members countrywide. Due to the situation the country is in, they relaxed their requirement that you be prior military or law enforcement."[57] Many other messages linked to the Oath Keepers' recruitment page on their website: "If you are not an Oath Keepers member . . . please join! Go to: www.oathkeepers.org/membership/. You don't have to be prior service to be a member . . . we welcome all patriots."[58]

A similar common theme in the Oath Keepers' Gab messaging included calls to join their protests to resist the election results. A few days after Joe Biden was announced the winner, the group advertised a large protest that they organized in Washington, D.C. In a message that they posted on Gab, they said: "Oath Keepers and patriots, duty calls! We must all march on Washington D.C. and directly back-up and defend President Trump as he fights against the ongoing coup that is attempting to steal the election."[59]

The largest event that the group organized was on January 6, 2021—the day the US Congress was scheduled to certify the vote of the Electoral College that would give Biden the presidency. The Oath Keepers' activity for this day included a public-facing protest as well as more secret activity that involved plans to storm Capitol Hill.[60] In many messages that the group posted on Gab, they called others to join their protest. "Now is the time to stand. It's not too late to go. Jump on a plane! Jump in your car!" they said. "Show Congress that we the people will not stand for the election being stolen. . . . Stand now, or kneel forever."[61]

GAB USERS' ENGAGEMENT WITH THE OATH KEEPERS' CONTENT

Was the audience on Gab receptive to the Oath Keepers' mobilization efforts? To examine users' engagement with the Oath Keepers' messaging on the platform, I examined whether the content they posted included mentions of the group. I identified posts that talked about the Oath Keepers by looking for Gab messages that included keywords commonly used to refer to the group on the platform.[62] I then examined how messages mentioning the Oath Keepers and their activity varied over time, and in particular whether they differed between individuals who were banned from Twitter and those who were not.

If deplatforming made Gab users more receptive to extremist messaging, we would expect to see those who were suspended from Twitter become more engaged with extremist content, such as the messages posted by the Oath Keepers, after their ban. Figure 5.7 shows time trends in Gab users' mentions of the Oath Keepers before and after Twitter's suspensions. I find that attention to the Oath Keepers was very low among suspended and nonsuspended

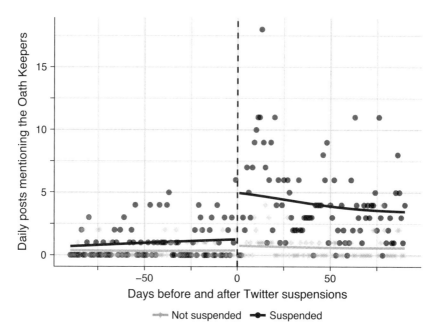

FIGURE 5.7. Engagement with the Oath Keepers' Messaging on Gab
Note: The figure shows time trends in mentions of the Oath Keepers on Gab before and after being deplatformed on Twitter. The *x*-axis shows the difference, in days, between the date of deplatforming and the date when individuals posted on Gab, and the *y*-axis shows the number of posts that mentioned the Oath Keepers. Suspended users became significantly more engaged with the Oath Keepers' content after deplatforming.

users before Twitter's deplatforming actions. The vast majority of individuals in my sample did not talk about the Oath Keepers at all, and if they did, they did so infrequently.

However, in the weeks and months after individuals in my dataset experienced Twitter's suspensions, they became significantly more engaged with the Oath Keepers' content—a trend that I do not observe for those who were not deplatformed (not even on Twitter; see the appendix for additional results). The change in banned users' attention to the Oath Keepers' messaging on Gab was quite significant: there was a threefold increase in mentions of the group in the post-suspension period.

To further examine the correlation between engagement with the Oath Keepers and anger about being deplatformed, I looked at whether mentions of the group varied between suspended users who expressed anger over being banned from Twitter and those whose posts conveyed a more neutral emotional tone. I found that individuals who were angry about Twitter's censorship were almost twice as likely to engage with the Oath Keepers' content on Gab than were those who expressed less anger. This finding further supports my argument that frustration from deplatforming can make individuals more receptive to extremist messaging on less-moderated social media sites.

Conclusion

This chapter has shown how militant and hate organizations use less-moderated platforms for mobilization and recruitment by focusing on the audience from which these groups seek to mobilize supporters. I argued that even though less-moderated platforms have smaller audiences, they can be useful for mobilization when users of these platforms find the content that they disseminate appealing. Drawing on novel cross-platform data, I showed that personal experiences with content moderation—in particular, deplatforming—can make individuals susceptible to extremist propaganda, especially when such messaging effectively targets their grievances.

The ability of extremist groups to mobilize supporters on less-regulated platforms is a direct result of the diversity in content policies across social media sites. When some platforms impose restrictions while others do not, efforts by some platforms to create safer spaces online are counteracted by the lack of moderation on other platforms.

In the context of the 2020 US elections, the increase in the moderation of election-related content by mainstream platforms such as Facebook and Twitter created spillover effects on platforms with more lenient policies, such as Gab, where deplatformed individuals found a "safe haven" in which they were exposed to greater levels of hate speech and extremist content. These findings point to the importance of taking into account the activity taking place on less-regulated platforms when considering content moderation as a policy tool to combat online harms.

6

Reaching the Masses
by Changing Messaging

Telegram is not a media platform for dawa [proselytization] . . . rarely would
you find someone from the general public following you. That's why our main
platform is where the General Public is found. Like on Twitter and Facebook.

—ISLAMIC STATE ACTIVIST, QUOTED IN BERGER
AND PEREZ, "THE ISLAMIC STATE'S DIMINISHING
RETURNS ON TWITTER," 2016

WHEN THE ISLAMIC STATE SHIFTED its activities to Telegram, a platform
with more lenient content moderation policies, it found new ways to advance
its cause online. The group's activists created a myriad of new channels on
which they discussed the latest events and propaganda releases, connected
with friends, and coordinated "offline" activities—even violent attacks. But what
Telegram lacked was a large audience. Unlike mainstream platforms that
hosted large swaths of the general public, Telegram was considered more
"niche"—only those already interested in the Islamic State would go out and
seek the group's channels on Telegram. The platform was insufficient for reaching the broader public. At the same time, large platforms like Twitter, Facebook, and YouTube placed strong restrictions on what could be posted on
their sites. Almost any piece of content that Islamic State activists wished to
post on these platforms was immediately removed, before it could reach the
intended audience. Thus, in order to continue operating on large but more
moderated platforms, the group's activists needed to change how they
communicated.

In the previous chapters, I explained how militant actors leverage diversity in platform policies to build resilience to moderation. I showed how groups identify platforms to which to migrate, mobilize supporters on less-moderated spaces, and exploit audience grievances from moderation to drive support for their cause. In this chapter, I explain how extremist groups adapt to moderation even on the most restrictive platforms by shifting their messaging strategies. In a multi-platform world, adapting messaging is complementary to migration: groups reach audiences not only by decamping to less-moderated platforms but also by retaining a presence on mainstream social media sites. In much the same way that a movie can reach a wider audience by removing age-inappropriate content and attaining a PG rating, dangerous organizations may be willing to trade off the "authenticity" of their message for the sake of accessing influential platforms. But adapting messaging to platform rules is not the only way by which groups access high-impact platforms. In addition to toning down violating content, dangerous organizations also increase their survivability on moderated platforms by engaging in threshold evasion: making strategic efforts to smuggle in prohibited messaging alongside seemingly innocuous content and thereby evade detection. I discuss each of these tactics in turn.

Content Adaptation

To publish on large, moderated platforms, actors must follow the rules. Content deemed harmful is subject to suspension and takedown. This is usually not a problem for political actors who rarely trigger moderation thresholds.[1] By contrast, militant groups tend to post prohibited content (such as depictions of violence), and some are subject to outright bans on any content they might produce. These actors have no choice but to adapt.

What does adaptation look like in practice? Chapter 2 described how militant and hate organizations identify the moderation thresholds of different platforms. Notwithstanding a general preference for posting freely without restrictions, groups sometimes opt for publishing modified versions of their material in order to remain influential on platforms that restrict content. To do so, they may censor certain types of content, post more compliant content, or embed messages in "innocent" material.

In this section, I describe the process of content adaptation, both within platforms and across platforms, by analyzing two case studies. First, I examine the Taliban's use of Twitter and its attempts to post content promoting violence on the platform. The case involving the Taliban is an interesting one because the group was banned on many mainstream social media platforms but not on Twitter. This provides an opportunity to examine how the group modified the content it produced to comply with Twitter's policies prohibiting the glorification of violence.

Second, I study how the QAnon movement responded to moderation policies when technology companies sought to limit its content on their sites. I show that after the policy change, QAnon activists disseminated milder versions of their message on platforms that embraced stricter moderation thresholds while keeping a more authentic version on less-moderated platforms. These cases illustrate how content adaptation allows groups to remain influential on social media by strategically adapting their messages to platforms' moderation rules.

The Taliban's Adaptation to Content Moderation

Wars today cannot be won without media. Media aims at the heart rather than the body, [and] if the heart is defeated, the battle is won.

—WEBSITE EDITOR FOR THE TALIBAN, QUOTED IN JOHNSON,
DUPEE, AND SHAAKER, "THE TALIBAN'S USE OF THE INTERNET,
SOCIAL MEDIA VIDEO, RADIO STATIONS, AND GRAFFITI," 2018

The Taliban's journey into social media is a fascinating story. From a group that had earlier banned the use of any media—including television and the internet—it transformed in the early years of the twenty-first century into a tech-savvy organization capable of exploiting social media platforms to promote its message online. The Taliban's influence operations on social media have been cited as one of the reasons the group was so successful in taking over Afghanistan's territory in the summer of 2021, and its online media teams have been particularly sensitive to platforms' content policies. To remain effective online in the face of growing regulation, the group has been careful to remain within the rules, providing a useful case with which to study content adaptation.

Compared to other militant groups banned from mainstream platforms, the Taliban has been given more leeway. While platforms like Facebook and YouTube outlawed the group for being a "dangerous organization," Twitter did not ban the Taliban. Instead, the platform took down content posted by the group only when it violated its policies against the glorification of violence and platform manipulation.[2] Thus, while any message that the Taliban posted on Facebook and YouTube was subject to automatic removal, the group's content was allowed to remain on Twitter as long as it complied with the rules. This has created an opportunity to study the Taliban's adaptation to Twitter's policies—in particular, the group's strategy of shifting its messaging to remain under Twitter's moderation threshold after experiencing suspensions.

Early Adoption of Online Media

Like many other militant organizations, the Taliban has been relying on propaganda to support its activities. Long before it embraced the virtual world, the group had been using propaganda to influence local populations through official print publications, pamphlets, audiocassettes, and DVDs, among other media. One of the group's most widely known influence efforts took the form of the "night letters" it disseminated in areas under its control to intimidate the local population into compliance. For example, in a night letter distributed in the Wardak province, the Taliban sought to deter families from sending their daughters to a government-run school. In another one, the group warned residents in Khost province against working with or supporting international forces and the Afghan government, threatening them with death if they failed to heed the warning.[3] Over time, it became clear that a more robust online presence would benefit the group's messaging efforts, not only locally but also in shaping global public opinion.

When social media platforms became prominent toward the end of the first decade of the 2000s, the Taliban began experimenting with disseminating content on those platforms as well. In 2009 the group launched its first YouTube channel to share videos that it then embedded on its website.[4] Even though it was initially apprehensive about using "Western" technology platforms, the group began trying out various features offered by these platforms, such as Facebook's "share" button, which allowed readers of its website to share content with their friends.[5] It was not until 2011 that the Taliban launched official accounts on Facebook and Twitter to directly disseminate its propaganda. Some argue that the official adoption of online platforms was inspired by successful mobilization during the Arab Spring and the growing popularity of social media among other militant groups in the region.[6]

In its early days, the Taliban attracted a relatively small number of followers on Facebook, Twitter, and YouTube. The group's first Twitter account, for example, had only about 5,000 followers in 2011, and its Facebook pages had just over 2,000 "likes."[7] Over time, however, the group's online networks grew substantially. As of March 2024, the Twitter account for the Taliban's spokesperson had over 960,000 followers, and the networks of the group's sympathizers on the platform consisted of over 92,000 users.

Online Amplification of Offline Activities

One of the most distinctive ways in which the Taliban has been using social media is in its amplification of military activities. As in its earlier "offline" propaganda campaigns, the group has been focused on using media to create an image of itself as a capable and strong militant actor. An analysis of tens of thousands of propaganda pieces created by the Taliban found that the vast majority focused on the group's military victories against Afghan forces, including details on battlefield events as well as more general imagery of the group's training in military preparedness.[8] The Taliban's propaganda included some nonmilitary topics, such as its ability to govern and its other civilian activities, but, perhaps more than other groups, it sharply focused its online campaigns on supporting its military offensive on the ground.

The group's agility in using social media was in sharp contrast to the Afghan government's methods for getting its message out. Upon launching an offensive on a city or region in Afghanistan, the Taliban was quick to publicize the event on social media, providing details about what had happened even before the Afghan government could deliver a formal announcement. This allowed the Taliban to shape the narrative around the event in its favor and present itself as a relatively reliable source of information, even for Western journalists.[9]

It is not surprising that the group used similar tactics to support its takeover of Afghanistan in the summer of 2021. In May of that year, when the United States started withdrawing troops from Afghanistan, the Taliban launched a large offensive to take over territory in the country. Alongside weapons, the group provided soldiers with smartphones and microphones, asking them to share real-time information about military actions through social media.[10]

The extensive use of online platforms helped the Taliban create an impression that its victory was inevitable. Even when its fighters were still engaged in combat in contested areas and it was unclear whether they would win, the group's activists disseminated thousands of social media posts declaring their victory. In August 2021, as the Taliban made advances in Mazar-i-Sharif, the fourth-largest city in Afghanistan, online activists launched a coordinated social media campaign to propagate the message of its growing strength. They disseminated content aimed at intimidating Afghan soldiers in the area, stating that the "Taliban were 'advancing rapidly' on the city, continuing to fight, and launching operations 'from all four sides of the city.'"[11] An investigation by the Atlantic Council's Digital Forensic Research Lab found that the Taliban's messages were not only shared by local fighters but also copied and pasted over a hundred times on Twitter by a cadre of online activists. The online narrative that the group was advancing focused attention on the weakness of the Afghan forces and strengthened the image of the Taliban as a victorious actor. Some have pointed to these kinds of online campaigns as an explanation for why many Afghan soldiers fled their posts in the summer 2021 campaign, leading to one of the most remarkable takeovers of territory by an insurgent group in recent history.[12]

Social Media Platforms and Moderation of the Taliban's Content

The ability of the Taliban to use social media so effectively that it could shape reality on the ground caught many by surprise. Even though experts were expecting the group to take over territory after the withdrawal of American forces, few, including President Biden, anticipated that the Taliban would advance so quickly.[13]

Since the Taliban became the de facto government of Afghanistan, some have wondered whether and how social media companies should moderate its activity online. As a group that has been known to have links to terrorism, should it be banned from online platforms? Or should social media companies allow it to use their services, as they would any other government? Different platforms have adopted different policies regarding the Taliban: some have decided to ban the group, while others have allowed it to operate more freely. This variation in content moderation has enabled the continued advancement of the group's message through less-moderated platforms.

The mainstream platforms with the most restrictive policies toward the Taliban were Facebook, Instagram, WhatsApp, and YouTube, all of which banned the group on the basis of its inclusion on the US government's list of Specially Designated Global Terrorists (SDGTs). As stated in its community standards, Facebook did not allow "organizations or individuals that proclaim a violent mission or are engaged in violence to have a presence on Facebook."[14] Instagram and WhatsApp, whose moderation is based on the same standards, followed suit. "We are relying on that policy to proactively take down anything that we can that might be dangerous or that is related to the Taliban in general," said the head of Instagram in an interview.[15]

YouTube similarly said that it removed content "produced by violent criminal or terrorist organizations" or content that "depicts the insignia, logos, or symbols of violent criminal or terrorist organizations in order to praise or promote them."[16] YouTube banned the Taliban from its platform because the US government had designated it a global terrorist group. Any message, video, or post that the group sought to upload was therefore subject to removal, regardless of the specific content.

But not all platforms took such a strict stance against the Taliban. Twitter, Telegram, and a range of smaller platforms did not impose actor-level bans. Twitter stood out in particular because its limited moderation of Taliban content contrasted with its treatment of other militant organizations, such as the Islamic State, Al-Shabaab, and Al-Qaeda. In a statement explaining Twitter's moderation decisions relating to the Taliban, a representative of the company said that "Twitter's top priority is keeping people safe, and we remain vigilant. We will continue to proactively enforce our rules and review content that may violate Twitter Rules, specifically policies against glorification of violence and platform manipulation and spam."[17]

In its policy against the glorification of violence, Twitter stated that it would ban content "glorifying, praising, condoning, or celebrating:

- violent acts committed by civilians that resulted in death or serious physical injury, e.g., murders, mass shootings;
- attacks carried out by terrorist organizations or violent extremist groups (as defined by [the] terrorism and violent extremism policy); and
- violent events that targeted protected groups."[18]

Under this rule, any content posted by the Taliban that promotes violent attacks is subject to removal from the platform. However, since the Taliban was not subject to an actor-level ban, content that did not publicize or promote violence remained on Twitter.

A Study of the Taliban's Adaptation to Content Moderation

The theoretical framework presented in chapter 2 shows that groups that build resilience to moderation not only migrate to platforms with more permissive content policies but also adapt their messaging to the rules of the platforms on which they seek to operate. Since the Taliban was subject to an actor-level ban on almost every large platform except Twitter, it is not surprising that the Taliban focused its messaging there. But Twitter's moderation policies required that the group refrain from posting content glorifying violence. Since the Taliban's online campaigns sought to emphasize its military victory against Afghan forces, limiting content describing violent attacks could make it harder to project an image of military strength.

I examined how the Taliban adapted to Twitter's policies by conducting an empirical study of its messaging around the time the platform began enforcing its rules against the group's glorification of violence. I employed several sources of data in examining what the Taliban posted on Twitter over time and whether its messages included content that violated the platform's rules; when Twitter enforced its policies against the glorification of violence; and finally, how the Taliban reacted—if at all—to Twitter's suspension of its accounts.

To collect data on the Taliban's activity on Twitter, I assembled a list of 190 handles used by the group on the platform. The list consisted of the account of the official spokesperson of the organization, Zabihullah Mujahid, as well as the accounts of other well-known Taliban activists.[19] To gather information on the content that these accounts posted on Twitter, as well as the accounts' status on the platform, I used an automated tracker that prospectively collected data from Twitter between March and December 2021. The real-time data collection allowed me to archive valuable information on the Taliban's messaging on the platform, even in cases where the content was later removed for violating the rules. Each day the tracker gathered information about the posts that Taliban accounts shared on Twitter and checked whether they were still active or suspended from the platform.

In total, I was able to capture 112,793 Twitter posts shared by Taliban accounts during this period. The vast majority of the content (over 77 percent) was in Pashto and Dari, the most popular languages in Afghanistan. The other languages used by the group on Twitter included Urdu, Arabic, and English. This language distribution is similar to what was found in other Taliban media: even though the group disseminated propaganda in multiple languages, it often focused on content that would be most relevant to the local populations in Afghanistan.[20]

To measure the extent to which these accounts posted content that violated Twitter's policy against the glorification of violence, I looked for messages in Taliban activists' Twitter posts that described violent attacks. Because the group used Twitter to amplify its military offensive on the ground, its activists often posted details about the Taliban's military activities in various locations in Afghanistan. For example, in a post from an account that was later suspended by Twitter, Taliban activists celebrated the detonation of a car bomb on an army camp that killed or injured more than twenty Afghan soldiers.[21] In another post that was later removed by Twitter, the group promoted its takeover of a district in Afghanistan and the killing and surrender of members of the Afghan army.[22]

Since such acts of violence were promoted by the Taliban in various ways—using different words in multiple languages—I created a list of keywords that could capture descriptions of violence in various forms. To ensure that the list included a diverse set of terms, I used a computational method called "word embeddings"; this method makes it possible to find various representations, or synonyms, of a given word in a given corpus of text. In allowing researchers to study the context in which words appear in a set of documents and to identify words that frequently co-occur, word embeddings have become a useful tool in many social science applications.[23] I used a skip-gram word embeddings model to find words that captured the concept of "attack" as conveyed in Taliban tweets in Pashto, Dari, Urdu, Arabic, and English. I found that the words "explosion," "bomb," "kill," "operation," "base," "troops," and "enemy" were most closely associated with "attack" across languages.[24] I used the top twenty words in each language to identify Taliban posts on Twitter that talked about violent attacks.[25]

In addition to studying the messages that Taliban activists posted on Twitter, I also collected data on their status on the platform. Between March and October 2021, 38 of the 190 Taliban accounts that I was tracking were suspended from Twitter. I do not have information on what exactly led to their suspension, but it is possible to examine whether the content that suspended accounts posted was more likely to violate Twitter's rules against the glorification of violence than content posted by accounts that were not banned.

Figure 6.1 shows the daily frequency of posts talking about violent attacks by Taliban accounts that were suspended from Twitter and those that were not. Although the time trends in posting about violence were similar for suspended and nonsuspended accounts, I find that banned Taliban activists were more likely to post about violence in the weeks before their suspension. The figure shows a steady increase in the number of posts describing violent attacks starting in April 2021, which roughly corresponds to the time when the group began its ground offensive to take over territory in Afghanistan.

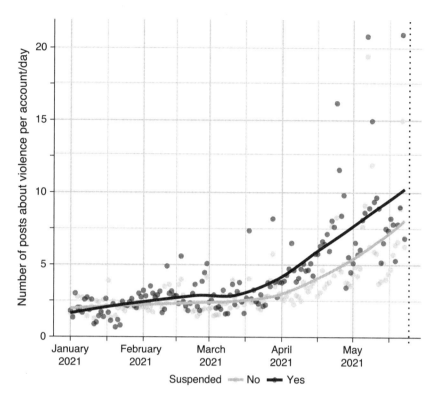

FIGURE 6.1. Taliban Accounts' Posts about Violence by Suspension Status
Note: The figure shows the daily frequency of Twitter posts about violent attacks by Taliban accounts that were suspended from Twitter (dark gray) and those that were not (light gray). The dotted vertical line marks the date of the first suspension wave (May 25, 2021).

Shifting Discourse on Violent Attacks

The suspension of certain Taliban Twitter accounts provides an opportunity to study how the rest of the group's activists who were not suspended reacted to Twitter's enforcement of its policies. In other words, the deplatforming of Taliban members' accounts from Twitter provides concrete information about the platform's moderation threshold. Even though Twitter did not change its policy against the glorification of violence during this period, it did take action to enforce its rules in a way that gives clues about the kind of content that was more likely to be removed. Thus, if the Taliban engaged in content adaptation in order to remain active on Twitter, we would expect to see its members tone down their messages promoting violence to avoid further suspensions.

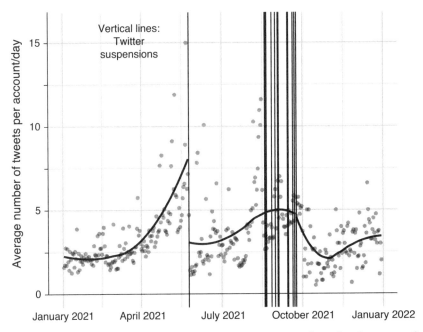

FIGURE 6.2. Adaptation to Twitter's Policy against the Glorification of Violence
Note: The figure shows the daily frequency of tweets about violent attacks by Taliban accounts before and after Twitter's suspension waves. The black lines represent smoothed versions of the raw data in three periods: (1) before the first deplatforming wave on May 25, 2021, (2) after the first wave and before the second wave in August 2021, and (3) after the second wave.

Figure 6.2 provides a clear picture of the Taliban's adaptation to Twitter's moderation. The figure shows the over-time trends in the group's posting about violent attacks, where the y-axis shows the average number of daily tweets about violence posted by each nonsuspended Taliban account. It can be seen that Taliban activists frequently talked about violence on Twitter, and many posted several times a day about attacks, a trend that intensified with the beginning of the group's military offensive in the spring of 2021.

However, the figure also shows that Taliban activists became more careful in their postings about violence after experiencing suspensions. In the figure, the vertical black lines show the dates on which Taliban Twitter accounts were suspended. The first suspension wave took place on May 25, 2021, when twenty Taliban accounts were banned from Twitter at once. After the takeover of

Kabul on August 15, Twitter suspended additional accounts associated with the group, but this time it spread the enforcement actions over several weeks.

The data show that Taliban activists shifted their messaging after experiencing bans on Twitter. Before the first suspension wave, the group's activists increased their violent discourse on the platform: the average number of daily posts talking about attacks more than doubled between April and May 2021. After the first wave of suspensions, the group sharply reduced content promoting violence. From an average of over fifteen daily posts per account on the day before the bans, Taliban activists decreased their posts about violence to less than two per account-day in the days after a suspension. In the following months, Taliban accounts continued to avoid posting frequently on the platform about violent attacks. But in August 2021, when the group engaged in its final offensive to take over Kabul, its members again intensified their posts about violence. This time, however, they were more careful with their content than they had been before the first suspension wave, posting only several tweets per account-day about violent attacks.

This decrease in the Taliban's messages about violence reflected a more general decline in the content that the group posted after Twitter's suspensions. When I examined the messages that Taliban activists posted during this period, I found increased awareness of content moderation. Some activists publicized their new accounts after their old accounts were suspended,[26] others lamented Twitter's removal of comments and "likes" on their posts,[27] and still others were frustrated that Twitter did not allow them to post photos and videos.[28]

Within two weeks after Twitter's first suspension wave in May 2021, the group's members started publicizing new handles. "[This is] the official Twitter page of the Islamic Emirate of Afghanistan. I hope you will help me to publish it," said one activist.[29] "Follow the official Twitter page of the Islamic Emirate of Da'wah," said another.[30] When it became clear that new accounts could be created without eliciting further suspensions, Taliban members rejoiced about their ability to use Twitter. "Twitter (@Twitter) is freer than Facebook (@Facebook)," said one Taliban member.[31] "This is Twitter, it's not hard to be a talib," said another.[32]

A Shift Away from Violence

When Twitter began suspending more Taliban accounts after the fall of Kabul, the group again toned down its discourse about violence, posting significantly less often about attacks than at any time during the study period.

The shift in messaging away from war-related content was identified in other Taliban media published around the same time; such shifts were likely to be related to the group's effort to project itself as a legitimate government actor after it had consolidated power over Afghanistan.[33] This sentiment was captured in a BBC interview with the Taliban's social media director: "Social media is [a] powerful tool to change public perception. . . . We want to change the perception of the Taliban."[34]

When examining Taliban activists' discourse about governance, I found that the group did increase its postings about government-related topics on Twitter after it consolidated its power over Afghanistan.[35] Although discourse on governance was present in Taliban tweets even before it took over the country, governance-related content increased by 65 percent after August 2021.[36] Disseminating posts about governance and civilian affairs not only helped the Taliban avoid moderation on Twitter but also facilitated the creation of a new public image for the group. By adapting its content to fit within Twitter's moderation rules, the group was able to maintain its presence on the platform while at the same time making itself more appealing to a larger audience.

The case of the Taliban shows how militant actors can "soften" their content in order to remain active on moderated platforms. Even though the group benefited from showcasing its military strength on Twitter, its members toned down their messages about violent attacks to avoid suspensions. However, even as Taliban activists exhibited careful adaptation to Twitter's moderation policies, the group's network of sympathizers were continuing to promote its violent activity on the platform, as I show later in the chapter. The Taliban adopted a strategy of threshold evasion to advance potentially objectionable content through unaffiliated accounts that were less likely to be detected and removed.

Adapting Messaging across Platforms: The Case of QAnon

Thus far, I have described content adaptation within a single platform. But messaging can also be adapted to conform to platform rules across multiple online spaces. Because social media platforms have different moderation thresholds, groups can disseminate adapted forms of their messages on each platform and thereby reach broader audiences. Tailoring content also allows groups to align their messages more closely with the preferences of each platform's audience, making those messages more appealing. Adapting to moderation thresholds *across platforms* can broaden a group's base of support.

Here I examine how extremist actors engage in cross-platform content adaptation by discussing the QAnon movement, whose rapid growth on social media was very much driven by its appeal to diverse audiences on different platforms. QAnon offers a particularly compelling case through which to study cross-platform content adaptation because it has maintained a presence on many platforms in parallel and experienced a dramatic shift in moderation over time. QAnon activists operated freely on mainstream social media in the movement's early years, but by mid-2020 technology companies were cracking down on the movement, heavily restricting the sort of content that activists could post online. The shift in moderation policies provides an opportunity to examine how QAnon adapted in the face of new forms of moderation—not only *within* mainstream platforms but also *across* other less-moderated sites.

From the Fringes of the Internet to Mainstream Social Media

In many ways, QAnon is a child of the internet. Unlike extremist organizations that were founded "offline" and later established a social media presence, QAnon arose in the digital world. The origins of the movement can be traced to posts that appeared in 2017 on the 4chan messaging board by an anonymous account called "Q Clearance Patriot"—or "Q." Q presented himself as a high-ranking member of the Trump administration who had access to classified information about the then-president's plan to fight against a group of Democratic leaders and Hollywood celebrities who, as Q argued, were operating a child sex trafficking ring. Q posted thousands of messages predicting that various ring leaders would soon be arrested for being "child-eating pedophiles."[37] Over time the range of conspiracies expanded to other actors and stories.[38]

As fringe as these ideas may sound, Q began attracting a large number of followers who were intrigued by his "insider" stories and predictions about the upcoming crackdown on corrupt elites. As the anonymous account continued posting content on messaging boards such as 4chan and 8chan, an online community of "Q believers" grew on these sites and soon expanded to mainstream platforms.[39] QAnon first established a presence on Reddit, a popular forum on which users can create "subreddits"—communities that they autonomously manage and moderate. Reddit helped QAnon supporters popularize Q's messages by making them accessible to a wider segment of the public. Since Reddit was a much larger platform that was easier to navigate than fringe messaging boards, it allowed the movement to disseminate its content to a broader audience and attract people closer to the mainstream.[40]

Indeed, after QAnon supporters moved to Reddit, the movement experienced almost exponential growth in the number of its followers. QAnon's subreddit reached more than seventy thousand subscribers within several months, and activists soon began publicizing Q's message on other platforms as well.[41] Some created YouTube videos explaining the movement's core beliefs, and others dedicated their Facebook and Twitter accounts to supporting QAnon's message. Soon enough, the movement's videos had attracted millions of views, and its sympathizers began engaging in enthusiastic conversations about Q's hidden messages and their meaning for the future.[42]

Over time, thousands of QAnon groups and pages proliferated on Facebook, Twitter, and YouTube, attracting millions of followers.[43] In addition to organic growth, the movement also used advertisements and coordinated campaigns to amplify its messages. An investigation by Graphika, a social media research firm that specializes in analyzing networks, found that QAnon-affiliated accounts on Twitter were densely connected to one another, often acting as "armies" pushing the movement's content on the platform. They were particularly effective at inserting QAnon-inspired messages into unrelated political conversations. When a news topic was trending on Twitter, QAnon activists would post hashtags related to the topic to inject Q's ideas into broader online discussions about the event.[44]

The rapid growth of QAnon communities online illustrates the power of social media—especially mainstream platforms—in facilitating the growth of even the most fringe ideologies. The messages advanced by Q moved so rapidly from niche platforms to mainstream media that by 2020 a significant portion of American citizens began believing in some aspects of the theory. For example, in a nationally representative poll conducted in December 2020, 17 percent of the respondents said that they believed that "a group of Satan-worshipping elites who run a child sex ring are trying to control our politics and media"—a core belief of the QAnon conspiracy.[45] QAnon even made its way into politics: in the 2020 US elections, over ninety individuals who ran for Congress publicly supported the movement, and two were elected to Congress.[46] Beyond the United States, QAnon also gained large followings in Europe, Latin America, and Japan.[47]

Platforms' Changing Policies toward QAnon

QAnon's rising influence on social media prompted criticism that technology companies were not taking action to moderate that content. As a matter of principle, many platforms adopted a policy of non-interference with user-generated content that did not violate their terms of service. QAnon's criticism of Washington elites was initially seen as speech that was perhaps outlandish but not harmful.[48]

However, as QAnon communities grew on social media, it became clear that their ideas were becoming increasingly extremist and had the potential to cause harm. Reddit was the first to observe the problem. In some Reddit communities, where QAnon sympathizers posted thousands of comments every day, there was a rapid increase in threats and calls for violence against Hillary Clinton and other members of the US government. In other Reddit communities, QAnon sympathizers maliciously shared personal information about individuals they thought were part of the trafficking ring and disseminated fabricated images of some of them eating children.[49] As the toxicity of QAnon communities increased on Reddit, the company decided to ban the movement from its platform. In September 2018, Reddit announced that it had outlawed several QAnon communities, stating that "posting content that incites violence, disseminates personal information, or harasses will get users and communities banned."[50]

But the Reddit ban did not prevent QAnon from promoting its violent ideology online. Shortly thereafter, the movement flocked to Facebook, Twitter, and YouTube, where it amassed even larger audiences. A wave of toxic posts, harassment, and incitement to violence soon followed. Between 2018 and 2020, numerous incidents were reported across the United States involving violence or attempted violence by QAnon supporters. Some engaged in armed standoffs with the police, others attempted kidnappings, and still others sought to assassinate individuals believed to be affiliated with the trafficking ring—including high-level government officials.[51] In 2019, the FBI warned that QAnon could become a serious domestic terrorist threat: "The FBI assesses [that] anti-government, identity based, and fringe political conspiracy theories very likely motivate some domestic extremists, wholly or in part, to commit criminal and sometimes violent activity."[52]

While the FBI's warning did not lead to an immediate change in platforms' moderation policies, the COVID-19 pandemic—which provided the movement with new mobilization opportunities that resulted in a dramatic growth in toxic content, harassment, and incitement of violence—led many companies to change their policies toward QAnon.

Among large platforms, Twitter was the first to act. On July 21, 2020, the company announced the suspension of over seven thousand QAnon accounts for violating its policies:

> This week we are taking further action on so-called "QAnon" activity across the service. We will permanently suspend accounts Tweeting about these topics that we know are engaged in violations of our multi-account policy, coordinating abuse around individual victims, or are attempting to evade a previous suspension—something we've seen more of in recent weeks.[53]

In addition to banning accounts, Twitter also announced that it would remove QAnon content from its automated recommendations, reduce its appearance in conversations and searches, and block URLs associated with QAnon from being shared on its site. These steps reflected a change in the platform's moderation threshold that now designated *any* QAnon material as a violation of its rules.

After Twitter changed its policies toward QAnon, other platforms followed. On August 19, 2020, Facebook announced that its policy banning dangerous individuals and organizations would extend to groups that "have demonstrated significant risks to public safety but do not meet the rigorous criteria to be designated as a dangerous organization."[54] Such groups included QAnon as well as far-left anarchist groups and militias in the United States. Initially, Facebook only took down posts that could be used by these groups to engage in organized violence but allowed ideologically supportive content to remain on the platform. However, it was soon criticized for not doing enough to curb QAnon's influence.[55] Subsequently, Facebook updated its policy again in October 2020 to ban "any Facebook Pages, Groups and Instagram accounts representing QAnon, even if they contain no violent content."[56] Facebook's new policies against QAnon aimed at preventing the movement from growing on its platform marked a sharp change in the company's moderation threshold.

Around the same time, other companies took similar actions. YouTube announced that the company was working to "curb hate and harassment by removing more conspiracy theory content used to justify real-world violence." To further this effort, the company removed tens of thousands of videos and suspended hundreds of channels promoting QAnon.[57] Pinterest also announced that it was "not a place for QAnon conspiracy theories or other harmful and misleading content," adding that its moderators would "proactively look for and remove content related to QAnon, in addition to taking action on content reported to [the platform]."[58] Efforts to ban QAnon continued on other platforms as well.[59]

But not all social networks outlawed QAnon. Smaller, less-moderated platforms continued to allow the movement to flourish. The CEO of Gab, for example, welcomed QAnon supporters on his platform after they were banned from Facebook. In a statement published on the platform's blog, he said:

> You can deplatform these people from legacy tech platforms and call them "racists" and "conspiracy theorists" in the legacy media, but nothing can stop what has already been started and it will only continue to grow. . . . Based on what I have observed for the past several months, the core philosophy of the QAnon community is to be inherently skeptical of what legacy media elites report, conduct your own research, and share the truth far and wide. I see nothing wrong with this and we gladly welcome it on Gab.com.[60]

The striking difference between Gab's approach and that of other platforms allowed QAnon to continue growing and exerting influence even after mainstream platforms banned the movement. Although QAnon content was removed from Facebook and Twitter, it continued to flourish on other platforms like Gab and Parler, and ultimately QAnon activists were able to mobilize hundreds of supporters to engage in real-world harm—for example, during the attack on the US Capitol on January 6, 2021. Much of the mobilization for January 6 took place on these less-moderated platforms, as numerous examples have shown.[61]

The variation between moderation thresholds allows us to examine how groups engage in content adaptation *across* platforms. Because QAnon was subject to a strict ban on mainstream platforms, supporters had to adapt content in a way that made their messages appear unrelated to QAnon. These supporters did so by employing vague rhetoric that allowed them initially to avoid triggering mainstream platforms' takedown policies while continuing to share the "more authentic" versions of their messages on fringe platforms with more lenient moderation thresholds.

QAnon's Content Adaptation across Platforms

To adapt content to these varying policies, QAnon supporters shared modified versions of their message on platforms with stricter moderation rules while keeping more authentic versions of their content on platforms where the movement was not banned. Since Twitter was among the first social media platforms to ban QAnon, I focus on Twitter to study content adaptation. But since QAnon activists used other platforms as well, I also examine how *these same activists* behaved on Gab, a platform with looser moderation rules. For this purpose, I draw on unique data that allow me to examine how QAnon supporters posted content on these two platforms simultaneously.

My data include information on the messages that over thirty thousand individuals with accounts on both Gab and Twitter posted between 2019 and 2021. Since my focus is on Twitter's policy change announced on July 21, 2020, I homed in on the months before and after the announcement. To examine the extent to which these users advanced QAnon content on Twitter and Gab, I measured their use of hashtags that were known to be affiliated with the movement during this period. These included #wwg1wga, which stands for "where we go one, we go all" (a statement used by QAnon activists to show solidarity with one another), and #thegreatawakening, which speaks to the time when, QAnon supporters believed, Q's prophecies would be revealed to the world.[62] I then measured how often these users posted QAnon hashtags like these before and after Twitter's policy change.

Figure 6.3 shows the proportion of posts containing QAnon hashtags that were posted on Twitter and Gab over time. The dark gray line shows the trends on Twitter, and the light gray line shows the trends on Gab. Prior to Twitter's policy change on July 21, 2020, these users posted content with QAnon hashtags in a roughly similar manner. Even though there was a slight difference in the overall prevalence of QAnon hashtags between the platforms prior to the policy change, the *trends* between the two platforms during that period were largely parallel. This is a somewhat technical point, but the presence of parallel time trends *prior* to Twitter's policy change suggests that the differences we observe *after* the policy change were probably caused by it—that is, these differences did not reflect ongoing processes that would have led to differences in the use of QAnon hashtags even if the policy change had not occurred.

After July 21, 2020, the pattern changed quite dramatically. On the day Twitter announced its ban on QAnon, hashtags related to the movement spiked on the platform, as can be seen in the large increase in the figure immediately following the vertical black line. This spike in hashtag mentions is likely to reflect discussion of the policy change itself. In the months that followed, however, the use of QAnon hashtags on Twitter began to steadily decrease.

By contrast, the prevalence of QAnon posts on Gab remained the same—and even increased slightly—in the months following Twitter's announcement.

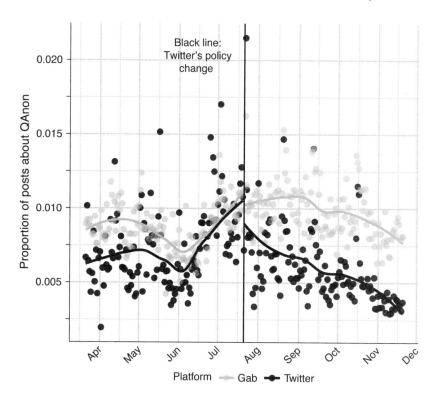

FIGURE 6.3. QAnon Content across Platforms before and after Twitter's Policy Change
Note: The numbers indicate the proportion of posts containing QAnon hashtags posted on Twitter and Gab in the months before and after Twitter's July 20, 2021 policy change banning QAnon content.

This shows that Twitter's policy change was effective at reducing QAnon content *on Twitter alone*: QAnon supporters continued to actively post content using QAnon hashtags on Gab, which had not prohibited that content.

One question that arises is whether the decline in QAnon-related hashtags on Twitter reflects a mere mechanical reduction in the *number* of QAnon-supporting accounts—after all, thousands were suspended by Twitter—as opposed to an adaptation of content to platform-specific thresholds, as suggested theoretically. To verify that these findings truly reflect content adaptation, I conducted a more rigorous statistical test to examine changes among the *same users* posting about QAnon over time.[63]

Figure 6.4 shows that even when we consider only changes in QAnon content by the same social media users, they employed fewer QAnon hashtags on

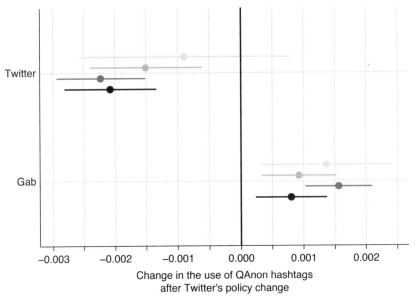

Change in the use of QAnon hashtags
after Twitter's policy change

Before/after window ⬤ One week ⬤ One month ⬤ Two months ⬤ Three months

FIGURE 6.4. QAnon Messaging on Twitter and Gab after Twitter's Policy Change
Note: The figure shows changes in posts using QAnon hashtags after Twitter's policy change. QAnon activists reduced their direct references to QAnon on Twitter, while increasing such references on Gab. Full results are reported in the appendix.

Twitter after the policy change.[64] This can be seen in the coefficients in the "Twitter" row, which show the difference in the use of QAnon hashtags on Twitter after the policy change when taking into account changes in the use of these hashtags on Gab. I also find that posts about QAnon increased on Gab to a statistically significant extent (see the "Gab" row in figure 6.4). This is further evidence that the decline in QAnon messaging on Twitter was driven by a choice to avoid mentioning the movement's hashtags—behavior that the same users did not exhibit on Gab.

Critically, my theoretical framework looks beyond the prediction that extremist content will decline on moderating platforms; instead, my framework anticipates that groups will not simply avoid posting banned content but will change the *form* of their messages to retain some presence on mainstream platforms while staying below moderating thresholds. In the case of QAnon, direct references to the movement were banned, but more subtle forms of QAnon content were less likely to be taken down, especially if the connection to the movement was unclear and vague. Indeed, when examining the overall activity of QAnon sympathizers on Twitter, I found that they did not stop using the platform after the policy change. They continued engaging on it, but in a different way.

It is often difficult to measure vague, modified, or indirect references to banned content, but the QAnon case provides a unique opportunity to examine this strategy. Around the same time that the movement was banned from Twitter, a completely unrelated campaign by a nonprofit organization called Save the Children was launched on the platform. Save the Children sought to raise funds for its humanitarian activities to help children who had experienced exploitation, and it created the hashtag #SaveTheChildren, which it used for its online campaign. Although the charity had nothing to do with Q's conspiracy theory, QAnon activists saw its campaign as an opportunity to advance their message indirectly on the platform.

After QAnon was banned from Twitter, its activists, who refrained from directly referencing the movement on Twitter, began promoting the QAnon ideology by, in effect, expropriating the #SaveTheChildren hashtag for their own campaign. The shift in messaging was quite remarkable: messages promoting #SaveTheChildren increased almost 300 percent among QAnon activists on Twitter. The move away from "authentic" QAnon content to a milder version focusing on child sex trafficking made QAnon much more appealing to a larger share of social media users, who became exposed to the movement's ideas—often for the first time—through the #SaveTheChildren campaign.

This strategic messaging shift occurred on other platforms as well. On Facebook, for example, QAnon activists created more than one hundred groups claiming to advance the fight against child trafficking, leading to a dramatic increase in membership to over five hundred thousand in a matter of weeks.[65] This example illustrates how adapting messages to platform moderation thresholds allows groups to avoid bans *and* make their ideology more appealing to larger segments of the population on mainstream platforms. Similar to the Taliban's content adaptation, QAnon activists learned how to fit their messaging to Twitter's moderation policies, thereby successfully reaching the masses on the platform with modified versions of their content.

Threshold Evasion

Beyond adapting content to social media platforms' moderation thresholds, dangerous organizations can evade bans on highly moderated platforms by embedding prohibited content within seemingly innocuous media, adding noise to propaganda to evade detection, or using supporter networks to spread their content unofficially. The goal of these tactics is to continue reaching audiences on highly moderated platforms by disseminating messages that *seem* to fall below the moderation threshold, but nonetheless promote violating content.

"Smuggling in" Banned Content

The Islamic State, for example, has recently used "content masking" to overcome Facebook's automated detection algorithms. Instead of disseminating officially branded content—which would automatically be taken down for violating Facebook's dangerous organization policies—the group embedded its messages within popular news clips (for example, clips from the BBC or France24) while editing out its logos.[66] In other instances, the group branded its material with Netflix and Amazon logos to appear innocuous.[67] Examples are given in figure 6.5. These modifications made the Islamic State's content appear to be legitimate and thus more resistant to moderation. Other groups have engaged in similar tactics: far-right groups in the United States advanced their content on social media while posing as youth organizations and journalists, and others disseminated content while posing as news organizations or "terrorism research centers" to promote propaganda.[68]

In other cases, activists of dangerous organizations were able to evade content bans on highly moderated platforms by adding "noise" to propaganda messages: they inserted dots or lines in their visual content or used broken text that made matches with known propaganda difficult.[69] For example, the word "kill" in Arabic, قَتْل, is often used as a predictor for violating content on social media platforms. To promote messages about violence, Islamic State activists have used English characters in place of Arabic characters to evade moderation on Facebook. Thus, instead of using the Arabic word, they used a modified version of the word for "kill," "لTQ," to publicize an attack that the group carried out in Iraq in August 2022. This effectively prevented Facebook's artificial intelligence algorithms from classifying the message as violent.[70]

Using Unaffiliated Accounts to Promote Violating Content

Beyond embedding propaganda in messages that seem innocuous, militant organizations also seek to use supporter networks to spread their message on highly moderated platforms. Since independent sympathizers are not formally affiliated with armed organizations, they are less likely to be subject to platform

FIGURE 6.5. Content Masking by Islamic State Activists on Facebook
Note: The screenshots capture Islamic State propaganda hidden behind innocuous-looking content. Top left: *BBC News* logo overlaid on official IS propaganda; top right: *France 24* news logo overlaid on official IS propaganda; bottom left: Amazon logo used to brand IS content; bottom right: Netflix logo used to brand IS content. Image credit: Moustafa Ayad, Institute for Strategic Dialogue.

bans and tend to have their posts taken down only when they share content that clearly violates the rules. Thus, militant groups banned from social media often seek to inspire follower networks to amplify their content indirectly.

The Taliban have been known to use this strategy. As the group began experiencing suspensions on Twitter, its official accounts carefully adapted to the platform's moderation policies by minimizing content promoting violent activity, as detailed earlier in this chapter. In parallel, however, its network of sympathizers continued to use Twitter to share information about Taliban attacks.

The benefit of using sympathizer networks to disseminate messages was particularly strong in the Taliban context because Twitter's moderation of content in Pashto and Dari—the languages most commonly used in Afghanistan—has been spotty. This made it easier for Taliban sympathizers to share information about the group's violent activity in those languages and go undetected. Enforcement of moderation policies can be particularly limited in contexts where content moderators lack deep familiarity with the languages or cultures in which the content is produced. The Institute for Strategic Dialogue found that non-English content, even when it violates content moderation rules, is much less likely to be taken down than English-language content.[71] Weak enforcement can be exploited by militant actors who seek to advance their agenda on mainstream platforms.

To shed light on these indirect evasion strategies, I examined the dissemination on Twitter by the group's large network of sympathizers of content promoting violent Taliban attacks.[72] I found many Pashto and Dari posts by Taliban sympathizers promoting the group's violence in Afghanistan. These posts had probably evaded content moderation because of the language barrier. Some of this content focused on the group's ground offensive, while some celebrated the Taliban's punishment of individuals in areas under its control. For example, in a post from April 2021 written in Pashto, a sympathizer shared a graphic video of the Taliban hanging a person who had been sentenced to death in a Taliban court, celebrating the act as a form of justice.[73] Posts publicizing the hangings of offenders were shared on Twitter by Taliban sympathizers and received hundreds of "likes."[74] At the time of writing, these posts had still not been removed from Twitter, notwithstanding the platform's rule against posting content that glorifies violence. These examples illustrate the benefits of using unaffiliated accounts to promote violating content for groups seeking to continue reaching audiences on large moderated platforms.

Conclusion

What do these patterns tell us about groups' ability to evade moderation on highly regulated platforms? I started this chapter by explaining the continuing importance of large platforms for militant and hate groups' online campaigns, even when they have less-regulated platforms to operate in. Mainstream social media sites provide access to the largest segments of the public and allow messages to reach wide audiences. It is therefore not a surprise that the supporter of the Islamic State cited in the beginning of the chapter called on his friends to continue reaching out to Twitter and Facebook, where the "General Public is found."

However, the moderation policies of the large, high-impact platforms are also the most restrictive. Social media sites with large user bases tend to be those most often targeted by government regulation, as well as the ones most likely to spend resources on moderating extremist content. Thus, in order to continue influencing audiences on these platforms, dangerous organizations need to change their communication strategies. Throughout this chapter, I have shown that militant actors are able to continue reaching the masses either by sacrificing message "authenticity"—for example, by toning down violating content—or by leveraging knowledge about how moderation is done to "smuggle in" prohibited content.

But the success of militant groups in evading moderation on large platforms is strongly influenced by their ability to operate on less-moderated sites. In these less-regulated spaces, militant actors coordinate messaging campaigns to be launched on mainstream platforms, mobilize supporter networks that can help spread violating content, and provide important knowledge on evading mainstream platforms' propaganda detection systems. Thus, in a manner similar to the other mechanisms discussed in chapters 4 and 5, divergence in content policies across platforms is what allows militant organizations to build resilience to moderation—even on large, highly regulated sites.

7

Is Convergence in Moderation a Solution?

Alignment in Moderation Thresholds

Up to now, I have discussed how extremist organizations adapt to content moderation in a context of policy divergence—that is, when social media platforms have different moderation thresholds. I have shown that divergence in content moderation enables militant and hate groups to build resilience online by migrating between platforms, mobilizing supporters in less-regulated spaces, and using less-moderated sites to organize messaging campaigns on larger platforms. In other words, when some platforms moderate harmful content and others do not, extremist groups can reach audiences on social media through platforms with more lenient moderation rules.

In this chapter, I return to the theoretical framework and ask: If divergence between platforms increases extremists' resilience to moderation, does convergence weaken their ability to do so? When we look at the two-dimensional depiction of the online information environment in panel A of figure 7.1, we can see that variation in moderation thresholds (the y-axis) facilitates migration and mobilization in less-moderated spaces. Different moderation thresholds also enable militant and hate organizations to create more robust, cross-platform information operations. Thus, an important driver of the persistence of harmful content on social media is the difference in moderation standards across platforms.

So, what might happen if we reduce this variation in moderation policies? Panel B in figure 7.1 shows a scenario in which the content policies of all platforms converge along a single, lower threshold.[1] In this scenario, moderation

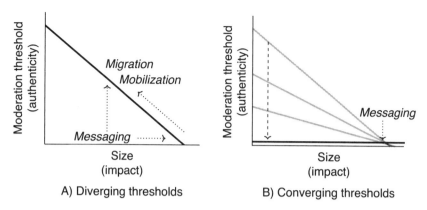

FIGURE 7.1. Adaptation to Diverging and Converging Moderation Thresholds
Note: The figure shows extremists' adaptation mechanisms when social media platforms have different moderation thresholds (panel A) and when their thresholds converge on a more restrictive level (panel B).

rules across social media sites are the same, regardless of platform size. Of course, perfect convergence in content moderation, as depicted in panel B of figure 7.1, is not realistic. There is no world in which each and every social media company adopts the same content standards. The point of thinking about such a scenario is to help us see the trade-off that extremist groups' face when the online information environment changes. When we collapse the "authenticity" dimension on the *y*-axis, what does this theoretical framework predict that militant and hate groups will do?

Recall that authenticity and impact are two important factors that shape extremist online behavior. When using social media, militant and hate organizations seek platforms that allow them to post content freely and to disseminate propaganda that reflects their ideology ("authenticity") while at the same time maximizing the reach of their online campaigns ("impact"). When moderation policies diverge, as shown in panel A of figure 7.1, the ability to post authentic content on social media and the potential to reach wide audiences are in tension. Thus, to maximize both dimensions, extremist actors leverage differences in content standards across platforms to build resilience to moderation.

But when there is no variation in moderation thresholds, some of the mechanisms that facilitate extremist resilience are no longer present. Consider the migration mechanism, for example. The goal of migrating between platforms is to find online spaces that are less likely to restrict an organization's content. Migration will thus reflect an "upward" move toward the upper-left end of panel A of figure 7.1, that is, toward smaller platforms with more lenient content policies. However, when all platforms—small and large—are governed by the same (restrictive) moderation standards, as shown in panel B, there are no places with higher thresholds to move to. In a similar manner, the mobilization mechanism, which relies on the existence of less-moderated sites to target potential recruits, is no longer relevant if platforms have the same moderation policies.

Thus, when social media companies align their content standards along a more restrictive threshold, migration and mobilization are no longer useful for building digital resilience. In such scenarios, the only relevant mechanism is messaging. Changing the content shared online in a way that can evade moderation may consist of making messages "less authentic," to fit the more restrictive moderation threshold, or smuggling violating content into messages that seem innocuous (see chapter 6 for examples).

In the case of threshold convergence, therefore, messaging is most likely to take place on larger social media sites. Since platforms of all sizes have the same moderation standards, groups would prefer to focus on the larger sites to maximize impact. For these reasons, convergence in content moderation across platforms is likely to shift extremist adaptation mechanisms away from migration and mobilization on smaller platforms toward greater sophistication in messaging strategies to evade moderation on larger sites.

What does this mean for extremist resilience online? From a theoretical perspective, we would therefore expect that changing the online information environment from divergence to convergence in content moderation will limit extremist actors' ability to exploit internet platforms to advance their goals online.

A Push toward Cross-Platform Cooperation

The idea that alignment between social media platforms can better prevent harmful content from spreading on the internet is behind many recent calls for cross-industry collaboration in combating extremism. Both governments and technology companies have become more aware that campaigns spreading harmful content online have become complex, involve many social media platforms, and increasingly leverage loopholes in companies' moderation systems.

Government Calls for Collaboration

One of the most ambitious efforts to increase multi-stakeholder collaboration is the Christchurch Call to Action, an initiative led by Jacinda Ardern of New Zealand and Emmanuel Macron of France that was launched after the Christchurch mosque shootings in March 2019.

What made the attack in Christchurch so horrifying—beyond the sheer hate, violence, and destruction targeting the Muslim community in New Zealand—was that it was livestreamed on Facebook by the perpetrator for seventeen minutes before it was taken down by the company. By the time Facebook removed the video, it had already spread to many other sites.[2] As one reporter explained, "The New Zealand massacre was livestreamed on Facebook, announced on 8chan, reposted on YouTube, commentated about on Reddit, and mirrored around the world before the tech companies could even react."[3]

Indeed, even days after Facebook deleted the livestream of the attack (including over 1.5 million copies) and blocked 1.2 million attempted uploads, thousands of copies of the video were still surfacing on other platforms.[4] YouTube in particular found it challenging to control the spread of content showing the attack. As the company's chief product officer said in an interview, when the platform "took down one [video], another would appear, as quickly as one per second."[5] Those who uploaded the video to YouTube were able to evade the platform's moderation systems by modifying the video's content— for example, by adding visual "noise," inserting random logos, and changing the video to look like animation.[6] It soon became clear that actions to remove harmful content by one platform were insufficient when copies could be shared on other sites.

Thus, many policymakers started believing that cooperation between platforms was the only viable solution to suppressing extremist content online.[7] "The events of Christchurch highlighted once again the urgent need for action and enhanced cooperation among [a] wide range of actors," said Prime Minister Ardern and President Macron in the aftermath of the attack.[8] To facilitate multi-stakeholder cooperation, they initiated the Christchurch Summit in Paris in May 2019, to which they invited government leaders and CEOs of technology companies. The goal was to come together to find collaborative solutions to terrorism and violent extremism on social media. "We all need to act," said Ardern in a statement before the summit. "It's critical that technology

TABLE 7.1: Signatories to and Partners in the Christchurch Call to Action

Countries

France	Croatia	Iceland	Luxembourg	Slovakia
New Zealand	Cyprus	India	Maldives	Slovenia
Argentina	Czech Republic	Indonesia	Malta	South Korea
Australia	Denmark	Ireland	Mexico	Spain
Austria	Estonia	Italy	Mongolia	Sri Lanka
Belgium	Finland	Ivory Coast	Norway	Sweden
Bulgaria	Georgia	Japan	Peru	Switzerland
Canada	Germany	Jordan	Poland	The Netherlands
Chile	Ghana	Kenya	Portugal	Tunisia
Colombia	Greece	Latvia	Romania	United Kingdom
Costa Rica	Hungary	Lithuania	Senegal	United States

International organizations

European Commission
Council of Europe*
United Nations Educational, Scientific and Cultural Organization (UNESCO)*
The Global Community Engagement and Resilience Fund (GCERF)*
Tech Against Terrorism*

Technology companies

Amazon	YouTube	Microsoft	LINE	MEGA
Meta	Zoom	Qwant	Twitter	Clubhouse
Google	Daily Motion	JV	Roblox	

Source: Christchurch Call to Action, "Partners," https://www.christchurchcall.com/our-community/partners.

*A partner organization that supports the objectives of the Christchurch Call to Action through its work.

platforms like Facebook are not perverted as a tool for terrorism, and instead become part of a global solution to countering extremism."[9]

The Christchurch Call to Action consisted of a plan that included voluntary commitments by governments and technology companies to address extremist content online in order to prevent events like the Christchurch shootings from happening again. Over sixty countries, international organizations, and technology companies signed the agreement (see table 7.1). Governments that signed the Christchurch pledge committed to investing in measures to make their countries more resistant to extremism, for example, by helping their societies become resistant to radical ideologies through educational programs and digital literacy initiatives; ensuring the enforcement of laws (if they existed) to prevent dangerous actors from producing and disseminating harmful content online; and helping to develop industry standards to remove extremist content through regulation.[10]

Technology companies that signed the agreement committed to taking "cooperative measures" that would limit the dissemination of terrorist and violent extremist content on their sites and to develop technology that would facilitate information sharing with other platforms. Companies also agreed to offer more transparency on their content moderation policies and to take steps to ensure that their algorithms were not used to "drive users towards and/or amplify terrorist and violent extremist content."[11]

The Christchurch Call to Action was thus the first initiative of its kind to seek—at least on paper—cooperation among a wide range of actors to prevent harmful content from spreading on the internet. However, such collaborative efforts had already been set in motion among some technology companies a few years before.

Industry Initiatives to Facilitate Cooperation

Indeed, one of the examples of industry collaboration cited most often is the Global Internet Forum to Counter Terrorism (GIFCT). GIFCT was founded in 2017 by Facebook, Microsoft, Twitter, and YouTube to facilitate collaboration in moderating extremist content. In its early days, GIFCT included only four companies, but today over twenty platforms are members. As discussed in its official mission statement, GIFCT's goals include providing technology companies with tools to prevent extremist use of their platforms, facilitating knowledge sharing between stakeholders, and helping with the development of counternarratives to serve as alternatives to extremist groups' online messaging.[12] GIFCT's mission is similar in many ways to the goals of international organizations that seek to facilitate cooperation between states in the international system (or their compliance with international agreements).[13]

GIFCT is best known for its hash-sharing database, a place where platforms can share information on content that they have taken down for violating their policies. This information sharing allows other platforms to act against similar content if it appears on their sites. A hash is a form of "digital signature"—a numerical representation of visual content that can be used to rapidly identify similar uploads of content across platforms.

Initiatives like GIFCT do not mandate that platforms change their moderation policies, but they do provide a framework that makes collaboration easier by sharing data on content that violates at least some rules of some of the platforms in the network. As the organization states on its official website: "At GIFCT, we respect that each member might operate a little differently. We don't tell our members how to use the hashes or how to apply their own policies. Rather, we are here to help our members collaborate, and together we can make terrorists ineffective online."[14] Although organizations like GIFCT do not formally dictate moderation policies, they nonetheless have immense influence on the de facto policies that platforms adopt because they provide an easy-to-replicate framework for moderating militant and hate groups' content. Smaller platforms that lack the resources to develop moderation rules often rely on the guidance of larger platforms; as a result, there is greater alignment between their moderation policies and those of more established sites.[15]

Another type of policy convergence takes place during the development of content moderation guidelines. For example, when Tech Against Terrorism, the nongovernmental organization that helps technology companies combat terrorists' use of their platforms, recognized that smaller platforms often struggle to moderate extremist content, it created a "mentorship program" to advise these platforms on policies for content moderation. The organization's recommendations are not identical for all platforms, but they are all based on the following general principles: encouraging platforms to moderate on the basis of specific terrorist designation lists, emphasizing the type of language that moderation policies should include, and ensuring that moderation rules respect human rights.[16]

To see how such efforts can align policies, consider the case of JustPaste.it, a small file-sharing platform operated by a young entrepreneur from Poland. When Islamic State activists began using JustPaste.it for propaganda dissemination, the owner of the platform struggled to moderate the group's content, as most of it was in Arabic, a language he did not understand. But instead of resorting to blunt measures like removing all Arabic content, he decided to join GIFCT, which enabled him to use tools developed by larger platforms to target Islamic State propaganda on his site.[17] Those who work on trust and safety on other small platforms similarly acknowledge their reliance on larger technology companies when moderating harmful content. For example, Clubhouse, an audio-based social media platform, praised Tech Against Terrorism for its assistance in providing policy recommendations and extolled the advantages of being able to draw on policy "templates" when developing moderation rules.[18]

When companies work together to ban harmful content from their platforms, whether by sharing information on violating content or by designing similar policies, the outcome is greater alignment in content moderation thresholds. This looks very different from a world with no collaboration. Platforms have their individual stakeholders, products, and audiences and therefore do not naturally arrive at the same policies to combat online harms. As Evelyn Douek explains, technology companies optimize their content moderation policies so differently that it is often difficult for them to reach a consensus.[19] But when governments put pressure on platforms and civil society organizations and other private-public initiatives make concentrated efforts to facilitate collaboration between them, the result may be more unity in moderation policies.

A Study of Convergence in Content Moderation across Platforms

Do efforts to increase collaboration between platforms facilitate greater similarity in moderation policies? To what extent do thresholds converge in the broader online ecosystem? And which social media companies are most closely aligned in content rules? In this section, I examine trends in threshold convergence by drawing on data that track changes in the moderation policies of sixty platforms.

Studying the evolution of technology companies' content policies is not a simple task, for several reasons. First, social media platforms do not always make their moderation rules available to the public. Even the most prominent platforms did not publish their content moderation policies until the mid-2010s. Second, it is not clear what policy convergence should look like: Is it similarity in the language of the policies? Agreement on more general standards? The existence of specific provisions to moderate harmful content in a certain way? Finally, when we think about the moderation thresholds that shape extremist actors' behavior online, are we talking about the policies or their enforcement? Although companies may have rules to limit harmful content on their websites, they may nonetheless fail to systematically enforce them.

Given the difficulty of systematically observing enforcement, I opted to take a simple approach to studying convergence between platforms that examines the *policies* that companies publish online. My focus is therefore on convergence in content standards, not on their enforcement. Drawing on my analysis in chapter 4, which examined technology companies' content rules along nine categories of harmful content, I created a variable that measured each company's moderation threshold from the first time that its policies appeared online.

To gather historical data on moderation policies, I used the Internet Archive's Wayback Machine to access historical versions of each company's content moderation rules, as described in its terms of service or community standards documentation.[20] Since the volume of text was very large (there were hundreds of historical "snapshots" of each company's moderation policies), I measured the existence of each policy using a dictionary approach. In text analysis applications, dictionaries are used to measure the presence, or the prevalence, of a particular topic by counting the number of times predefined keywords are found in the document. I created lists of keywords for each of the nine moderation categories that commonly appeared in companies' content moderation policies.[21] Table 7.2 shows examples of keywords for each policy, and the appendix shows the full lists of keywords.

Using this dictionary, I created a measure for the moderation threshold of each platform in each historical version of its content policies. To keep this measure consistent with my analysis in the previous chapters, I constructed the threshold by counting the number of content moderation categories that were included in each historical version of the companies' policies. As before, I inverted the scale of the moderation threshold such that higher (lower) values reflected less (more) moderation and rescaled it to range between zero and one. Since this dictionary-based measure relied on keywords (and not on close reading of each historical version of companies' moderation policies, as I did in chapter 4), I examined the correlation between my qualitative measure of companies' thresholds and the keywords-based approach. I found that both measures were highly correlated, validating the use of the dictionary to measure companies' content moderation rules.[22]

Measuring Convergence in Moderation

With data documenting the historical evolution of each platform's moderation policies, I was able to examine convergence in moderation thresholds. According to my theory, convergence reflects a shift toward similar policy standards across platforms. This shift can happen along various levels of the moderation threshold, but my theoretical interest is particularly in convergence on more restrictive levels.

TABLE 7.2: Example Keywords to Measure the Moderation of Harmful Content

Category	Keywords
1. Dangerous actors	violent organization, dangerous organization, violent extremist, criminal terrorist, terrorist organization, organized hate group, armed group, terrorist activity, terrorist, violent extremism, dangerous individuals, foreign terrorist organizations, nonstate actors
2. Violent events	harmful activity, coordination cause harm, harmful activities, promoting violent crimes, coordinating harm, violent events, glorifying violent tragedies, promote attack, glorifying violent events, violent acts, dangerous activities, criminal activities, physical violence
3. Hateful ideologies	hateful ideologies, extremist ideologies, chauvinism, nationalism, hatred, hostility, fascism, racial superiority, ideologies, nazism, white supremacy
4. Glorification of violence	glorify violence, celebrate suffering, graphic content, gory, depict violence, shocking, sadistic, gruesome violence, glorifying extreme violence, bodily injury, graphic violence, disturbing scenes
5. Threats and incitement	incite violence, threatening, intimidating, instigating, promote violence, advocate violence, encourage terrorism, incite hatred, calls to violence, inspire violence, promotes violence, promotes harm, promote extreme
6. Harassment and bullying	harassment, targeted harassment, abusive behavior, harass, intimidate, malicious contact, threaten, bully, personal attack, abusive language, doxing, promote hate, harassing
7. Hate speech	hateful, harmful stereotypes, protected characteristics, dehumanizing, profanity, derogatory, malicious, racism, sexism, lewd, vulgar, bigoted, slurs, statements of inferiority, expressions of contempt, dismissal
8. Misinformation	misinformation, misleading content, deceptive, manipulated media, distortions, falsehoods, misrepresentations, conspiracy, disinformation, malinformation, inauthentic, falsify information
9. Platform manipulation	deceptive, mislead, fabricate, manipulative behavior, spam, scam, fake engagement, impersonation, fake profile, fraudulent

I measured convergence in two ways. First, I counted the number of plat-forms with which each company shared policies in each time period in my historical data.[23] Platforms' policies converged if they moderated harmful content along similar categories. For example, a social media company that restricted content relating to dangerous actors (category 1), the glorification of violence (category 4), and hate speech (category 7) was in greater align-ment with companies that moderated content along these three categories than with those that restricted other types of harmful content. I examined convergence among all platforms by averaging the convergence scores for each time period.

In addition, I studied the distribution of the moderation threshold (the one that counts the number of moderation categories in each company's historical policies) across platforms by calculating its mean and variance over time. The average level of the moderation threshold gives us information about the over-all restrictions that platforms placed on harmful content in each time period. The variance provides information on the distribution of the threshold over time: if the variance is higher, then platform moderation thresholds are more different from each other. If it is lower, then they are more similar—that is, they exhibit greater convergence.

These measures gave me rich information to examine, specifically: (1) how many companies converged in their policies over time; (2) whether convergence was happening at lower or higher levels of the moderation threshold; and (3) if there was convergence, which companies were aligning their moderation policies. The appendix provides more details on these measures.

Trends in Platform Convergence

Figure 7.2 shows how convergence varied over time. Panel A shows the average number of platforms that aligned their moderation policies in each period. I find that convergence doubled during the years of my data—rising from around ten converging platforms in 2018 to about twenty in 2022. In other words, the number of platforms with similar moderation standards has grown over time. This may be the result of the recent push for multi-stakeholder col-laboration, industry-led initiatives to facilitate cooperation between platforms such as the GIFCT, or even growing regulatory pressures to restrict harmful content on social media.

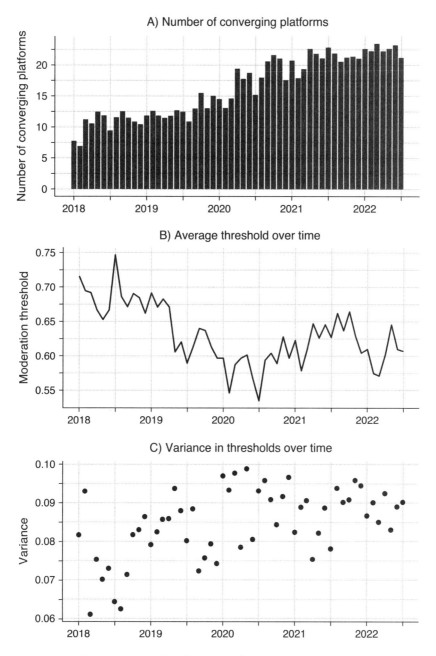

FIGURE 7.2. Convergence in Moderation Policies over Time
Note: Panel A shows the average number of platforms whose policies converged in each time period. Panel B shows the average level of the moderation threshold over time. Panel C shows the variance in moderation thresholds in each time period.

But did this convergence decrease threshold levels in the broader online ecosystem? Panel B in figure 7.2 shows the average levels of the moderation threshold in each time period, taking into account all sixty platforms in my data. While moderation policies became more restrictive between 2018 and 2020, the average levels of the threshold began increasing in mid-2020, suggesting that the higher number of converging platforms has not made the information environment more restrictive overall. This finding is further corroborated by the trends in panel C, which shows that the variance in the moderation thresholds increased over time. What might explain these patterns?

Only Some Platforms Align Their Moderation Policies

To understand why, on the one hand, we see more social media platforms converging and, on the other, the average levels of the moderation threshold not going down (and variance going up), I conducted a deeper investigation to identify the platforms that aligned their content policies and the platforms that did not. It is possible that the findings in figure 7.2 reflect two phenomena that happened in parallel. First, a push for cross-platform cooperation led some technology companies to invest in moderation, leading to greater alignment in their content policies. Second, as these platforms began moderating more content, others popped up to provide alternative spaces with less restrictions.

Indeed, as I show in chapter 5, greater moderation by mainstream social media companies aggravated users who were subject to content bans. It is possible, therefore, that the demand for more "free speech platforms" facilitated the creation of new social media sites with more lenient content policies at the same time that other platforms became more restrictive in their rules.

Figure 7.3 supports this interpretation. Panel A shows examples of converging platforms—those that were more similar to other platforms in their content policies—and panel B shows examples of nonconverging platforms. I find a clear pattern of divergence: while Twitter, Pinterest, YouTube, Tumblr, TikTok, and Facebook decreased their moderation thresholds over time (made them more restrictive), other platforms, such as Parler, Gab, Telegram, Rumble, and Rocket.Chat, generally did not change their (already lenient) moderation rules—except to make them *less* restrictive. The data thus suggest that platform convergence did take place, but that it was limited to a certain part of the online ecosystem.

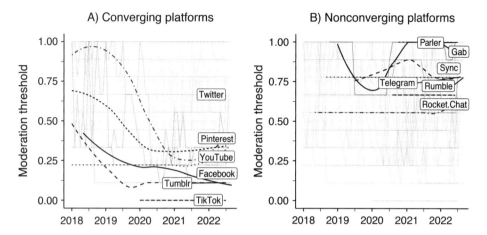

FIGURE 7.3. Converging and Nonconverging Platforms
Note: Panel A shows examples of converging platforms—those that were similar to other platforms in their content policies. Panel B shows examples of nonconverging platforms—those that showed greater difference from other platforms in their content moderation policies.

Does Collaboration Limit Extremist Activity on Social Media?

To what extent did these patterns shape the behavior of militant and hate groups online? Based on my theoretical analysis in the first section, "Alignment in Moderation Thresholds," convergence should limit extremist activity on social media, at least to some degree. When platforms pose similar restrictions on harmful content, the mechanisms that facilitate the resilience of extremist organizations should become more limited. Thus, in a world of convergence, extremist actors should move away from migration and mobilization on smaller platforms toward more sophistication in messaging strategies on larger sites.

Of course, as I showed earlier, the online environment did not exhibit complete convergence. While some companies became more similar in how they moderated content, others did not and remained lenient in their moderation rules. This provides an opportunity to study the relationship between convergence and extremist activity on social media by comparing organizations' presence on platforms that aligned their policies with their presence on those that did not.

To do so, I went back to the data that I presented in chapter 4, which tracked the public presence of over a hundred militant and hate groups on different social media sites. The data included information on accounts that were officially and unofficially linked to these organizations on various platforms, as well as information on the suspension status of their accounts. If convergence facilitates better moderation of harmful content, then we would expect to see groups struggle to maintain their presence on platforms that align their moderation thresholds. We might also see converging platforms engaging in more enforcement—for example, by deplatforming more accounts.

Using my analysis of platforms' policy convergence from the previous section, I identified the companies that exhibited alignment in moderation and those that did not.[24] I then matched this information with data on militant and hate groups' social media presence and tested the correlation between convergence and these organizations' online activity on various platforms.

Panel A in figure 7.4 shows the relationship between convergence and extremist groups' social media presence. The points reflect coefficients from a regression analysis in which I regressed the variables listed in the rows on an indicator variable that captured whether or not a platform converged its moderation policies with other platforms. To account for the "impact" dimension, I controlled for platform size in all regressions.[25]

I find that militant and hate organizations' official accounts were significantly less likely to be present on platforms that aligned their moderation policies. Official accounts consisted of social media handles that belonged to the organizations' leadership or used groups' official insignia. Convergence was associated with an almost 40 percent decrease in these groups' official presence. The figure also shows that militant and hate organizations' accounts were more than twice as likely to be suspended by converging platforms than by those that did not align their moderation policies. This suggests that convergence may facilitate greater enforcement of moderation rules, as illustrated in the GIFCT case discussed earlier.

Finally, I find that these groups were significantly more *unofficially* present—via accounts that were not formally affiliated with the organizations but helped publicize their content on the platform—on converging platforms. This suggests that groups that were banned from platforms that aligned their moderation policies may have shifted to advancing their propaganda on these sites using unofficial accounts. The pattern is consistent with the messaging mechanism in which groups change how they disseminate content to adapt to platforms' moderation rules. Indeed, using unofficial handles to disseminate pro-

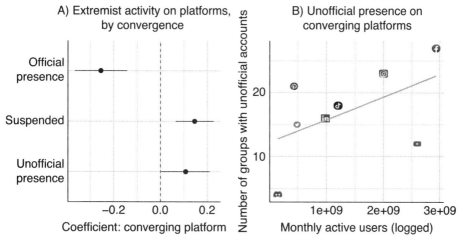

FIGURE 7.4. Extremist Presence by Platform Convergence
Note: Panel A shows the correlation between convergence and the activity of militant and hate groups on social media platforms. Panel B shows the relationship between the size of converging platforms and the number of groups operating unofficial accounts on them.

paganda on social media is an adaptation tactic that I discuss in more detail in chapter 6.

So what does extremist activity look like on converging platforms? Earlier in the chapter, I argued that in the case of "perfect" convergence (when there is no variation in the "authenticity" dimension), extremist organizations would prefer to operate on larger platforms that allow them to maximize the impact of their online campaigns (see panel B of figure 7.1). We can test this hypothesis by examining whether militant and hate groups prefer to use larger converging platforms as opposed to smaller ones. Since official accounts were more likely to be banned on platforms that aligned their moderation policies, I examined the use of unofficial accounts—those that enabled groups to push propaganda indirectly—between smaller and larger converging sites.

Panel B in figure 7.4 shows that militant and hate organizations were significantly more likely to operate unofficial accounts on converging platforms with large user bases (measured with monthly active users) as opposed to smaller ones. This supports the theoretical idea that groups prefer to maximize impact when authenticity is held constant. In other words, when choosing between platforms with similar moderation rules, extremist organizations prefer to advance their content (albeit informally) on platforms with larger audiences.

Thus, convergence in moderation thresholds does seem to limit the activity of extremist organizations on social media, at least to some extent. My analysis shows that militant and hate groups seeking to operate on platforms that align their content policies find it harder to maintain official accounts and are more likely to experience bans. At the same time, these groups adapt to the more restrictive environment by advancing their content on these platforms informally. And as convergence reduces the diversity in moderation among aligning platforms, extremist organizations prefer to operate on larger sites to maximize impact. Whether this is a linear process that would continue with greater levels of convergence remains an open question.

The Costs of Convergence to Nonharmful Speech

The potential of cross-platform collaboration to combat online extremism has brought many to see it as *the* solution to harmful content on social media. In this section, I raise several ethical and practical considerations to underscore the limitations of this approach. The first problem with convergence in moderation is that it can inadvertently limit nonharmful speech. Although aligning moderation thresholds can help technology companies create a "united front" to combat militant and hate groups' exploitation, it can also give too much power over online speech to a small number of actors. As Douek explains, "The fear that a single actor can decide what can or cannot be said in large parts of the online public sphere has led to growing calls for measures to promote competition between digital platforms." Indeed, many have pointed to the incredible power that technology companies have in multiple areas of social and political life, highlighting the potential risks of such centralization.[26]

In the context of online extremism, the main concern over aligning policies is the exacerbation of the "collateral damage" problem: removing harmful content inevitably also entails inadvertently removing nonharmful content from many online sites.[27] Since the line between violating and nonviolating content can be blurry, platforms sometimes make errors in their determination of harmful content. These mistakes can be the outcome of insensitive automated algorithms that are trained to err on the side of over-inclusion (for example, deeming any content that mentions a certain keyword to be violating). Mistakes can also arise from human error and inadequate understanding of the context in which messages are shared. Scholars who study how content moderation affects civil liberties note that technology companies based in Western countries often struggle to consider local cultural nuances when moderating content in non-Western contexts; as a result, they unintentionally remove nonharmful messages posted by marginalized groups. The lack of understanding of local languages can be a problem as well, leading to the removal of benign content in languages that moderators do not know well.[28]

When moderation thresholds across platforms converge, the effect of erroneous content removals may be much harsher because actors whose content is mistakenly deleted from one platform are removed from other platforms as well. Take the case of civil rights activists seeking to document human rights abuses in conflict settings around the world. Since the visual representation of the messages that they share may look similar to extremist propaganda disseminated by violent groups (for example, depictions of violence and atrocities or other conflict-related scenes), activists' messages are sometimes incorrectly classified as militant group propaganda in hash-sharing databases like the one operated by GIFCT. Facebook, for example, made several errors in its classification of harmful content in a large enforcement action in May 2020 that resulted in the takedown of the accounts of eighty-seven Syrian and Palestinian journalists and civil rights activists sharing news about human rights violations.[29] If these sorts of determinations were to be copied by other platforms, activists would be even more limited in their ability to share their messages online, raising ethical questions about banning protected speech through cross-platform collaboration.[30]

Another concern about more centralized moderation relates to the widening scope of content that is subject to removal. When social media platforms operate independently of one another, the content that they remove is determined by their own moderation policies, which, as described in chapter 2, are in large part a function of the preferences of their stakeholders. However, when platforms work together to moderate harmful content, there may be a "feedback effect" in the development of moderation policy as platforms share ideas with each other, potentially resulting in an expansion of the types of content that each platform moderates. This kind of expansion is what Danielle Citron calls "censorship creep"—a phenomenon where moderation extends beyond its initial set of categories. As she explains when discussing the moderation of harmful content:

> Companies' TOS [terms of service] policies could be interpreted to prohibit speech far beyond speech inciting hatred of (or calling for violence against) vulnerable groups or violent extremist content. They could result in the global deletion of a government official's tweets. They could lead to

the worldwide removal of websites criticizing political candidates. They could result in the global suspension of civil rights activists' Facebook profiles.[31]

Scholars worry about an ever-growing list of banned categories because it is often difficult to precisely define these types of content. Even in the large literature on terrorism, scholars tend to debate definitions, and the rules that define extremist content, hate speech, and other harmful materials are even harder to agree upon. These definitional challenges are one of the main reasons for technology companies' initial reluctance to moderate militant and hate groups' content: they were concerned that ambiguity regarding the definition of "terrorist speech" would lead to the removal of content that should be protected from censorship.[32]

Nevertheless, many platforms ended up harmonizing their policies on banning jihadist groups like the Islamic State, Al-Shabaab, and Al-Qaeda. Less agreement has been reached on the moderation of far-right and far-left extremist groups. This discrepancy is partly driven by how governments define terrorism in criminal law. For example, the fact that many far-right and far-left actors are not legally considered terrorist groups in the United States leads to certain limitations on platforms that rely on the government's terrorist designation lists to ban dangerous organizations. Some platforms started putting more fringe groups on their banned actor lists after the Christchurch attack in New Zealand, but many did not. As a result, policy alignment in moderating extremist groups' content tends to heavily focus on jihadist, non-Western organizations. For example, the vast majority of GIFCT's hash-sharing database consists of material posted by jihadist groups, while the moderation of far-right or far-left content is far less centralized.[33] Thus, militant and hate groups adhering to these ideologies are able to advance their cause more easily because they operate under much more lenient thresholds on many online platforms.

A related, much broader concern is authoritarian misuse of the term "terrorism" for the purpose of suppressing dissent. A large literature on liberation technologies and digital authoritarianism has shown that the rise in the use of social media has led nondemocratic governments to take harsher repressive actions against activists who challenge their rule.[34] Scholars have shown, for example, that governments use internet shutdowns and filtering tools to control information flows within their jurisdictions;[35] monitor and censor content that they consider harmful (using almost the exact same methods that technology companies use to moderate content in more democratic contexts);[36] and flood the internet with propaganda and online harassment to manipulate the online information space.[37]

Since centralizing moderation across platforms can be so powerful, free speech advocates worry that anti-democratic governments will take advantage of regulations to influence what gets added to hash-sharing databases to facilitate the rapid removal of content posted by dissidents.[38] Saudi Arabia, for example, revised its penal laws relating to terrorism in 2017 to include the use of the internet to "disturb public order" and "undermine state reputation or status."[39] China has similarly defined online messages as illegal if they "harm the nation's honor and interests," "subvert" the Chinese Communist Party regime, or challenge the government's social, ethnic, religious, or economic policies.[40] Russia similarly expanded its counterterrorism legislation in 2018 to require that social media companies share information about users to enable more surveillance.[41] Convergence of moderation thresholds facilitates the efficient removal of extremist content, but it also comes at a cost to human rights and civil liberties, at least in certain settings.

In addition to the normative concerns over centralized moderation, there are practical problems with its use in combating online extremism. When discussing threshold alignment earlier in this chapter, I described a world in which *all platforms* in the online ecosystem would participate in cross-platform collaboration. In reality, however, only a fraction of platforms take part in these efforts. For example, in 2023 the twenty-eight platforms that were members of GIFCT comprised fewer than half of the platforms militant actors are known to use.[42] And this does not even account for extremist groups' own websites, which saw growth in the early 2020s.[43]

Although more technology companies are expected to join cross-platform initiatives in the future, many other platforms will not, either because such participation requires resources they do not have or because aligning moderation with other platforms conflicts with their core mission. Social media sites like Gab and Parler, for example, have long championed largely unmoderated speech in their communities, precisely in response to the stricter moderation on other platforms. Thus, even efforts to centralize moderation, while promising in theory, can be less effective in practice if not all parts of the online ecosystem choose to cooperate.

8

Conclusion

THE FUTURE OF ONLINE HARMS

WHEN I STARTED WORKING ON THIS BOOK, I was in the midst of monitoring networks of militant and hate groups on several social media platforms. I studied the propaganda that these groups created to mobilize supporters, the content dissemination tactics that they employed online, and the ways in which their audiences reacted to their information campaigns. Like many other researchers and policy professionals working on trust and safety issues on social media, I was fascinated with how rapidly these organizations adapted to changing standards in content moderation. I saw militant and hate groups attempting to use new handles to reappear on platforms that had banned them; I observed changes in the ways in which they communicated; and I also saw growth in the use of unaffiliated accounts that promoted these groups' messages unofficially.

But what I quickly discovered was that the activity of militant and hate organizations on platforms that moderate extremist content provides only part of the picture. Adaptation to content moderation is far more complex and expansive, and it happens in many other online spaces that scholars do not traditionally study. I also found that policymakers, technology companies, and researchers tend to bring a narrow, within-platform perspective to the moderation of harmful content. In other words, many evaluate content moderation and its effectiveness "one platform at a time," without considering how one technology company's actions can shape activity on other platforms.

As I dug deeper to understand extremist organizations' behavior on less-studied platforms, I found many adaptation strategies that linked one platform to another. It became clear that what we observe by studying social media platforms like Facebook, Twitter, and YouTube in isolation is only a fraction of what is happening in the broader online ecosystem. Way more is taking place on smaller, less-regulated spaces that we simply do not study. This discovery made me realize that in order to understand why online extremism persists, we need to examine digital behavior from a broader, cross-platform perspective. That is, not only do we need to expand research on online activity to examine less-moderated sites, but we also need to understand how the behavior of extremist organizations is linked across platforms.

The Effects of Different Standards for Governing Digital Spaces

In this book, I have shown that a key factor driving the digital resilience of militant and hate organizations is divergence in the way technology companies police speech online. In the first two decades of the 2000s, the number of companies that offered services for user-generated content mushroomed around the world. Social media platforms cater to different audiences, have different features and tools, and are also governed by a range of different content policies. Although many recognize that the moderation of harmful content varies between platforms, little attention has been given to the drivers and consequences of this variation.

This book has offered a framework to understand the properties of this new and diverse online information environment by tracing the process that leads technology companies to restrict harmful content on their sites. I have shown that content moderation is strongly related to the level of the regulatory pressures that technology companies face, and that government demands to remove harmful content often center on companies that are perceived to have the largest impact on society. I have explained how this approach creates an online environment in which platforms with large user bases face heavy regulatory burdens and therefore moderate harmful content to a much greater extent than do platforms with fewer users.

This systematic relationship between the size of social media platforms and their level of moderation creates an important trade-off for militant and hate organizations. On the one hand, these actors wish to maximize the authenticity of their messaging campaigns, and on the other, they seek to have a large impact on target audiences. Since the platforms with lenient policies are also those with the smallest user bases, and since platforms with high impact also have the most restrictive moderation policies, extremist organizations' adaptation strategies often take place on several platforms in parallel and are, by design, interlinked across online sites.

Throughout the book, I have described different ways in which extremist organizations build resilience on social media when platforms are governed by different moderation standards. I explained that migration enables groups to continue their information operations in the face of bans on moderating platforms. By examining the logic of migration in a diverse online environment and drawing on empirical data on the multi-platform presence of over a hundred different organizations, I showed in chapter 4 that social media sites that provide the best mix of content authenticity and audience reach are most often the destination of extremist migration.

I have also explained how different moderation standards facilitate mobilization and recruitment on less-moderated platforms. In chapter 5, I illustrated the usefulness for mobilization when users of social media sites with more lenient moderation policies find appealing the content disseminated by militant and hate groups. By collecting cross-platform data that link user behavior to technology companies' moderation actions, I showed how individuals' personal experiences with content moderation—in particular, with having their account suspended—can make them susceptible to extremist propaganda.

Finally, I explained how variation in moderation policies across platforms allows dangerous organizations to overcome moderation by shifting their messaging strategies based on platform rules. I presented several case studies in chapter 6 of extremist actors posting content in parallel on platforms with different content policies in order to share "mild" messages on regulated platforms while disseminating more extreme material on less-moderated sites.

These findings have important implications for debates on the regulation of social media, which have largely ignored the ways in which the structure of the online information environment—in particular, the different standards for moderating harmful content—shapes dangerous organizations' online behavior. The analysis in this book also speaks to calls to increase multi-stakeholder collaboration in combating online harms, such as the Christchurch Call to Action. In chapter 7, I showed that when social media platforms align their policies along more restrictive standards, they force a shift away from migration and mobilization on smaller platforms toward greater sophistication in messaging strategies on larger sites. By combining information on platform convergence with data on extremist online presence, I showed that cross-platform alignment in moderation limits militant and hate actors' activity on social media, at least to some extent.[1]

More generally, the book has highlighted the importance of independent, "outside" research on social media platforms. The ability to observe and systematically study cross-platform adaptation to content moderation requires access to social media data from multiple platforms. Technology companies are often motivated to "clean up" their own sites, but they do not observe, or study, the consequences of their actions in other online spaces.[2] Independent research that examines these questions from a cross-platform perspective would allow us to observe patterns in adaptation to moderation in the broader information environment.

The Fall of Twitter, the Rise of X, and the Future of Content Moderation

The framework that I have offered in this book provides insights into the future of online harms as platform policies continue to evolve, new social media sites emerge, and regulations pressure companies to moderate harmful content. I have focused on cases that illustrate what happens to militant and hate organizations when social media companies shift their policies toward more restrictive thresholds. But policy changes regarding content moderation can also shift in the opposite direction—toward more lenient moderation.

The case of Twitter/X provides a useful example. On October 27, 2022, after months of negotiations, Elon Musk purchased Twitter. The process of the company's acquisition had begun months earlier, in April of that year, when Musk made an unsolicited offer to buy Twitter for $44 billion. The company's board initially resisted the offer, but ended up accepting it. What followed was the most significant change in the leadership of a social media company in recent years.[3]

There were many reasons for Elon Musk's interest in purchasing Twitter. He saw the company's large user base—more than 300 million monthly active users—as an important "digital town square" where a "wide range of beliefs can be debated in a healthy manner."[4] He believed that by acquiring the company he would be able to prevent echo chambers.[5] But most of all, Musk saw Twitter as too restrictive in its content moderation policies. He was determined to change the company's approach to content moderation to make it more open to free speech. "I am against censorship that goes far beyond the law," said Musk in a tweet a day after the company accepted his offer. "If people want less free speech, they will ask government to pass laws to that effect. Therefore, going beyond the law is contrary to the will of the people."[6]

After acquiring the company, Musk made several important changes to Twitter's engagement in content moderation. Although the official "Twitter Rules" remained largely the same, Musk changed how they were enforced.[7] He dramatically reduced the number of people who worked on content moderation and laid off a large number of contractors who had played an important role in enforcing the company's rules against harmful content.[8] He also disbanded Twitter's Trust and Safety Council, an advisory group consisting of civil and human rights organizations that had helped the company address harassment, hate speech, child exploitation, and other types of harmful content.[9] He "unsuspended" many accounts that had been banned from the platform, including former president Donald Trump and figures associated with far-right and white supremacist groups.[10] Musk also limited the company's commitment to combating misinformation by leaving the European Union's Code of Practice on Disinformation and disabling a feature that allowed users to report misinformation about elections.[11]

Elon Musk's Twitter/X is a case where a large platform with a significant user base becomes more lenient in how it addresses harmful content—the opposite trend from what I have documented in the book. My theoretical framework suggests that this change in direction makes Twitter/X a prime target for extremist organizations. The company's lower investment in content moderation allows users to post more "authentic" content. Although the company's policies have remained largely the same, content that violates the policies is more likely to remain online because of its limited enforcement of the rules.[12] At the same time, X's large user base allows users to reach a much wider audience than they could on fringe platforms with a similarly lenient approach to content moderation. Thus, by allowing both greater content authenticity and audience reach, X is likely to attract extremist actors.

Although not enough evidence has accumulated, initial examples show that the platform has indeed become populated with more harmful content since Musk's acquisition of Twitter. Hate speech targeting African Americans, the LGBTQ+ community, and the Jewish community grew by over 60 percent, according to studies by the Center for Countering Digital Hate and the American Defense League.[13] Hate speech against Muslims has risen dramatically as well, based on analysis by the Institute for Strategic Dialogue.[14] The European Union found that X had the highest ratio of disinformation posts across all large social media platforms.[15] And research examining the prevalence of jihadi groups on social media found that Islamic State accounts on Twitter went up by 69 percent in the first weeks of Musk's tenure.[16]

These examples show the high value of large platforms with lenient moderation practices to actors that produce harmful content online and they provide clues as to what might happen when sites that reach millions of users become less restrictive in their moderation. They also point to the role of influential leaders of tech companies in shaping their platforms' content moderation policies.

But it remains an open question whether extremism on sites such as X will continue if the growing regulatory pressures persist. In September 2023, a prominent European Union regulator said that "Mr. Musk knows he is not off the hook. . . . There are obligations under the hard law. . . . My message for Twitter/X is you have to comply. We will be watching what you do."[17] As this book has shown, regulatory pressure has pushed technology companies to moderate more in the past. But whether the EU's regulations will encourage Musk to address harmful content on X remains to be seen.

From a broader perspective, the trends that I identified in the book—the convergence in content moderation policies of some platforms and the parallel divergence of other platforms—are likely to continue driving extremist actors' use of digital media in the future. On the one hand, as more technology companies become more restrictive in how they address harmful content, we are likely to see more limited extremist activity on social media. At the same time, the growth of new platforms whose content moderation does not converge—or the loosening of moderation practices among platforms that do engage in it—will keep providing these actors with new avenues for disseminating propaganda.[18] Inconsistency in how harmful content is regulated is likely to continue providing extremist organizations with opportunities to advance their goals online.

Implications for Other Areas of Harmful Content

The theoretical framework offered in this book provides insights into the success (or failure) of other online campaigns, such as mis- or disinformation operations, state-led domestic and foreign influence campaigns, and content promoting child sexual abuse material (CSAM).

Information Operations and Digital Propaganda

Like extremist organizations, state actors advancing information operations often seek to reach a wide audience in order to have a large impact. This is why they often spend many resources on the largest social media sites. But since many large technology companies have been increasing their efforts to remove disinformation from their platforms, state actors face a similar trade-off to the trade-off facing extremist organizations, as documented in this book. On the one hand, they can share their content on more lenient platforms, but that limits their audience reach. On the other, they can try to stay on the large platforms, but then they have to adapt their content to make it seem innocuous. The need to maximize audience reach while overcoming content moderation has led actors who engage in information operations to increasingly use multiple platforms and deploy tactics that are similar to those documented in this book.

For example, in August 2023, Meta said that it uncovered and disrupted a large influence operation by the Chinese government. The campaign used a network of accounts operating on over fifty online sites, including Facebook, Instagram, YouTube, X, TikTok, and Reddit. The goal was to promote China's strategic objectives by disseminating content supporting China and attacking accounts that criticized the Chinese Communist Party's policies. To overcome Facebook's and Instagram's content moderation actions, the network promoted the campaign via "spamouflaging"—embedding the content within messages that looked like spam.[19] This content adaptation tactic is very similar to the Islamic State's masking of its propaganda on Facebook (described in chapter 6). Meta identified the campaign and took down over five hundred thousand accounts associated with it, but the network continued to operate on platforms that did not remove its content.

In a similar manner, a recent campaign launched by Russia to support its military invasion of Ukraine used several platforms to overcome moderation. The campaign was cited as the largest and most complex information operation since the start of the war.[20] Aimed at undermining international support for Ukraine, it was particularly focused on convincing Europeans to stop supporting sanctions against Russia and the supply of weapons to Ukraine. The operation consisted of an elaborate network of fake websites that mimicked well-known European news outlets, such as *The Guardian* and *Der Spiegel*, and used a network of thousands of humanlike accounts that were created with AI-generated images on several platforms to disseminate links to these websites in an effort to generate engagement.[21] When platforms like Facebook and Instagram removed these accounts, the campaign increased its use of smaller sites like Telegram to promote its message, redirecting traffic from mainstream platforms to these less-regulated spaces.[22] The choice of sites like Telegram (a medium-sized platform with a relatively high moderation threshold) illustrates the value of sites that maximize both content authenticity and audience reach for these actors as well.

Child Sexual Abuse Material

Another area to which the theoretical framework is relevant is the promotion of child sexual abuse on social media. In many countries around the world, such content is considered illegal: over 130 national governments have banned the possession and spread of CSAM in their jurisdictions.[23] While the definitions vary between countries, most define CSAM as "the visual representation or depiction of a child" (that is, anyone under the age of eighteen) "engaged in a (real or simulated) sexual display, act, or performance."[24]

The rise of social media has led to a rapid growth in CSAM content online. A report by the National Center for Missing and Exploited Children showed that between 2019 and 2020 there was a 90 percent increase in notifications of child sexual abuse material on online platforms.[25] Similarly, in 2022, Facebook removed 92.2 million posts promoting child sexual exploitation—an almost 30 percent increase from the previous year.[26] Even more content was found on YouTube and TikTok, which together removed over 450 million videos promoting CSAM in the same year. Other social media platforms, such as Instagram and Snapchat, have also found millions of pieces of such content on their sites.[27]

But despite efforts to address child sexual abuse material, this content has remained widely available online—both on platforms that have policies against it and on those that do not. As with other categories of harmful content, policies to address CSAM vary across social media sites.[28] Although some technology companies, such as Meta and TikTok, have many categories to use in addressing CSAM, other companies, such as Discord and Telegram, have many fewer restrictions.[29] This inconsistency in how platforms address child sexual abuse material provides opportunities for CSAM-producing actors to build resistance to moderation.

And indeed, online networks that advance CSAM, perhaps not surprisingly, have been operating across many platforms—in a similar manner to extremist organizations. On social media sites with stricter policies against child sexual abuse material, these actors have been engaging in content adaptation: making their messages seem harmless by using words that do not violate platform rules, posing as other personas that appear unrelated to CSAM, and even masking their content with visual noise to avoid being detected by moderators.[30] At the same time, these actors have been making available more explicit content (which is often outlawed) on platforms that do not have strict moderation.[31] Thus, just like extremist organizations, CSAM-producing actors have become active on multiple platforms.

These examples show that my analytical approach adds to our understanding of the incentives of other actors that produce harmful content and provides insights into their strategies in a regulated online environment. Observing online activity from a cross-platform perspective allows us to see how platforms relate to each other and the important dimensions along which they vary. This approach thus generates important insights into the strategies and tactics of content creators on social media—especially those that produce content considered harmful.

Liberation Technologies

The theoretical approach that I advance here can also shed light on the online activity of a completely different set of actors: those who resist repression in authoritarian contexts. Throughout the book, I have focused on regulation of content largely taking place in democratic countries. In such contexts, content moderation limiting the activity of extremist organizations is often framed as a "good" action to fight "bad actors." However, if we switch the adjectives describing those seeking to overcome repression from negative valence to positive valence, we can see that this book's theoretical logic also helps explain the digital resilience of pro-democracy actors in authoritarian contexts.

A large literature on liberation technologies documenting the activity of pro-democracy activists has pointed to the important role of social media in resisting repression. By using information and communication technologies, these actors have been able to challenge authoritarian governments by mobilizing protests, exposing corruption, and monitoring abuse.[32] Pro-democracy activists have used digital media to mobilize protests in the Orange Revolution in Ukraine in 2004; in the Cedar Revolution in Lebanon in 2005; in the Green Movement protests in Iran in 2009; and in Egypt, Tunisia, Syria, Bahrain, and Libya during the Arab Spring.[33] Anti-regime activists have also used social media to express dissent in Saudi Arabia and to mobilize resistance to the Chinese government during high salience events.[34] Even though authoritarian governments have increased their efforts to suppress dissent through censorship and internet shutdowns, activists have remained resilient online.[35]

My theoretical framework can thus help explain the ability of pro-democracy activists to resist authoritarian repression. Although more research is needed to examine the activity of these actors in a multi-platform environment, there is already growing evidence that these actors adapt their messaging on different social media sites to avoid detection and punishment.[36] Thus, the existence of small platforms and diversity in content moderation rules is critical for organizations seeking social change—whether such change is seen as positive or negative by the societies in which they operate.

Important Areas for Future Research

There are still many open questions about online extremism and about harmful content more generally. First, we need more research on the digital information environment. The approach I took here of studying social media platforms as units within a broader ecosystem would be fruitful for future work on online regulation and content moderation. As governments continue to advance legislation to regulate harmful content on the internet, more research will be needed to understand where these approaches work well, and where they do not.

For example, while the hard law can dictate what social media companies ought to do, there is often a gap between regulatory requirements and their enforcement. Today almost every large social media company has strict policies against the spread of content that glorifies violence. However, the enforcement of these policies is often spottier than many would expect. In the war between Israel and Hamas that started after Hamas's terrorist attack against Israel in October 2023, an unprecedented number of social media posts glorifying the murder of civilians spread to millions of people around the world on Facebook, Instagram, X, YouTube, and TikTok.[37] Many of these messages first appeared on Telegram (where moderation policies are most lenient) and were then uploaded to other platforms where they "spread like wildfire."[38]

The viral dissemination of violent content from the war alerted many. Some worried about the exposure of children and teenagers to scenes of gore and inhumane violence, especially on TikTok.[39] Others worried that the violent content would radicalize and inspire some people to perpetrate similar acts elsewhere.[40] Still others were concerned about the mental health implications for social media users whose timelines became filled with violent scenes of war.[41] And indeed, the response from regulators came fast. Within days of the start of the conflict, the EU issued warnings to many social media companies to take down the violent content, as required by the Digital Services Act. Thierry Breton, the EU commissioner for internal market, wrote letters to Meta, X, YouTube, and TikTok (platforms on which the violent content was spreading rapidly), demanding that they step up their efforts to remove such content.[42]

However, technology companies did not follow through—or at least not fast enough. Some took many hours, or even days, to remove the images and videos. Others did not have sufficient resources to detect so much harmful content in so short a time frame. As a result, large amounts of violent content from the war remained online and spread to many other sites. What could have facilitated better enforcement of the EU's regulation? The tragic example of the Israel-Hamas war illustrates the need to better understand what can facilitate effective enforcement of policies to address harmful content online, especially in fast-moving situations like active wars.

Second, we need to have a better picture of what the moderation of harmful content would look like in a world where more content is generated by artificial intelligence, such as large language models. The rapid growth of generative AI has opened a new frontier for online content generation—in text, image, video, and audio formats. Here I have focused on cases in which harmful content was produced by humans, but we still do not know much about how dangerous organizations will act in a world where massive amounts of content can be generated by artificial intelligence.

Although it is early to say whether extremist actors will use these new tools extensively, initial evidence shows that some have already started. In March 2023, Meta's advanced AI model, whose use was supposed to be restricted, was leaked on the far-right forum 4chan.[43] Shortly thereafter, 4chan users began sharing tutorials on how to customize the model to bypass safety features that Meta put in place in order to allow the model to generate hateful and xenophobic messages and content glorifying violence.[44] In August 2023, researchers found another network of extremist accounts that used generative AI to advance an information operation on social media. The network used artificial intelligence to generate images that seemed realistic to the natural eye, as well as video and audio clips that very closely resembled human-created content. The AI-generated messages received more than five hundred million views on TikTok and over three hundred thousand subscribers on YouTube.[45] We need more research on the use of AI by dangerous actors to understand whether these examples will generalize to other extremist campaigns.

In addition, we are still just scratching the surface of what we need to know in order to prevent AI models from creating and disseminating harmful

TABLE 8.1: Harmful Content Production and Dissemination in the Era of Generative AI

		Dissemination	
		Humans	AI
Production	Humans	A. Humans produce, humans disseminate	C. Humans produce, machines disseminate
	AI	B. Machines produce, humans disseminate	D. Machines produce, machines disseminate

content. The existing paradigm of content moderation largely assumes that human actors are responsible for the dissemination of harmful information on the internet. There is currently no systematic framework to address harmful content generated by machines. Here I'd like to point to several areas that future research should pursue in this space, and I offer a conceptual way to organize such research.

When it comes to moderating harmful content in the era of generative AI, we should consider two important dimensions: the *production* of content and its *dissemination*, as depicted in table 8.1. In this book, I have analyzed cases of harmful content being produced by humans and disseminated by humans on social media (quadrant A).[46] But there are other scenarios that we should consider as generative AI models become widespread. The first is harmful content produced by AI and disseminated by humans (quadrant B). The examples described earlier, of extremist actors using AI to create misinformation that they then shared on social media, illustrates such a scenario.

The second case is when content produced by humans is replicated and disseminated by AI models in the course of their interaction with users (quadrant C). Chatbots like OpenAI's ChatGPT, Microsoft's Bing AI, or Google's Gemini draw on information posted by humans on the internet to share information with people who interact with them. Without restrictions, there is nothing that prevents chatbots from disseminating harmful content to users. Technology companies that own AI-powered chatbots started introducing measures that would limit the dissemination of harmful content on their systems, but we still have limited knowledge on whether such measures actually work and on what can be done to circumvent them.[47] We need more research on these sorts of scenarios to better understand how to prevent the misuse of generative AI technologies in the future.

The final scenario is AI models autonomously both producing and disseminating harmful content (quadrant D). This is a particularly challenging scenario for existing content moderation frameworks, which assume that human actors are those who produce harmful content. Do AI models have agency? Can we think of them as actors? If not, how should we update current content moderation policies to address such cases? These potential scenarios show that there is much more that needs to be studied on the intersection between AI and content moderation. In particular, how do we devise effective regulation of these emerging technologies? If there is anything that this book has shown it is that future regulation of artificial intelligence will have to take into account different standards to address harmful content. After all, the internet has always been—and will continue to be—an interconnected ecosystem.

Policy Takeaways

So, does content moderation work? The analysis in this book shows that it does, but only in a limited way if content policies are applied inconsistently across platforms. Technology companies' success in shifting the activity of extremist organizations away from their sites—as I have illustrated in the cases of the Islamic State, the Proud Boys, the Taliban, and QAnon—shows that moderation is able to curb harmful content on platforms that engage in it. However, the lack of consistency in moderation across platforms inhibits its effectiveness as a policy solution for harmful content in the broader online ecosystem. Thus, investing in mechanisms that facilitate convergence in platform policies—in a way that does not restrict nonharmful speech—would be a fruitful way to address extremist activity online.

In addition, it will be important to identify ways to make content moderation more legitimate in the eyes of social media users. As I have shown here, a large driver of the radicalization of deplatformed users on less-moderated platforms is their feeling that content moderation is unjustified. This reaction might be avoided if policies to address harmful content were communicated to social media users in a way that facilitates the support of the "online public." If content moderation is viewed as a legitimate policy solution to online harms, then social media users would perhaps be less vulnerable to extremism.

9

Appendix

Additional Information for Chapter 3

Countries and Regulations Included in the Dataset

Australia, Online Safety Bill, July 23, 2021

Austria, Communication Platforms Act (KoPl-G), January 1, 2021

Belgium, Digital Services Act (EU), November 16, 2022

Brazil, Bill 2630/Fake News Law, June 30, 2020

Bulgaria, Digital Services Act (EU), November 16, 2022

Croatia, Digital Services Act (EU), November 16, 2022

Cyprus, Digital Services Act (EU), November 16, 2022

Czech Republic, Digital Services Act (EU), November 16, 2022

Denmark, Digital Services Act (EU), November 16, 2022

Estonia, Digital Services Act (EU), November 16, 2022

Ethiopia, Hate Speech and Disinformation Prevention and Suppression Proclamation, March 23, 2020

Finland, Digital Services Act (EU), November 16, 2022

France, Avia Law, May 13, 2020; Digital Services Act (EU), November 16, 2022

Germany, Act to Improve Enforcement of the Law in Social Networks (Network Enforcement Act, NetzDG) June 30, 2017; Digital Services Act (EU), November 16, 2022

Greece, Digital Services Act (EU), November 16, 2022

Hong Kong, The Law of the People's Republic of China on Safeguarding National Security in the Hong Kong Special Administrative Region, June 30, 2020

Hungary, Digital Services Act (EU), November 16, 2022

India, 2021 Intermediary Guidelines and Digital Media Ethics Code,
  February 25, 2021
Indonesia, Regulation of the Minister of Communication and Informat-
  ics Number 5 of 2020 on Private Electronic System Operators,
  November 24, 2020
Ireland, Digital Services Act (EU), November 16, 2022
Italy, Digital Services Act (EU), November 16, 2022
Jordan, A Strategy to Regulate Social Media to Protect Users from
  Harmful and Illegal Content, in progress
Kazakhstan, On Amendments and Additions to Certain Legislative Acts
  of the Republic of Kazakhstan on the Protection of the Rights of the
  Child, Education, Information, and Informatization, May 3, 2022
Kenya, The Kenya Information and Communication (Amendment) Bill,
  in progress
Latvia, Digital Services Act (EU), November 16, 2022
Lithuania, Digital Services Act (EU), November 16, 2022
Luxembourg, Digital Services Act (EU), November 16, 2022
Malta, Digital Services Act (EU), November 16, 2022
Mexico, Proposed amendment to the Federal Telecommunications and
  Broadcasting Law, in progress
Netherlands, Digital Services Act (EU), November 16, 2022
New Zealand, Films, Videos, and Publications Classification (Urgent
  Interim Classification of Publications and Prevention of Online
  Harm) Amendment Bill 2020 268-1, November 2, 2021
Nigeria, Code of Practice for Interactive Computer Service Platforms/
  Internet Intermediaries and Conditions, in progress
Pakistan, Citizens Protection (Against Online Harm) Rules, October 20,
  2020
Poland, Digital Services Act (EU), November 16, 2022
Portugal, Digital Services Act (EU), November 16, 2022
Romania, Digital Services Act (EU), November 16, 2022
Singapore, Online Safety (Miscellaneous Amendments) Act, November 24,
  2022
Slovakia, Digital Services Act (EU), November 16, 2022
Slovenia, Digital Services Act (EU), November 16, 2022
Spain, Digital Services Act (EU), November 16, 2022
Sweden, Digital Services Act (EU), November 16, 2022
Thailand, Suppression of Dissemination and Removal of Computer Data
  from the Computer System B.E. 2565, December 25, 2022

Turkey, Bill Amending Law No. 5651 on Regulating Internet Publications and Combating Crimes Committed by Means of Such Publications, July 29, 2020

United Kingdom, Draft of Online Safety Bill, in progress

Venezuela, Law Against Hatred, November 8, 2017

Vietnam, Regulations to Deal with "False" Content on Social Media Platforms, November 3, 2022

Additional Information for Chapter 4

Groups from the Mapping Militants Project (N = 59)

Ahrar al-Sham, Hay'at Tahrir al-Sham (formerly Jabhat al-Nusra), Hezbollah, Kata'ib Hezbollah, The Islamic State, Bandas Criminales, National Liberation Army (Colombia), Revolutionary Armed Forces of Colombia–People's Army, Abu Sayyaf Group, al-Qaeda, al-Qaeda in the Arabian Peninsula, al-Qaeda in the Indian Subcontinent, Ahlu Sunna wal Jama, al-Qaeda in the Islamic Maghreb, Tehreek Nifaz-e-Shariat Mohammadi, The Islamic State–Sinai Province, al-Qaeda Kurdish Battalions, al-Shabaab, Boko Haram, Haqqani Network, Harakat-ul-Mujahedeen, Harkat-ul-Jihadi al-Islami, Islamic Army in Iraq, Jaish-e-Mohammed, Jemaah Islamiyah, Lashkar-e-Jhangvi, Lashkar-e-Taiba, Lashkar-e-Zil, Moroccan Islamic Combatant Group, Mujahideen Army, Tehrik-i-Taliban Pakistan, the Taliban, Ansar al-Shariah (Tunisia and Libya), Bangsamoro Islamic Freedom Fighters, Ansar al-Sunna Shariah, Asa'ib ahl al-Haq, Badr Organization of Reconstruction and Development, Islamic Movement of Kurdistan, Jaysh Rijal al-Tariqa al-Naqshbandia (JRTN), Kata'ib Sayyid al-Shuhada, Mahdi Army, Ansar Dine, Caucasus Emirate, Al Akhtar Trust, Balochistan Liberation Army, Balochistan Liberation Front, Balochistan Republican Army, Islami-Jamiat-Taliba, Jamaat-ul-Ahrar, Lashkar-e-Islam, Nazir Group, Sipah-e-Sahaba Pakistan, Zain Group, Communist Party of the Philippines–New People's Army, Moro Islamic Liberation Front, Moro National Liberation Front, Ras Kamboni Movement, Jaysh al-Islam, The Southern Front.

Groups in the Southern Poverty Law Center's Extremist Files Database (N = 55)

The Right Stuff, The Base, Revolt Through Tradition, Patriot Front, National Reformation Party, International Conservative Community, American Identity Movement, American Freedom Party, Vinlanders Social Club, United

Skinhead Nation, Firm 22, Blood and Honour Social Club, American Front, American Defense Skinheads, AC Skins, Wolves of Vinland, Asatru Folk Assembly, Nationalist Social Club (NSC-131), National Socialist Movement, National Alliance, Folks Front/Folkish Resistance Movement, Atomwaffen Division, American Nazi Party, 14 First, League of the South, Identity Dixie, United Klan Nation, Patriotic Brigade Knights of the Ku Klux Klan, Order of the Ku Klux Klan/White Christian Brotherhood, Loyal White Knights of the Ku Klux Klan, American Christian Dixie Knights of the Ku Klux Klan, United Nuwaubians Worldwide, All Eyes on Egipt, True Nation Israelite Congregation, Sicarii 1715, Revolutionary Black Panther Party, Proud Boys, New Black Panther Party for Self Defense, New Black Panther Party, Israelite Saints of Christ, Israelite School of Universal Practical Knowledge, Israel United in Christ, House of Israel, Great Millstone, Black Riders Liberation Party, Ambassadors of Christ, Nation of Islam, Committee for Open Debate on the Holocaust, Soldiers of Odin, Act for America, Sure Foundation Baptist Church, Stedfast Baptist Church, Revival Baptist Church, Pacific Justice Institute, Mass Resistance, American Family Association.

Replication of Figure 4.3 with NGOs

In chapter 4, I present an analysis showing how militant and hate groups' presence on social media varies with platform moderation and size. To check whether the findings shown in figure 4.3 capture something specific to groups that are impacted by content moderation (and not to any organization that seeks to use social media platforms to accomplish its goals), I repeated this analysis by focusing on nongovernmental organizations. I collected data on the online presence of eleven organizations that work in the area of humanitarian relief, peace, security, and development: Action Against Hunger, CARE, Doctors Without Borders, International Medical Corps, Islamic Relief Worldwide, International Rescue Committee (IRC), International Committee of the Red Cross, Oxfam International, Refugees International, World Jewish Relief, and World Vision.

Using the methodology described in chapter 4, I collected data on the official social media handles of these NGOs on the following twelve platforms (the same ones that I examine in chapter 4): Facebook, Instagram, LinkedIn, Parler, Pinterest, Reddit, Telegram, TikTok, Twitter, YouTube, Discord, and Gab.

Figure 9.1 shows how NGOs' online presence varies with specific moderation policies. The figure displays the average number of organizations with

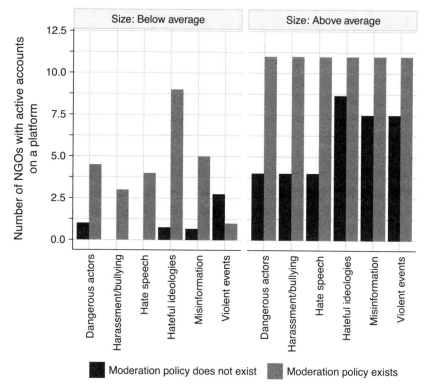

FIGURE 9.1. Nongovernmental Organizations' Accounts by Moderation Policy and Size

Note: The figure shows the number of NGOs with active accounts on social media platforms. The gray bars show the prevalence of NGOs on platforms that include the policies listed in the *x*-axis, and the black bars show the patterns for platforms that do not include these rules. The left panel shows platforms with smaller-than-average user bases and the right panel shows platforms with larger-than-average user bases.

active accounts on social media platforms that vary in their moderation and size. The gray bars show groups' presence on platforms that include the policies listed in the *x*-axis, and the black bars show the patterns for platforms that do not include these rules. To examine whether moderation interacts with platform size, I break down the data by platforms whose user bases are below average (left-side panels) or above average (right-side panels).

Unlike militant and hate organizations, which are often subject to content bans on social media, I find that the online presence of NGOs tends to be

higher on platforms that *do* include the moderation policies listed on the
x-axis. NGOs are more (not less!) likely to be actively present on platforms
that ban dangerous organizations, harassment and bullying, hate speech and
hateful ideologies, as well as misinformation, than on platforms that do not
include these policies. As expected—and consistent with the argument that
actors prefer platforms with larger audiences—I also find that NGOs have a
more active presence on larger sites. These results support my theoretical predictions that only actors that produce content that is likely to be acted upon
will prefer larger platforms with more lenient moderation policies.

Additional Information for Chapter 5

Collecting Gab and Twitter Data

To collect Gab data, my first step was to download all posts that were publicly
available on the platform, without any filtering. Using the API of the Mastodon social network, on which Gab has been operating since July 2019, I collected information on all posts that were viewable on Gab's public timeline.[1]
This initial collection allowed me to obtain data on Gab users who had been
active on the platform since October 2019. In June 2020, Gab disabled the
public timeline. To continue collecting data, I moved to a retrospective collection from which I obtained all historical posts by Gab users who were in my
dataset by that point, that is, users who had made a public post prior to
June 2020. After January 2021, I was again able to access Gab's public timeline
and to resume both prospective and retrospective data collection. The total
number of unique Gab users in my sample is 93,004.

My second step was to identify Gab users with Twitter accounts. My approach was simple: I queried the Twitter API for screen names used by Gab
users. Matching screen names is a popular approach to finding user linkages
across platforms. Other methods are available, some of which draw on the
similarity in the content that users post across platforms, as well as similarity
in user metadata (profile pictures, profile descriptions, and so on).[2] Although
matching screen names probably undercounts users who do not use the same
name across platforms, this approach is less likely to include accounts of unrelated users. Using the matched screen name approach, I identified 30,444
Gab users who had active Twitter accounts (33 percent of the Gab users in my
sample), and downloaded all available posts by these users on both platforms.
Manual validation of the matched accounts confirmed that these were owned
by the same individuals.

Measuring Hate Speech

The next step was to measure the extent to which users on both platforms engaged with hate speech. Since the volume of Gab and Twitter posts was high, I used automated text analysis to measure hate speech. Definitions of hate speech vary, but many capture a similar concept. I used the description in the *Encyclopedia of Political Communication* to define online hate speech:

> Comments containing speech aimed to terrorize, express prejudice and con-tempt to- ward, humiliate, degrade, abuse, threaten, ridicule, demean, and discriminate based on race, ethnicity, religion, sexual orientation, national origin, or gender. . . . Also including pejoratives and group-based insults, that sometime comprise brief group epithets consisting of short, usually negative labels or lengthy narratives about an out group's alleged negative behavior.[3]

I focused on two categories in my definition of hateful content: (1) posts ex-pressing prejudice and contempt toward individuals from a nonwhite social group, including African Americans, Jews, Muslims, Asians, individuals from Latin American countries, and immigrants; and (2) content expressing support for or sympathy with white nationalism in the United States. To create a training set for the model, I randomly sampled 124,006 Twitter and Gab posts from the full post-level data that I downloaded from both platforms. I then worked with a team of research assistants to label this sample along the following categories:

1. **Hateful language**: Posts expressing prejudice and contempt toward individuals from a nonwhite social group, including pejoratives and group-based insults that could appear as negative labels for or narra-tives about the group's alleged negative behavior.
2. **Anti-Black**: Posts expressing hate toward individuals from a Black and/or African American background, including comments criticizing interracial marriage.
3. **Anti-Jewish**: Posts expressing hate toward individuals from a Jewish background, including comments criticizing marriage between whites and Jews.
4. **Anti-Muslim**: Posts expressing hate toward individuals from a Muslim background, including comments criticizing marriage between whites and Muslims.
5. **Anti-Asian:** Posts expressing hate toward individuals from an Asian, East Asian, or South Asian background, including comments criticiz-ing marriage between whites and Asians.

6. **Anti-Latinx**: Posts expressing hate toward individuals from a Latin American background, including comments criticizing marriage between whites and those of Latino descent.

7. **Anti-immigrant**: Posts expressing hate toward immigrants (refugees, asylum seekers, and other types of migrants), including posts criticizing open borders and liberal immigration policies.

8. **Endorsing white nationalism/white supremacy**: Posts expressing support for or sympathy with the white nationalist movement, its ideology, and its activities, including comments related to the theme "make (white) America great again."

To classify hate speech in unlabeled posts, I used a recurrent neural network with an LSTM (Long Short-Term Memory) layer. Table 9.1 shows the model's architecture. The input consisted of an embedding layer that took in sequences of 250 integers and embedded them into dense vectors of eight dimensions. The embedding layer had 400,000 parameters that were learned during training. The output layer was a dense layer with a single unit that outputted a single binary classification value (0 or 1) for whether the tweet expressed hate speech or not. I trained the model using the Adam optimization algorithm with a learning rate of 0.001 and a binary cross-entropy loss function. The model was trained with eight epochs and a batch size of 64. In the training process, I set aside 10 percent of the training data as a validation set to ensure that the model did not overfit over the course of training. The model performed well at detecting hate speech in the data, as can be seen in the out-of-sample performance metrics reported in table 9.1. Summary statistics for the matched sample are shown in table 9.2.

TABLE 9.1: LSTM Model Architecture and Performance

Model Architecture		
Layer	Output Shape	Parameters (number)
Input (embedding)	(None, 250, 8)	400,000
LSTM	(None, 8)	544
Output (dense)	(None, 1)	9

Out-of-Sample Model Performance
Accuracy: 0.89; recall: 0.89; precision: 0.88; F1: 0.89

TABLE 9.2: Summary Statistics for Gab Posts by Matched Sample

Variable	Mean	Standard Deviation	Minimum	Maximum
Post by a suspended user	0.62	0.49	0	1
Post posted after suspension	0.43	0.49	0	1
Post expresses hate speech	0.07	0.26	0	1
Post expresses anger	0.003	0.06	0	1
Post expresses frustration with Big Tech censorship	0.018	0.13	0	1
Post mentions the Oath Keepers	0.001	0.03	0	1
Number of friends on Twitter	4,623.09	8,216.19	0	211,447
Number of followers on Twitter	7,320.33	18,158.41	0	338,332
Number of friends on Gab	3,155.46	4,796.12	0	37,356
Number of followers on Gab	7,568.99	30,253.89	0	309,473

TABLE 9.3: Difference-in-Differences Analysis for Number of Gab Posts

	(1) Number of Gab Posts per Day	(2) Number of Gab Posts per Day
Suspended	−1.804*** (0.597)	
Post	1.719** (0.675)	
Suspended x Post	1.843** (0.798)	2.078*** (0.628)
Constant	14.309*** (0.495)	
Observations	28,238	28,238
R^2	0.003	0.562
User fixed effects	No	Yes
Time fixed effects	No	Yes
Before/after window	90 days	90 days

$^{**}p < .05; ^{***}p < .01$

TABLE 9.4: Difference-in-Differences Analysis for Hate Speech and Anger

	(1) Hate Speech	(2) Hate Speech	(3) Anger	(4) Anger
Suspended	−0.397*** (0.052)		−1.225*** (0.172)	
Post	−0.361*** (0.059)		−1.521*** (0.194)	
Suspended x Post	0.383*** (0.069)	0.354*** (0.063)	1.283*** (0.229)	1.156*** (0.201)
Constant	1.234*** (0.043)		4.434*** (0.142)	
Observations	28,238	28,238	28,238	28,238
R^2	0.002	0.415	0.003	0.460
User fixed effects	No	Yes	No	Yes
Time fixed effects	No	Yes	No	Yes
Before/after window	90 days	90 days	90 days	90 days

***$p < .01$

TABLE 9.5: Difference-in-Differences Analysis for Big Tech Censorship and the Oath Keepers

	(1) Big Tech Censorship	(2) Big Tech Censorship	(3) Oath Keepers	(4) Oath Keepers
Suspended	0.061*** (0.020)		0.002 (0.004)	
Post	0.005 (0.022)		0.004 (0.005)	
Suspended x Post	0.013 (0.026)	0.058** (0.027)	0.014** (0.006)	0.003 (0.006)
Constant	0.219*** (0.016)		0.009*** (0.004)	
Observations	28,238	28,238	28,238	28,238
R^2	0.001	0.239	0.002	0.154
User fixed effects	No	Yes	No	Yes
Time fixed effects	No	Yes	No	Yes
Before/after window	90 days	90 days	90 days	90 days

**$p < .05$; ***$p < .01$

TABLE 9.6: Suspended User's Anger over Being Deplatformed by User's Follower Count

	(1) Anger	(2) Anger	(3) Big Tech Censorship	(4) Big Tech Censorship
Post-suspension	−0.28593		−0.00274	
	(0.35571)		(0.05403)	
Number of Twitter followers	0.000001***		0.00000	
	(0.0000000)		(0.00000)	
Post-suspension x Number of Twitter followers	0.00002**	0.00002**	0.000004***	0.000003**
	(0.00001)	(0.00001)	(0.000001)	(0.000001)
Constant	2.66794***		0.38672***	
	(0.26831)		(0.04075)	
Observations	2,058	2,058	2,058	2,058
R²	0.21873	0.59834	0.00531	0.43725
User fixed effects	No	Yes	No	Yes
Time fixed effects	No	Yes	No	Yes
Before/after window	7 days	7 days	7 days	7 days

$**p < .05; ***p < .01$

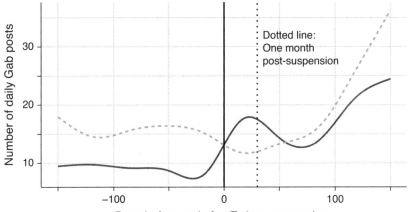

FIGURE 9.2. Number of Gab Posts by All Suspended Users
Note: The figure shows the number of posts that all users who were suspended from Twitter (including those who were not included in the matched study) posted on Gab before and after Twitter suspensions. The figure shows that users increased their overall usage of Gab in the months after being deplatformed. Although some suspended users reduced their Gab posting in the month after suspension (gray dashed line), they increased their Gab activity in the following months. This illustrates that Twitter deplatforming increased overall usage of Gab, even among users who did not enter my matched study.

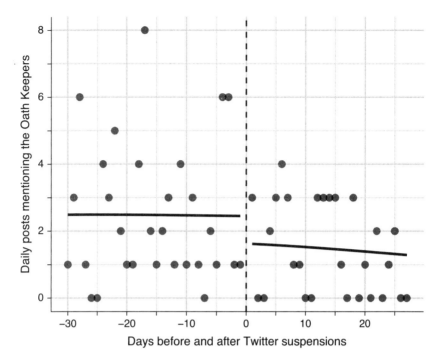

FIGURE 9.3. Engagement with the Oath Keepers' Messaging on Twitter
Note: The figure shows time trends in mentions of the Oath Keepers on Twitter
by nonsuspended users before and after Twitter's deplatforming. The *x*-axis shows
the difference, in days, between the date of deplatforming and the date when
individuals posted on Twitter, and the *y*-axis shows the number of posts that
mentioned the Oath Keepers. Nonsuspended users' engagement with the Oath
Keepers' content on Twitter declined slightly after deplatforming.

Additional Information for Chapter 6

TABLE 9.7: Top Words Associated with "Attack" in Taliban Tweets
across Languages

Pashto	Dari	Urdu	Arabic	English
برید	مجاهدين	فوجی	لقوات	killed
وروسته	محافظ	حمله	العملاء	forces
موټر	ضربات	ضلع	قافلة	military
چاودنه	کوبندهء	بمباری	استشهد	civilians
بم	تلفات	لوگوں	هجوم	base

TABLE 9.7: (*continued*)

Pashto	Dari	Urdu	Arabic	English
وشو	حمله	امریکی	عسکرية	soldiers
ترسره	كشته	ربائی	جنديا	raid
چاودنی	دشمن	مجاہد	الأمريكية	troops
مجاهدينو	زخمی	حملے	القوات	strike
باندي	اساس	لابور	للقوات	operation
عسکرو	انفجار	رسالت	أمنية	airstrike
دښمن	حملات	میڈیا	استشهادية	mercenary
هوايي	نیروی	فورسز	مركز	army
ملکي	عملیاتی	حکومت	رتل	withdrawal
شو	عساکر	سنگین	قاعدة	gunmen
دروند	پولیس	ردعمل	جنود	convoy
شوی	مه	بلمند	التابعة	invaders
موټربم	قرارگاه	گورنر	القبض	force
وحشي	نیرو	تحریک	معسکر	enemy
بریدونه	وحشی	عہد	هجومي	killing

TABLE 9.8: QAnon Messaging on Twitter and Gab after Twitter's Policy Change

	Dependent Variable			
	Use of QAnon Hashtags in a Post			
	(1)	(2)	(3)	(4)
	One Week	One Month	Two Months	Three Months
After Twitter's policy change (Post is on Gab)	0.001** (0.001)	0.001*** (0.0003)	0.002*** (0.0003)	0.001*** (0.0003)
Post is on Twitter	−0.003 (0.002)	−0.005*** (0.001)	−0.005*** (0.001)	−0.004*** (0.001)
After Twitter's policy change *x* Post is on Twitter	−0.001 (0.001)	−0.002*** (0.0005)	−0.002*** (0.0004)	−0.002*** (0.0004)
Observations	117,267	529,681	1,064,517	1,608,040
R^2	0.494	0.383	0.367	0.337
User fixed effects	Yes	Yes	Yes	Yes
Clustered standard errors	User	User	User	User

**$p < .05$; ***$p < .01$

Additional Information for Chapter 7

Collecting Historical Versions of Platforms'
Content Moderation Policies

I obtained historical versions of 60 social media platforms' content moderation policies using the Internet Archive's Wayback Machine (https://archive.org). The data include 1,802 historical versions of 60 platforms from January 1, 2018, to September 1, 2022. Since the volume of text was very large (there were hundreds of historical "snapshots" of each company's moderation policies), I measured the existence of each policy using a dictionary approach. Table 9.9 shows the keywords for each policy.

TABLE 9.9: Keywords to Measure Moderation of Harmful Content

Category	Keywords
1. Dangerous actors	violent organization, dangerous organization, criminal organization, extremist group, violent extremist, violent organizations, dangerous organizations, criminal organizations, extremist groups, violent extremists, violent criminal, criminal terrorist, terrorist organization, organized hate groups, nonstate armed groups, armed groups, armed group, terrorist activity, terrorist, terrorist organizations, terrorist content, dangerous actors, extremists, violent extremism, perpetrators, prohibited entities, terrorism, gangs, trafficking rings, hate group, hate groups, dangerous individuals, designate individuals, offline harms, specially designated narcotics trafficking kingpins, foreign terrorist organizations, engage in violence, nonstate actors
2. Violent events	harmful activity, coordination cause harm, harmful activities, promoting violent crimes, coordinating harm, violent events, glorifying violent tragedies, promote attacks, promote attack, glorifying violent events, violent acts, dangerous activities, criminal activities, physical violence, advocates violence, acts of violence
3. Hateful ideologies	hateful ideologies, hateful ideology, extremist ideologies, extremist ideology, chauvinism, nationalism, hatred, hostility, fascism, racial superiority, ideologies, nazism, white supremacy

TABLE 9.9: (*continued*)

Category	Keywords
4. Glorification of violence	glorify, violent crime, violent crimes, violent events, violent event, glorify violence, glorifies violence, celebrates the suffering, celebrate suffering, humiliation, graphic content, gory, shock, disgust, gratuitously, shocking, sadistic, gruesome, glorifies extreme, extreme violence, suffering, shocking, bodily injury, graphic violence, disturbing scenes, gore, excessive violence, glorification, glorification of violence, graphic deaths, dismembered, mutilated, charred, human remains, depict violence, violence-glorifying, violence glorifying, glorifying violence, depictions of violence, self-harm, self harm, violent content, gratuitous violence, realistic violence
5. Threats and incitement	inflict violence, incite violence, threats, physical harm, threatening, threaten, intimidating, intimidate, offensive, instigate, instigating, commit violent, commit violence, promote violence, incites, intent to commit, commit act, lawless action, harm others, incitement to violence, intimidation, advocates violence, advocate violence, encourage terrorism, incite hatred, calls to violence, encourages acts of violence, encourage acts of violence, fosters terrorism, foster terrorism, inspire violence, inspire violent, promotes violence, threaten violence, promotes harm, promote harm, promote extreme, incitement of violence
6. Harassment and bullying	harassment, targeted harassment, abusive behavior, harass, intimidate, malicious contact, threatening, threaten, bully, bullied, personal attack, abusive language, doxing, promote hate, bullying, harassing, promote violence
7. Hate speech	race, ethnicity, national origin, caste, sexual orientation, gender, gender identity, religious affiliation, disability, serious disease, directly attack, threaten, hate, hate speech, direct attack, protected characteristics, harmful stereotypes, statements of inferiority, expressions of contempt, disgust, dismissal, cursing, calls for exclusion, segregation, dehumanizing, obscene, defamatory, hateful, racially offensive, ethnically offensive, hatred, discrimination, hateful behavior, denigrates, dehumanizes, discriminatory action, disability status, slurs, vulnerable groups, protected classifications, cultural identity, ethnic background, religious beliefs, epithets, profanity, abusive, racist, insult, defame, slander, disparage, discriminate, hostility, dehumanization, derogatory, malicious, inflammatory, racism, sexism, discriminatory, lewd, vulgar, bigoted, immigration status, demeans, defames

(*continued*)

TABLE 9.9: (*continued*)

Category	Keywords
8. Misinformation	misleading content, deceptive, confusing, manipulated, manipulated media, distortions, falsehoods, falsehood, misrepresentations, misrepresentation, misleading statements, misleading, mislead, inaccurate, false, disinformation, mal-information, malinformation, misinform, inauthentic, falsified, conspiracy
9. Platform manipulation	deceptive, mislead, fake, identities, identity, fabricated, fabricate, manipulative, manipulative behavior, spam, scam, integrity, authenticity, fake engagement, impersonation, falsify information, fake profile, real name, impersonate, manipulation, misrepresent, false, fraudulent, deceive, manipulating, misappropriate

Measuring Convergence in Content Moderation Policies

My first convergence measure consisted of a count of the number of platforms with which each technology company shared policies in each time period in my historical data. To create this measure, I first identified all the unique time periods for which I had historical content moderation policy pages from the Wayback Machine. Then, for each time period, I calculated the cosine similarity between each pair of platforms along the nine categories of harmful content that made up the moderation threshold. This gave me a rough measure of the similarity in the language of moderation policies across platforms. After obtaining cosine similarity measures for each pair of platforms in each time period, I then counted, for each platform, the number of other platforms with which its cosine similarity score was higher than the average for that time period.

My second measure was the average of the moderation threshold—across all platforms—over time. I created this measure by computing the mean of the moderation threshold scores for all platforms with available policies in a given time period. This measure allowed me to examine the overall "restrictiveness" of harmful content in the broader online information ecosystem. Finally, I calculated the variance in platforms' moderation thresholds in each time period in my data. Low variance would mean that moderation thresholds were more similar to each other, and higher variance reflected greater diversity in moderation.

TABLE 9.10: Extremist Presence by Platform Convergence

	Dependent Variable		
	Official Presence	Suspended	Unofficial Presence
	(1)	(2)	(3)
Converging platform	−0.255***	0.146***	0.108**
	(0.057)	(0.041)	(0.053)
Monthly active users	0.139**	−0.028	−0.111*
	(0.069)	(0.050)	(0.065)
Constant	0.672***	0.058*	0.271***
	(0.041)	(0.030)	(0.038)
Observations	578	578	578
R^2	0.035	0.026	0.008

*$p < .10$; **$p < .05$; ***$p < .01$

NOTES

1: Introduction

1. Elias Groll, "Islamic State Releases Video Showing Jordanian Pilot Being Burned Alive," *Foreign Policy*, February 3, 2015, https://foreignpolicy.com/2015/02/03/islamic_state_releases_video_showing_jordanian_pilot_being_burned_alive/.

2. Tamar Mitts, Gregoire Phillips, and Barbara F. Walter, "Studying the Impact of ISIS Propaganda Campaigns," *Journal of Politics* 84, no. 2 (2022): 1220–25.

3. Data from CrowdTangle, a public insights tool owned and operated by Facebook (http://crowdtangle.com/).

4. Ravi Somaiya, "ISIS Video Presents Grim Choice for News Media," *New York Times*, February 3, 2015, https://www.nytimes.com/2015/02/04/business/execution-video-presents-grim-choice-for-news-media.html; Nicky Woolf, "Fox News Site Embeds Unedited ISIS Video Showing Brutal Murder of Jordanian Pilot," *Guardian*, February 4, 2015, https://www.theguardian.com/media/2015/feb/04/fox-news-shows-isis-video-jordan-pilot.

5. Amnesty International, "The Social Atrocity: Meta and the Right to Remedy for the Rohingya," Amnesty International, September 29, 2022, https://www.amnesty.org/en/documents/ASA16/5933/2022/en/; Jenifer Whitten-Woodring, Mona S. Kleinberg, Ardeth Thawnghmung, and Myat The Thitsar, "Poison if You Don't Know How to Use It: Facebook, Democracy, and Human Rights in Myanmar," *International Journal of Press/Politics* 25, no. 3 (2020): 407–25.

6. Yochai Benkler, Robert Faris, and Hal Roberts, *Network Propaganda: Manipulation, Disinformation, and Radicalization in American Politics* (Oxford: Oxford University Press, 2018); Pablo Barberá, "Social Media, Echo Chambers, and Political Polarization," in *Social Media and Democracy: The State of the Field, Prospects for Reform*, edited by Joshua A. Tucker and Nathaniel Persily, 34–55 (Cambridge: Cambridge University Press, 2020); Kate Starbird, Renée DiResta, and Matt DeButts, "Influence and Improvisation: Participatory Disinformation during the 2020 US Election," *Social Media + Society* 9, no. 2 (2023): 20563051231177943; Ella Busch and Jacob Ware, "The Weaponisation of Deepfakes: Digital Deception by the Far-Right," International Centre for Counter-Terrorism, December 2023, https://www.icct.nl/sites/default/files/2023-12/The%20Weaponisation%20of%20Deepfakes.pdf.

7. Sapna Maheshwari, "Young TikTok Users Quickly Encounter Problematic Posts, Researchers Say," *New York Times*, December 14, 2022, https://www.nytimes.com/2022/12/14/business/tiktok-safety-teens-eating-disorders-self-harm.html; Center for Countering Digital Hate, "Deadly by Design: TikTok Pushes Harmful Content Promoting Eating Disorders and

Self-Harm into Young Users' Feeds," December 15, 2022, https://counterhate.com/research/deadly-by-design/; Luis Ferré-Sadurní, "New York Seeks to Limit Social Media's Grip on Children's Attention," *New York Times*, October 11, 2023, https://www.nytimes.com/2023/10/11/nyregion/tiktok-instagram-algorithm-children.html.

8. Sean Ingle, "Sports Bodies to Boycott Social Media for Bank Holiday Weekend over Abuse," *Guardian*, April 29, 2021, https://www.theguardian.com/sport/2021/apr/29/major-sports-bodies-84-hour-social-media-boycott-over-online-abuse-facebook-twitter; Cameron White and Damola Odeyemi, "The Social Media Boycott Garnered Momentum. Now It's Time for Change," *Varsity*, May 8, 2021, https://www.varsity.co.uk/sport/21363.

9. Todd Spangler, "YouTube Hit with Another Ad Scandal, Even as P&G Returns to the Platform," *Variety*, April 20, 2018, https://variety.com/2018/digital/news/youtube-ad-scandal-racist-nazi-procter-gamble-1202770250/; Tiffany Hsu and Gillian Friedman, "CVS, Dunkin', Lego: The Brands Pulling Ads from Facebook over Hate Speech," *New York Times*, June 26, 2020, https://www.nytimes.com/2020/06/26/business/media/Facebook-advertising-boycott.html; Tiffany Hsu and Eleanor Lutz, "More than 1,000 Companies Boycotted Facebook. Did It Work?" *New York Times*, August 1, 2020, https://www.nytimes.com/2020/08/01/business/media/facebook-boycott.html.

10. Dan Milmo, "Rohingya Sue Facebook for £150bn over Myanmar Genocide," *Guardian*, December 6, 2021, https://www.theguardian.com/technology/2021/dec/06/rohingya-sue-facebook-myanmar-genocide-us-uk-legal-action-social-media-violence; Cara Anna (Associated Press), "Ethiopians File Lawsuit against Meta over Hate Speech in Tigray War," *PBS News Hour*, December 14, 2022, https://www.pbs.org/newshour/world/ethiopians-file-lawsuit-against-meta-over-hate-speech-in-tigray-war; David McCabe, "Supreme Court to Hear Case That Targets a Legal Shield of Tech Giants," *New York Times*, February 20, 2023, https://www.nytimes.com/2023/02/20/technology/supreme-court-tech-section230.html.

11. New Zealand Government, "PM House Statement on Christchurch Mosques Terror Attack," Beehive.gov.nz, March 19, 2019, https://www.beehive.govt.nz/release/pm-house-statement-christchurch-mosques-terror-attack.

12. Damien Cave, "Countries Want to Ban 'Weaponized' Social Media. What Would That Look Like?" *New York Times*, March 31, 2019, https://www.nytimes.com/2019/03/31/world/australia/countries-controlling-social-media.html.

13. European Commission, "Digital Services Act: EU's Landmark Rules for Online Platforms Enter into Force," November 16, 2022, https://ec.europa.eu/commission/presscorner/detail/%20en/ip_22_6906.

14. Twitter Transparency (now X Transparency), "Removal Requests: Latest Data: Legal Demands," December 2021, https://transparency.twitter.com/en/reports/removal-requests.html#2021-jul-dec; TikTok, "Government Removal Requests Report," November 10, 2023, https://www.tiktok.com/transparency/en-us/government-removal-requests-2023-1/; Meta, "Community Standards Enforcement Report," Transparency Center, fourth quarter 2023, https://transparency.fb.com/reports/community-standards-enforcement/.

15. European Parliament, "Verbatim Report of Proceedings," Parliamentary Debate, January 19, 2022, https://www.europarl.europa.eu/doceo/document/CRE-9-2022-01-19_EN.html; Tiffany Hsu, "News on Fringe Social Sites Draws Limited but Loyal Fans, Report Finds," *New York Times*, October 6, 2022, https://www.nytimes.com/2022/10/06/technology/parler-truth-social-telegram-pew.html.

16. See Meta, "Facebook Community Standards," https://transparency.fb.com/policies/community-standards/.

17. TikTok, "Community Guidelines Enforcement Report: January 1, 2023–March 31, 2023," June 30, 2023, https://www.tiktok.com/transparency/en-us/community-guidelines-enforcement-2023-1/.

18. Sarah T. Roberts, "Content Moderation," in *Encyclopedia of Big Data*, edited by Laurie A. Schintler and Connie L. McNeely (Cham: Springer, 2017), 1–4.

19. Bennett Clifford, "Migration Moments: Extremist Adoption of Text-Based Instant Messaging Applications," Global Network on Extremism and Technology, November 9, 2020, https://gnet-research.org/2020/11/09/migration-moments-extremist-adoption-of-text-based-instant-messaging-applications/.

20. Jared Holt, "After the Insurrection: How Domestic Extremists Adapted and Evolved after the January 6 US Capitol Attack," Atlantic Council Digital Forensic Research Lab, January 2022, https://www.atlanticcouncil.org/wp-content/uploads/2022/01/After-the-Insurrection.pdf. See also chapter 6.

21. This research includes Matteo Cinelli, Walter Quattrociocchi, Alessandro Galeazzi, Carlo Michele Valensise, Emanuele Brugnoli, Ana Lucia Schmidt, Paola Zola, Fabiana Zollo, and Antonio Scala, "The COVID-19 Social Media Infodemic," *Scientific Reports* 10, no. 1 (2020): 1–10; and Yingdan Lu, Jack Schaefer, Kunwoo Park, Jungseock Joo, and Jennifer Pan, "How Information Flows from the World to China," *International Journal of Press/Politics* (2022): 1940161221117470.

22. David A. Lake, "Rational Extremism: Understanding Terrorism in the Twenty-First Century," *Dialogue IO* 1, no. 1 (2002): 15–28.

23. Barbara F. Walter, "The Extremist's Advantage in Civil Wars," *International Security* 42, no. 2 (2017): 7–39.

24. Renanah Miles Joyce and V. Page Fortna, "Extremism and Terrorism: Rebel Goals and Tactics in Civil Wars," *Perspectives on Politics*, forthcoming.

25. John M. Berger, *Extremism* (Cambridge, MA: MIT Press, 2018), 39.

26. Berger 2018, 39.

27. Miles Joyce and Fortna, forthcoming; William Stephens, Stijn Sieckelinck, and Hans Boutellier, "Preventing Violent Extremism: A Review of the Literature," *Studies in Conflict and Terrorism* 44, no. 4 (2021): 346–61; Minerva Nasser-Eddine, Bridget Garnham, Katerina Agostino, and Gilbert Caluya, *Countering Violent Extremism (CVE) Literature Review*, Defense Technical Information Center, March 1, 2011, https://apps.dtic.mil/sti/citations/ADA543686.

28. Alia Braley, Gabriel S. Lenz, Dhaval Adjodah, Hossein Rahnama, and Alex Pentland, "Why Voters Who Value Democracy Participate in Democratic Backsliding," *Nature Human Behaviour* 7 (May 22, 2023): 1282–93.

29. Ruth E. Appel, Jennifer Pan, and Margaret E. Roberts, "Partisan Conflict over Content Moderation Is More than Disagreement about Facts," *Science Advances* 9, no. 44 (November 3, 2023), https://doi.org/10.1126/sciadv.adg6799.

30. Ève Dubé, Jeremy K. Ward, Pierre Verger, and Noni E. MacDonald, "Vaccine Hesitancy, Acceptance, and Anti-Vaccination: Trends and Future Prospects for Public Health," *Annual Review of Public Health* 42, no. 1 (2021): 175–91; Lisa Hagen, "As the Pandemic Winds Down, Anti-Vaccine Activists Are Building a Legal Network," *Morning Edition*, NPR, May 4, 2023, https://www.npr.org/2023/05/04/1173697394/as-the-pandemic-winds-down-anti-vaccine-activists-are-building-a-legal-network.

31. Linda Qiu, "Trump Ads Attack Biden through Deceptive Editing and Hyperbole," *New York Times*, August 15, 2020, https://www.nytimes.com/2020/08/15/us/politics/trump -campaign-ads-biden.html; Asma Khalid and Tamara Keith, "Trump and Biden Wage an Uneven Virtual Campaign," NPR, May 21, 2020, https://www.npr.org/2020/05/21/859932268 /trump-and-biden-wage-an-uneven-virtual-campaign; Eric Zeng, Miranda Wei, Theo Gregersen, Tadayoshi Kohno, and Franziska Roesner, "Polls, Clickbait, and Commemorative $2 Bills: Problematic Political Advertising on News and Media Websites around the 2020 US Elections," *Proceedings of the 21st ACM Internet Measurement Conference*, 2021, 507–25.

32. Andrew Torba, "A Discussion with Business Insider about QAnon," *Gab News*, November 30, 2020, https://news.gab.com/2020/11/30/a-discussion-with-business-insider-about -qanon/.

33. Christopher St. Aubin and Jacob Liedke, "Most Americans Favor Restrictions on False Information, Violent Content Online," Pew Research Center, July 20, 2023, https://www .pewresearch.org/short-reads/2023/07/20/most-americans-favor-restrictions-on-false -information-violent-content-online/.

34. Ken Yeung, "Telegram Delivers 12B Messages a Day, CEO Pavel Durov Says WhatsApp Sucks," *VentureBeat*, September 21, 2015, https://venturebeat.com/social/telegram-delivers-12b -messages-a-day-ceo-pavel-durov-says-whatsapp-sucks/.

35. Yeung 2015.

36. Abdel Bari Atwan, *Islamic State: The Digital Caliphate* (Berkeley: University of California Press, 2019); Stephane J. Baele, Katharine A. Boyd, and Travis G. Coan, eds., *ISIS Propaganda: A Full-Spectrum Extremist Message* (Oxford: Oxford University Press, 2019); Richard A. Nielsen, *Deadly Clerics: Blocked Ambition and the Paths to Jihad* (Cambridge: Cambridge University Press, 2017); Daniel Byman, *Spreading Hate: The Global Rise of White Supremacist Terrorism* (Oxford: Oxford University Press, 2022); Cynthia Miller-Idriss, *Hate in the Homeland: The New Global Far Right* (Princeton, NJ: Princeton University Press, 2020); Mitts, Phillips, and Walter 2022; Brody McDonald, "Extremists Are Seeping Back into the Mainstream: Algorithmic Detection and Evasion Tactics on Social Media Platforms," Global Network on Extremism and Technology, October 31, 2022, https://gnet-research.org/2022/10/31/extremists-are-seeping-back -into-the-mainstream-algorithmic-detection-and-evasion-tactics-on-social-media-platforms; Tamar Mitts, "Countering Violent Extremism and Radical Rhetoric," *International Organization* 76, no. 1 (2022): 251–72.

37. Clifford 2020; Cody Buntain, Martin Innes, Tamar Mitts, and Jacob Shapiro, "Cross-Platform Reactions to the Post–January 6 Deplatforming," *Journal of Quantitative Description: Digital Media* 3 (2023).

38. Séraphin Alava, Divina Frau-Meigs, and Ghayda Hassan, *Youth and Violent Extremism on Social Media: Mapping the Research* (Paris: UNESCO Publishing, 2017); Mattias Ekman, "Anti-Refugee Mobilization in Social Media: The Case of Soldiers of Odin," *Social Media + Society* 4, no. 1 (2018): 2056305118764431; Jade Hutchinson, Amarnath Amarasingam, Ryan Scrivens, and Brian Ballsun-Stanton, "Mobilizing Extremism Online: Comparing Australian and Canadian Right-Wing Extremist Groups on Facebook," *Behavioral Sciences of Terrorism and Political Aggression* 15, no. 2 (2023): 215–45; Tamar Mitts, "From Isolation to Radicalization: Anti-Muslim Hostility and Support for ISIS in the West," *American Political Science Review* 113, no. 1 (2019): 173–94.

39. Margaret E. Roberts, *Censored: Distraction and Diversion inside China's Great Firewall* (Princeton, NJ: Princeton University Press, 2018); Margaret E. Roberts, "Resilience to Online Censorship," *Annual Review of Political Science* 23 (2020): 401–19; Jennifer Pan and Alexandra A. Siegel, "How Saudi Crackdowns Fail to Silence Online Dissent," *American Political Science Review* 114, no. 1 (2020): 109–25.

40. Baele, Boyd, and Coan 2019.

41. Miller-Idriss 2020.

42. Mitts 2019.

43. Nathaniel Persily and Joshua A. Tucker, *Social Media and Democracy: The State of the Field, Prospects for Reform* (Cambridge: Cambridge University Press, 2020); Thomas Zeitzoff, "How Social Media Is Changing Conflict," *Journal of Conflict Resolution* 61, no. 9 (2017): 1970–91; Gary King, Jennifer Pan, and Margaret E. Roberts, "How Censorship in China Allows Government Criticism but Silences Collective Expression," *American Political Science Review* 107, no. 2 (2013): 326–43; Joshua A. Tucker, Andrew Guess, Pablo Barberá, Cristian Vaccari, Alexandra Siegel, Sergey Sanovich, Denis Stukal, and Brendan Nyhan, "Social Media, Political Polarization, and Political Disinformation: A Review of the Scientific Literature," prepared for the Hewlett Foundation, March 2018, https://hewlett.org/wp-content/uploads /2018/03/Social-Media-Political-Polarization-and-Political-Disinformation-Literature -Review.pdf.

44. Tamar Mitts and Kylan Rutherford, "The PIC Framework: Understanding the New Information Environment," working paper, Columbia University, n.d.

45. Kiran Garimella and Dean Eckles, "Images and Misinformation in Political Groups: Evidence from WhatsApp in India," *Harvard Kennedy School Misinformation Review* 1, no. 5 (July 7, 2020), https://doi.org/10.37016/mr-2020-030; Simon Chauchard and Kiran Garimella, "What Circulates on Partisan WhatsApp in India? Insights from an Unusual Dataset," *Journal of Quantitative Description: Digital Media* 2 (2022).

46. Binny Mathew, Anurag Illendula, Punyajoy Saha, Soumya Sarkar, Pawan Goyal, and Animesh Mukherjee, "Hate Begets Hate: A Temporal Study of Hate Speech," *Proceedings of the ACM on Human-Computer Interaction* 4, no. CSCW2 (2020): 1–24; Andrea Sipka, Aniko Hannak, and Aleksandra Urman, "Comparing the Language of QAnon-Related Content on Parler, Gab, and Twitter," *Proceedings of the 14th ACM Web Science Conference 2022* (2022): 411–21.

47. Nika Aleksejeva, Lukas Andriukaitis, Luiza Bandeira, Donara Barojan, Graham Brookie, Eto Buziashvili, Andy Carvin, Kanishk Karan, Ben Nimmo, Iain Robertson, and Michael Sheldon, "Operation 'Secondary Infektion': A Suspected Russian Intelligence Operation Targeting Europe and the United States," Atlantic Council Digital Forensic Research Lab, August 2019, https://www.atlanticcouncil.org/wp-content/uploads/2019/08/Operation-Secondary-Infektion _English.pdf.

48. Rebecca Tan, "Terrorists' Love for Telegram, Explained," *Vox*, June 30, 2017, https://www .vox.com/world/2017/6/30/15886506/terrorism-isis-telegram-social-media-russia-pavel -durov-twitter.

49. Louise Matsakis, "Pittsburgh Synagogue Shooting Suspect's Gab Posts Are Part of a Pattern," *Wired*, October 27, 2018, https://www.wired.com/story/pittsburgh-synagogue -shooting-gab-tree-of-life/.

50. Holt 2022.

51. New Zealand Government, "NZ and France Seek to End Use of Social Media for Acts of Terrorism," April 24, 2019, https://www.beehive.govt.nz/release/nz-and-france-seek-end-use -social-media-acts-terrorism; White House, "Statement by Press Secretary Jen Psaki on the Occasion of the United States Joining the Christchurch Call to Action to Eliminate Terrorist and Violent Extremist Content Online," May 7, 2021, https://www.whitehouse.gov/briefing-room /statements-releases/2021/05/07/statement-by-press-secretary-jen-psaki-on-the-occasion-of -the-united-states-joining-the-christchurch-call-to-action-to-eliminate-terrorist-and-violent -extremist-content-online/.

52. Danielle Keats Citron, "Extremist Speech, Compelled Conformity, and Censorship Creep," *Notre Dame Law Review* 93 (2017): 1035.

53. Aleksejeva et al. 2019.

54. Esteban Ponce de León and Daniel Suárez Pérez, "Multi-Platform Troll Farm Linked to Nicaraguan Government," Atlantic Council Digital Forensic Research Lab, November 5, 2021, https://medium.com/dfrlab/multi-platform-troll-farm-linked-to-nicaraguan-government -be79121d55b4.

55. Citron 2017; Evelyn Douek, "The Rise of Content Cartels," Columbia University, Knight First Amendment Institute, February 11, 2020, https://knightcolumbia.org/content/the-rise-of -content-cartels.

2: A Theory of Digital Resilience

1. Tarleton Gillespie, *Custodians of the Internet* (New Haven, CT: Yale University Press, 2018), 5.

2. To be sure, the policies that platforms make known to the public do not reflect all of a platform's (internal) policies that govern content moderation. Here I focus on the public version of the policies, as that is what matters most for understanding extremist groups' behavior. As I show in later chapters, militant and hate organizations draw on this sort of public information that technology companies publicize on their websites to build resilience to content moderation.

3. Jack Snyder, *Human Rights for Pragmatists: Social Power in Modern Times* (Princeton, NJ: Princeton University Press, 2022).

4. Loránd Bodó, "Decentralised Terrorism: The Next Big Step for the So-Called Islamic State (IS)?" *Voxpol*, December 12, 2018, https://www.voxpol.eu/decentralised-terrorism-the-next-big -step-for-the-so-called-islamic-state-is/; Adam Hadley, "Terrorists Are Hiding Where They Can't Be Moderated," *Wired*, May 31, 2021, https://www.wired.co.uk/article/terrorists-dweb.

5. Kate Klonick, "The New Governors: The People, Rules, and Processes Governing Online Speech," *Harvard Law Review* 131 (2017): 1598.

6. It is important to note that maximizing authenticity does not mean posting the most extreme content all the time. As my earlier work on Islamic State propaganda videos shows, extremist organizations post a diverse range of content, ranging from relatively "mild" messages to the most violent content. See Tamar Mitts, Gregoire Phillips, and Barbara F. Walter, "Studying the Impact of ISIS Propaganda Campaigns," *Journal of Politics* 84, no. 2 (2022): 1220–25. The idea behind posting the "most authentic" content—which can be extreme, or less extreme—is that it allows a group to test the boundaries of allowable content on a moderating platform.

7. Chris Sonderby, "Update on New Zealand," Meta, March 18, 2019, https://about.fb.com /news/2019/03/update-on-new-zealand/; Graham Macklin, "The Christchurch Attacks: Livestream Terror in the Viral Video Age," *CTC Sentinel* 12, no. 6 (2019): 18–29.

8. Matthew Newman, "Internet Platforms May Get Caught in Patchwork of Global Terror-Content Rules," *LexisNexis*, April 25, 2019, https://mlexmarketinsight.com/news-hub/editors -picks/area-of-expertise/data-privacy-and-security/internet-platforms-may-get-caught-in -patchwork-of-global-terror-content-rules.

9. Christchurch Call to Eliminate Terrorist and Violent Extremist Content Online, "Christchurch Call Text," https://www.christchurchcall.com/about/christchurch-call-text.

10. For documents leaked by whistleblower Frances Haugen, see https://drive.google.com /file/d/1mYY_1ark6wyNmwmAXp5MMynus0h4fcWj/view.

11. Germany Bundestag, "Act to Improve Enforcement of the Law in Social Networks (Network Enforcement Act)," July 12, 2017, https://perma.cc/7UCW-AA3A.

12. United Kingdom, "Online Safety Act 2023," legislation.gov.uk, October 26, 2023, https:// www.legislation.gov.uk/ukpga/2023/50/contents/enacted.

13. Tech Against Terrorism, "The Online Regulation Series: The Handbook," July 16, 2021, https://www.techagainstterrorism.org/2021/07/16/the-online-regulation-series-the-handbook/.

14. See Tech Against Terrorism's discussion of "beacon channels," which allow groups to signal where their content can be found on other parts of the web. Tech Against Terrorism, "Terrorist Content Analytics Platform: Year 1: 1 December 2020–30 November 2021," March 2022, https://www.techagainstterrorism.org/wp-content/uploads/2022/03/Tech-Against -Terrorism-TCAP-Report-March-2022_v6.pdf.

15. Bennett Clifford, "Migration Moments: Extremist Adoption of Text-Based Instant Messaging Applications," Global Network on Extremism and Technology, November 2020, https:// gnet-research.org/wp-content/uploads/2020/11/GNET-Report-Migration-Moments -Extremist-Adoption-of-Text%E2%80%91Based-Instant-Messaging-Applications_V2.pdf.

16. Cody Buntain, Martin Innes, Tamar Mitts, and Jacob Shapiro, "Cross-Platform Reactions to the Post–January 6 Deplatforming," *Journal of Quantitative Description: Digital Media* 3 (2023); Jared Holt, "After the Insurrection: How Domestic Extremists Adapted and Evolved after the January 6 US Capitol Attack," Atlantic Council Digital Forensic Research Lab, January 2022, https://www.atlanticcouncil.org/in-depth-research-reports/report/after-the -insurrection-how-domestic-extremists-adapted-and-evolved-after-the-january-6-us-capitol -attack/; Jared Holt and Max Rizzuto, "QAnon's Hallmark Catchphrases Evaporating from the Mainstream Internet," Atlantic Council Digital Forensic Research Lab, May 26, 2021, https:// medium.com/dfrlab/qanons-hallmark-catchphrases-evaporating-from-the-mainstream -internet-ce90b6dc2c55.

17. Lella Nouri, Nuria Lorenzo-Dus, and Amy-Louise Watkin, "Following the Whack-a-Mole: Britain First's Visual Strategy from Facebook to Gab," Global Network on Extremism and Technology, January 7, 2020, https://gnet-research.org/2020/01/07/following-the-whack-a -mole-britain-firsts-visual-strategy-from-facebook-to-gab/.

18. Bennett Clifford and Helen Christy Powell, "De-platforming and the Online Extremist's Dilemma," *Lawfare*, June 6, 2019, https://www.lawfaremedia.org/article/de-platforming-and -online-extremists-dilemma; Jacob N. Shapiro, *The Terrorist's Dilemma* (Princeton, NJ: Princeton University Press, 2013).

19. Loretta E. Bass, "What Motivates European Youth to Join ISIS?" *Syria Comment*, November 20, 2014, https://bit.ly/2AsjhFH; Sarah Lyons-Padilla, Michele J. Gelfand, Hedieh Mirahmadi, Mehreen Farooq, and Marieke Van Egmond, "Belonging Nowhere: Marginalization and Radicalization Risk among Muslim Immigrants," *Behavioral Science and Policy* 1, no. 2 (2015): 1–12; Tamar Mitts, "From Isolation to Radicalization: Anti-Muslim Hostility and Support for ISIS in the West," *American Political Science Review* 113, no. 1 (2019): 173–94.

20. Far-right recruits to the Azov movement, for example, radicalized on alternative platforms after being banned from mainstream platforms. See Simon Shuster and Billy Perrigo, "Like, Share, Recruit: How a White-Supremacist Militia Uses Facebook to Radicalize and Train New Members," *Time*, January 7, 2021, https://time.com/5926750/azov-far-right-movement-facebook/.

21. Clifford 2020.

22. Holt 2022; see also chapter 6.

23. Aaron Smith, "Public Attitudes toward Technology Companies," Pew Research Center, June 28, 2018, https://www.pewresearch.org/internet/2018/06/28/public-attitudes-toward-technology-companies/.

24. Ted Robert Gurr, *Why Men Rebel* (New York: Routledge, 2015); Richard A. Nielsen, *Deadly Clerics: Blocked Ambition and the Paths to Jihad* (Cambridge: Cambridge University Press, 2017).

25. Margaret E. Roberts, *Censored: Distraction and Diversion inside China's Great Firewall* (Princeton, NJ: Princeton University Press, 2018).

26. It should be noted that in the social media landscape, where content is generated by users, there is no strict "control" over what is being posted on behalf of a group. Extremist organizations often have members who manage their social media presence, but they also have unaffiliated supporters who push out their content. Thus, any strategy that a group is pursuing on social media will be subject to the decisions of individual supporters and members to post whatever they want. Since extremist groups seek the attention they receive from amplification by these individuals, they are willing to risk being subject to content moderation when messages posted by their sympathizers sometimes cross the moderation bar.

27. Mitts, Phillips, and Walter 2022.

28. Tamar Mitts, "Countering Violent Extremism and Radical Rhetoric," *International Organization* 76, no. 1 (2022): 251–72.

29. SITE Intelligence Group, "A SITE Study on the ICT Platforms Used to Spread ISIS and AQ Media," *Technology and Terrorism*, October 1, 2018, https://ent.siteintelgroup.com/inSITE-Report-on-Technology-and-Terrorism/insite-report-on-technology-and-terrorism-october-2018.html.

30. Global Internet Forum to Counter Terrorism, "Transparency Report," July 2021, https://gifct.org/wp-content/uploads/2021/07/GIFCT-TransparencyReport2021.pdf.

31. Tech Against Terrorism, March 2022.

32. Margaret E. Roberts, "Resilience to Online Censorship," *Annual Review of Political Science* 23 (2020): 401–19.

33. See chapter 6; see also Charlie Winter and Abdullah Alrhmoun, "Mapping the Extremist Narrative Landscape in Afghanistan," *Extrac*, November 2020, https://public-assets.extrac.io/reports/ExTrac_Afghanistan_1120.pdf.

34. Holt 2022; Holt and Rizzuto 2021.

35. Tech Against Terrorism, "Tracking Violent Far-Right Behavior Online," March 15, 2022, https://tech-against-terrorism-podcast.podcastpage.io/episode/tracking-violent-far-right -behaviour-online.

36. Clifford and Powell 2019.

37. Katie Tarasov, "Why Content Moderation Costs Billions and Is So Tricky for Facebook, Twitter, YouTube and Others," *CNBC*, February 27, 2021, https://www.cnbc.com/2021/02/27 /content-moderation-on-social-media.html; Rafael Jiménez-Durán, "The Economics of Content Moderation: Theory and Experimental Evidence from Hate Speech on Twitter," Working Paper 324, George J. Stigler Center for the Study of the Economy & the State (2023).

38. Dave Gershgorn and Mike Murphy, "Facebook Is Hiring More People to Moderate Content than Twitter Has at Its Entire Company," *Quartz*, October 12, 2017, https://qz.com/1101455 /facebook-fb-is-hiring-more-people-to-moderate-content-than-twitter-twtr-has-at-its-entire -company; Sam Levin, "Google to Hire Thousands of Moderators after Outcry over YouTube Abuse Videos," *Guardian*, December 5, 2017, https://www.theguardian.com/technology/2017 /dec/04/google-youtube-hire-moderators-child-abuse-videos.

3: Regulating Social Media Platforms

1. Joshua A. Tucker, Yannis Theocharis, Margaret E. Roberts, and Pablo Barberá, "From Liberation to Turmoil: Social Media and Democracy," *Journal of Democracy* 28, no. 4 (2017): 46–59.

2. Mary Anne Franks, "Beyond the Public Square: Imagining Digital Democracy," *Yale Law Journal* 131 (2021): 427.

3. US Senate Committee on Interstate Commerce, "Study of Communications by an Interdepartmental Committee: Letter from the President of the United States to the Chairman of the Committee on Interstate Commerce"(Washington: US Government Printing Office, 1934), https://docs.fcc.gov/public/attachments/DOC-328553A1.pdf.

4. US Government, "Communications Act of 1934," https://transition.fcc.gov/Reports /1934new.pdf.

5. Federal Communications Commission, "Appendix before the Federal Communications Commission in the Matter of Editorializing by Broadcast Licensees: Report of the Commission," June 8, 1949, https://docs.fcc.gov/public/attachments/DOC-295673A1.pdf.

6. Fred W. Friendly, *The Good Guys, the Bad Guys, and the First Amendment: Free Speech vs. Fairness in Broadcasting* (New York: Random House, 2013); Penny Pagano, "Reagan's Veto Kills Fairness Doctrine Bill," *Los Angeles Times*, June 21, 1987, https://www.latimes.com/archives/la -xpm-1987-06-21-mn-8908-story.html.

7. For example, in the Supreme Court ruling in FCC v. League of Women Voters, Justice William Brennan stated that expanding communication technologies made the fairness doctrine unnecessary: "Technological developments have advanced so far that some revision of the system of broadcast regulation may be required." US Supreme Court, "FCC v. League of Women Voters, 468 U.S. 364 (1984)," Justia Law, https://supreme.justia.com/cases/federal/us/468/364/#T11.

8. Federal Communications Commission, UNT Digital Library, "FCC Record," vol. 2, no. 17, pp. 5002–5398, August 17–28, 1987, https://digital.library.unt.edu/ark:/67531/metadc1594/.

9. Robert D. Hershey, "FCC Votes Down Fairness Doctrine in a 4–0 Decision," *New York Times*, August 5, 1987, https://web.archive.org/web/20120316054128/http://www.nytimes.com/1987/08/05/arts/fcc-votes-down-fairness-doctrine-in-a-4-0-decision.html.

10. Jeff Kosseff, *The Twenty-Six Words That Created the Internet* (Ithaca, NY: Cornell University Press, 2019).

11. *Congressional Record*, "Personal Explanation," *Congressional Record*, vol. 141, no. 129, August 4, 1995, H-8471, https://www.congress.gov/congressional-record/volume-141/issue-129/house-section/article/H8460-1.

12. *Congressional Record* 1995, H-8470.

13. *Congressional Record* 1995, H-8469.

14. *Congressional Record* 1995, H-8470.

15. Hannah Ritchie, Edouard Mathieu, Max Roser, and Esteban Ortiz-Ospina, "Internet," Our World in Data, 2023, https://ourworldindata.org/internet.

16. Ani Petrosyan, "Number of Internet and Social Media Users Worldwide as of January 2024 (in Billions)," Statista, January 31, 2024, https://www.statista.com/statistics/617136/digital-population-worldwide.

17. Karen Yourish, Derek Watkins, and Tom Giratikanon, "Where ISIS Has Directed and Inspired Attacks around the World," *New York Times*, March 2, 2016, https://www.nytimes.com/interactive/2015/06/17/world/middleeast/map-isis-attacks-around-the-world.html.

18. Ellen Nakashima, "Obama's Top National Security Officials to Meet with Silicon Valley CEOs," *Washington Post*, January 7, 2016, https://www.washingtonpost.com/world/national-security/obamas-top-national-security-officials-to-meet-with-silicon-valley-ceos/2016/01/07/178d95ca-b586-11e5-a842-0feb51d1d124_story.html.

19. David Lauer, "Facebook's Ethical Failures Are Not Accidental; They Are Part of the Business Model," *AI and Ethics* 1, no. 4 (2021): 395–403; Brandy Zadrozny, "'Carol's Journey': What Facebook Knew about How It Radicalized Users," *NBC News*, October 22, 2021, https://www.nbcnews.com/tech/tech-news/facebook-knew-radicalized-users-rcna3581.

20. Brian Fishman, "Dual-Use Regulation: Managing Hate and Terrorism Online before and after Section 230 Reform," Brookings, March 14, 2023, https://www.brookings.edu/articles/dual-use-regulation-managing-hate-and-terrorism-online-before-and-after-section-230-reform.

21. Fishman 2023.

22. Monica Bickert and Brian Fishman, "Hard Questions: How We Counter Terrorism," Meta, June 15, 2017, https://about.fb.com/news/2017/06/how-we-counter-terrorism/.

23. Meta Transparency Center, "Community Standards Enforcement Report," 2023, https://transparency.meta.com/reports/community-standards-enforcement/.

24. X (Twitter) Transparency, "Rules Enforcement," December 2021, https://transparency.twitter.com/en/reports/rules-enforcement.html.

25. Google, "Transparency Report: YouTube Community Guidelines Enforcement," September 2023, https://transparencyreport.google.com/youtube-policy/removals?hl=en.

26. YouTube Team, "Our Ongoing Work to Tackle Hate," YouTube Official Blog, June 5, 2019, https://blog.youtube/news-and-events/our-ongoing-work-to-tackle-hate/.

27. X (Twitter) Safety, "Updating Our Rules against Hateful Conduct," X (Twitter) Blog, July 9, 2019, https://blog.twitter.com/en_us/topics/company/2019/hatefulconductupdate.

28. Fishman 2023.

29. Georgia Wells, Ian Talley, and Jeff Horwitz, "'Trump or War': How the Capitol Mob Mobilized on Social Media," *Wall Street Journal*, January 7, 2021, https://www.wsj.com/articles/trump-or-war-how-the-capitol-mob-mobilized-on-social-media-11610069778; Cat Zakrzewski, Cristiano Lima, and Drew Harwell, "What the Jan. 6 Probe Found Out about Social Media, but Didn't Report," *Washington Post*, January 17, 2023, https://www.washingtonpost.com/technology/2023/01/17/jan6-committee-report-social-media/.

30. Sara Morrison, "How the Capitol Riot Revived Calls to Reform Section 230," *Vox*, January 11, 2021, https://www.vox.com/recode/22221135/capitol-riot-section-230-twitter-hawley-democrats.

31. Derek E. Bambauer, "What Does the Day after Section 230 Reform Look Like?" Brookings, January 22, 2021, https://www.brookings.edu/articles/what-does-the-day-after-section-230-reform-look-like/.

32. Anna M. Kaplan, "Kaplan Bill Combating Hate on Social Media Signed into Law with Landmark Legislative Package to Prevent Gun Violence," New York State Senate, June 6, 2022, https://www.nysenate.gov/newsroom/press-releases/2022/anna-m-kaplan/kaplan-bill-combating-hate-social-media-signed-law.

33. Rebecca Kern, "Push to Rein in Social Media Sweeps the States," *Politico*, July 1, 2022, https://www.politico.com/news/2022/07/01/social-media-sweeps-the-states-00043229.

34. *Congressional Record*, "H.R.5596: Justice against Malicious Algorithms Act of 2021," October 18, 2021, https://www.congress.gov/bill/117th-congress/house-bill/5596; (Office of) Mark R. Warner, "Warner, Hirono, Klobuchar Announce the SAFE TECH Act to Reform Section 230," February 5, 2021, https://www.warner.senate.gov/public/index.cfm/2021/2/warner-hirono-klobuchar-announce-the-safe-tech-act-to-reform-section-230; (Office of) Brian Schatz, "Schatz, Thune Reintroduce Legislation to Strengthen Rules, Transparency for Online Content Moderation, Hold Internet Companies Accountable," February 16, 2023, https://www.schatz.senate.gov/news/press-releases/schatz-thune-reintroduce-legislation-to-strengthen-rules-transparency-for-online-content-moderation-hold-internet-companies-accountable.

35. Joe Biden, "Republicans and Democrats, Unite against Big Tech Abuses," *Wall Street Journal*, January 11, 2023, https://www.wsj.com/articles/unite-against-big-tech-abuses-social-media-privacy-competition-antitrust-children-algorithm-11673439411?mod=opinion_lead_pos5.

36. Administration of Donald J. Trump, "Executive Order 13925—Preventing Online Censorship," May 28, 2020, https://www.govinfo.gov/content/pkg/DCPD-202000404/pdf/DCPD-202000404.pdf; Anshu Siripurapu, "Trump and Section 230: What to Know," Council on Foreign Relations, December 2, 2020, https://www.cfr.org/in-brief/trump-and-section-230-what-know.

37. Ted Cruz, "Sen. Cruz: Big Tech Poses the Single Greatest Threat to Our Free Speech and Democracy," October 1, 2020, https://www.cruz.senate.gov/newsroom/press-releases/sen-cruz-big-tech-poses-the-single-greatest-threat-to-our-free-speech-and-democracy.

38. *Congressional Record*, "H.R.874: Abandoning Online Censorship Act," February 8, 2021, https://www.congress.gov/bill/117th-congress/house-bill/874/text; *Congressional Record*, "H.R.3827: Protect Speech Act," June 14, 2021, https://www.congress.gov/bill/117th-congress/house-bill/3827/text.

39. Daphne Keller, "Lawful but Awful? Control over Legal Speech by Platforms, Governments, and Internet Users," *University of Chicago Law Review Online*, June 28, 2022, https://lawreviewblog.uchicago.edu/2022/06/28/keller-control-over-speech/.

40. John Villasenor, "Social Media Companies and Common Carrier Status: A Primer," Brookings, October 27, 2022, https://www.brookings.edu/articles/social-media-companies-and-common-carrier-status-a-primer/.

41. Fishman 2023.

42. "Tech Firms Must Do More on Extremism: World Economic Forum," *Reuters*, October 30, 2017, https://www.reuters.com/article/idUSKBN1CZ0B5/.

43. *Congressional Record*, "Disinformation Nation: Social Media's Role in Promoting Extremism and Misinformation," March 25, 2021, https://www.congress.gov/event/117th-congress/house-event/111407; US Senate Select Committee on Intelligence, "Hearing on Social Media Influence in the 2016 United States Elections," 115th Cong., 1st sess., November 1, 2017, https://www.govinfo.gov/content/pkg/CHRG-115shrg27398/pdf/CHRG-115shrg27398.pdf.

44. The Texas law applied to sites with more than 50 million monthly active users in the United States, and the Florida law applied to platforms with at least 100 million monthly active users globally. See Cain et al., "Texas House Bill 20 (H.B.20)," August 30, 2021, https://capitol.texas.gov/tlodocs/872/billtext/html/HB00020S.htm; Florida Senate, "Bill 7072 (S.B.7072)," July 1, 2021, https://www.myfloridahouse.gov/Sections/Documents/loaddoc.aspx?FileName=_s7072er.DOCX&DocumentType=Bill&BillNumber=7072&Session=2021.

45. Anu Bradford, *The Brussels Effect: How the European Union Rules the World* (Oxford: Oxford University Press, 2020), 159.

46. European Court of Human Rights. "Chamber Judgment: Erbakan v. Turkey," July 6, 2006, https://hudoc.echr.coe.int/eng#{%22itemid%22:[%22003-1728198-1812055%22]}.

47. Jenny Gesley, "Germany: Network Enforcement Act Amended to Better Fight Online Hate Speech," Library of Congress, Global Legal Monitor, July 6, 2021, https://www.loc.gov/item/global-legal-monitor/2021-07-06/germany-network-enforcement-act-amended-to-better-fight-online-hate-speech/.

48. Robert Gorwa, *The Politics of Platform Regulation* (Oxford: Oxford University Press, 2024).

49. Janosch Delcker, "Germany's Balancing Act: Fighting Online Hate While Protecting Free Speech," *Politico*, October 1, 2020, https://www.politico.eu/article/germany-hate-speech-internet-netzdg-controversial-legislation/.

50. Katrin Bennhold, "Germany Acts to Tame Facebook, Learning from Its Own History of Hate," *The New York Times*, May 19, 2018, https://www.nytimes.com/2018/05/19/technology/facebook-deletion-center-germany.html.

51. Lucas G. Drouhot, Karen Schönwälder, Sören Petermann, and Steve Vertovec, "Who Supports Refugees? Diversity Assent and Pro-Refugee Engagement in Germany," *Comparative Migration Studies* 11, no. 1 (2023): 4.

52. Patrick Zurth, "The German NetzDG as Role Model or Cautionary Tale? Implications for the Debate on Social Media Liability," *Fordham Intellectual Property, Media, and Entertainment Law Journal* 31, no. 4 (2021): 1101, https://ir.lawnet.fordham.edu/cgi/viewcontent.cgi?article=1782&context=iplj.

53. Karsten Müller and Carlo Schwarz, "Fanning the Flames of Hate: Social Media and Hate Crime," *Journal of the European Economic Association* 19, no. 4 (2021): 2131–67; Katrin Bennhold, "Chemnitz Protests Show New Strength of Germany's Far Right," *New York Times*, August 30, 2018, https://www.nytimes.com/2018/08/30/world/europe/germany-neo-nazi-protests-chemnitz.html.

54. Müller and Schwarz 2021.

55. "German Justice Minister Takes Aim at Facebook over Racist Posts," *Reuters*, August 27, 2015, https://www.reuters.com/article/us-facebook-germany-racism-idUSKCN0QW1SG 20150827.

56. *Reuters*, "German Justice Minister Takes Aim," 2015.

57. Simone Rafael, "Task Force against Hateful Content on the Internet: It's a Lot to Do" (translated from German), *Bell Tower News*, December 15, 2015, https://www.belltower.news /task-force-gegen-hassinhalte-im-internet-es-gibt-noch-viel-zu-tun-41028/.

58. Rafael 2015.

59. Federal Ministry of Justice and Consumer Protection, "The Initiative against Hate Crime on the Internet" (translated from German), September 2017, https://web-archive-org .translate.goog/web/20170930061101/http://www.fair-im-netz.de/WebS/NHS/DE/Home /home_node.html?_x_tr_sl=auto&_x_tr_tl=en&_x_tr_hl=en&_x_tr_pto=wapp.

60. Federal Ministry of Justice and Consumer Protection, "Together against Hate Messages: Ways to Tackle Hate Content Online Proposed by the Task Force on Dealing with Illegal Hateful Messages Online" (translated from German), December 15, 2015, https://www.fair-im-netz .de/SharedDocs/Downloads/DE/News/Artikel/12152015_TaskForceErgebnispapier.pdf?_ _blob=publicationFile&v=2.

61. Federal Ministry of Family Affairs, Senior Citizens, Women, and Youth, "Deletion of Punishable Hate Comments on the Internet Is Not Yet Sufficient" (translated from German), September 26, 2016, https://www.bmfsfj.de/bmfsfj/aktuelles/presse/pressemitteilungen /loeschung-von-strafbaren-hasskommentaren-im-netz-noch-nicht-ausreichend-111512.

62. Federal Ministry of Family Affairs, Senior Citizens, Women, and Youth 2016.

63. William Echikson and Olivia Knodt, "Germany's NetzDG: A Key Test for Combatting Online Hate," CEPS Policy Insight, Centre for European Policy Studies, November 2018, http://wp.ceps.eu/wp-content/uploads/2018/11/RR%20No2018-09_Germany's%20 NetzDG.pdf.

64. Article 19, "Germany: The Act to Improve Enforcement of the Law in Social Networks," August 2017, https://www.article19.org/wp-content/uploads/2017/09/170901-Legal-Analysis -German-NetzDG-Act.pdf.

65. Article 19, 2017.

66. Gesley 2021.

67. Gesley 2021.

68. The full list of offenses can be found in the German Criminal Code, https://www.gesetze -im-internet.de/englisch_stgb/englisch_stgb.html.

69. Amélie Pia Heldt, "Reading between the Lines and the Numbers: An Analysis of the First NetzDG Reports," *Internet Policy Review* 8, no. 2 (2019).

70. Human Rights Watch, "Germany: Flawed Social Media Law," February 14, 2018, https:// www.hrw.org/news/2018/02/14/germany-flawed-social-media-law.

71. Gesley 2021.

72. Oliver Noyan, "Germany's Online Hate Speech Law Slammed by Opposition, Commission," *Euractiv*, May 10, 2021, https://www.euractiv.com/section/internet-governance/news /germanys-online-hate-speech-law-slammed-by-opposition-commission/.

73. Melissa Eddy and Mark Scott, "Delete Hate Speech or Pay Up, Germany Tells Social Media Companies," *New York Times*, June 30, 2017, https://www.nytimes.com/2017/06/30 /business/germany-facebook-google-twitter.html.

74. Eddy and Scott 2017.

75. Susan Wojcicki, "Expanding Our Work against Abuse of our Platform," YouTube Official Blog, December 5, 2017, https://blog.youtube/news-and-events/expanding-our-work-against -abuse-of-our/.

76. Max Hoppenstedt, "A Visit to Facebook's Recently Opened Center for Deleting Content," *Vice*, January 2, 2018, https://www.vice.com/en/article/qv37dv/facebook-content -moderation-center.

77. Twitter, "Twitter Network Enforcement Law Report: January–June 2018" (translated from German), https://cdn.cms-twdigitalassets.com/content/dam/transparency-twitter/data /download-netzdg-report/netzdg-jan-jun-2018.pdf; Twitter, "Twitter Network Enforcement Law Report: January–June 2021," https://transparency.twitter.com/content/dam/transparency -twitter/country-reports/germany/netzdg-jan-jun-2021.pdf.

78. Epicenter Works, "First Analysis of the Austrian Anti-Hate Speech Law (NetDG/ KoPlG)," EDRi, September 10, 2020, https://edri.org/our-work/first-analysis-of-the-austrian -anti-hate-speech-law-netdg-koplg/.

79. Angelique Chrisafis, "French Online Hate Speech Bill Aims to Wipe Out Racist Trolling," *Guardian*, June 29, 2019, https://www.theguardian.com/world/2019/jun/29/french -online-hate-speech-bill-aims-to-wipe-out-racist-trolling.

80. James Vincent, "Google, Meta, and Others Will Have to Explain Their Algorithms under New EU Legislation," *The Verge*, April 23, 2022, https://www.theverge.com/2022/4/23 /23036976/eu-digital-services-act-finalized-algorithms-targeted-advertising.

81. Freedom House, "Freedom on the Net Report 2016: France," https://freedomhouse.org /country/france/freedom-net/2016#footnote27_ctxxokh.

82. Jane Kilpatrick, "When a Temporary State of Emergency Becomes Permanent," Transnational Institute, November 5, 2020, https://www.tni.org/en/stateofemergency; Reference for Paris terrorist attacks: "November 2015 Attacks: A Timeline of the Night That Shook the French Capital," *France 24*, September 8, 2021, https://www.france24.com/en/france/20210908-paris -november-2015-attacks-a-timeline-of-the-night-that-shook-the-city; Daniel Severson, "France's Extended State of Emergency: What New Powers Did the Government Get?" *Lawfare*, November 22, 2015, https://www.lawfareblog.com/frances-extended-state-emergency-what -new-powers-did-government-get.

83. National Assembly, "Draft Law Aimed at Combating Hate Content on the Internet" (aka "Avia Law"), https://ecnl.org/sites/default/files/files/Text-of-Avia-Bill-EN.pdf; Jacob Schulz, "What's Going On with France's Online Hate Speech Law?" *Lawfare*, June 23, 2020, https://www .lawfareblog.com/whats-going-frances-online-hate-speech-law; for Section 222-33 of the French Penal Code, see https://www.legifrance.gouv.fr/codes/article_lc/LEGIARTI000037289662/.

84. Schulz 2020.

85. Schulz 2020.

86. "Saisine CC—PPL Avia lutte contre les contenus haineux sur internet" submission to the Constitutional Council), https://cdn2.nextinpact.com/medias/saisine-lr-18-mai-2020.pdf.

87. Constitutional Council of France, "Decision No. 2020-801 DC of June 18, 2020" (press release translated from French), https://www.conseil-constitutionnel.fr/decision/2020 /2020801DC.htm.

88. Nicolas Boring, "France: Constitutional Court Strikes Down Key Provisions of Bill on Hate Speech," Library of Congress, June 29, 2020, https://www.loc.gov/item/global-legal-monitor/2020-06-29/france-constitutional-court-strikes-down-key-provisions-of-bill-on-hate-speech/. For example, the Commission nationale consultative des droits de l'homme (CNCDH) (National Consultative Commission on Human Rights), an independent administrative authority, issued an advisory opinion opposing the bill, explaining that the threat of very high fines, combined with a short window in which to evaluate the illegal nature of flagged content, would cause online platform providers to err toward over-censorship. The CNCDH also objected to the idea that algorithms and moderators with little training would judge the legality of content instead of the judiciary. Additionally, the CNCDH believed that the Avia Law would reinforce the dominance of large platform providers, as smaller providers might not have the means to apply the law. See Commission nationale consultative des droits de l'homme (CNCDH), "Avis relatif à la proposition de loi visant à lutter contre la haine sur internet," CNCDH, July 9, 2019, https://perma.cc/HR2L-GH9Q.

89. Emma Beswick, "Demonstrations Throughout France in Tribute to Beheaded Teacher," *Euronews*, October 19, 2020, https://www.euronews.com/2020/10/16/man-decapitated-near-paris-police-confirm-to-euronews.

90. *Euronews*, "Samuel Paty: French Teacher's Beheading Directly Linked to Social Media Campaign, Say Prosecutors," October 21, 2020, https://www.euronews.com/my-europe/2020/10/21/samuel-paty-french-teacher-s-beheading-directly-linked-to-social-media-campaign-say-prosec.

91. The Cube, "'We Need to Go a Step Further': French MP Laetitia Avia Says More Action Is Needed on Online Hate," *Euronews*, October 24, 2020, https://www.euronews.com/my-europe/2020/10/23/we-need-to-go-a-step-further-french-mp-laetitia-avia-says-more-action-is-needed-on-online-.

92. The Cube 2020.

93. The Cube 2020.

94. European Commission, "European Commission and IT Companies Announce Code of Conduct on Illegal Online Hate Speech" (press release), May 31, 2016, https://ec.europa.eu/commission/presscorner/detail/en/IP_16_1937.

95. Jillian C. York, "European Commission's Hate Speech Deal with Companies Will Chill Speech," Electric Frontier Foundation, June 3, 2016, https://www.eff.org/deeplinks/2016/06/european-commissions-hate-speech-deal-companies-will-chill-speech.

96. European Parliament, Legislative Train Schedule, "Preventing the Dissemination of Terrorist Content Online," April 20, 2022, https://www.europarl.europa.eu/legislative-train/theme-area-of-justice-and-fundamental-rights/file-preventing-the-dissemination-of-terrorist-content-online.

97. Jillian C. York and Christoph Schmon, "The EU Online Terrorism Regulation: A Bad Deal," Electric Frontier Foundation, April 7, 2021, https://www.eff.org/deeplinks/2021/04/eu-online-terrorism-regulation-bad-deal; EDRi, "Open Letter: Civil Society Urges Member States to Respect the Principles of Law in Terrorist Content Online Regulation," March 27, 2020, https://edri.org/our-work/open-letter-civil-society-urges-member-states-to-respect-the-principles-of-the-law-in-terrorist-content-online-regulation/.

98. European Union, "Directive (EU) 2017/541 of the European Parliament and of the Council of 15 March 2017 on Combating Terrorism and Replacing Council Framework Decision 2002/475/JHA and Amending Council Decision 2005/671/JHA," *Official Journal of the European Union*, March 31, 2017, https://eur-lex.europa.eu/legal-content/EN/ALL/?uri =CELEX%3A32017L0541; European Union, "Regulation (EU) 2021/784 of the European Parliament and of the Council of 29 April 2021 on Addressing the Dissemination of Terrorist Content Online," *Official Journal of the European Union*, May 17, 2021, https://eur-lex.europa.eu /legal-content/EN/TXT/PDF/?uri=CELEX:32021R0784.

99. European Union, "Regulation (EU) 2021/784," 2021.

100. Macklin 2019.

101. *Eureporter*, "Security Union: EU Rules on Removing Terrorist Content Online Enter into Force," *Eureporter*, June 8, 2021, https://www.eureporter.co/world/terrorism-world/2021 /06/08/security-union-eu-rules-on-removing-terrorist-content-online-enter-into-force/.

102. European Commission, "Shaping Europe's Digital Future: The Digital Services Act Package," updated February 16, 2024, https://digital-strategy.ec.europa.eu/en/policies/digital -services-act-package.

103. European Commission, "Digital Services Act: Commission Welcomes Political Agreement on Rules Ensuring a Safe and Accountable Online Environment" (press release), April 23, 2022, https://ec.europa.eu/commission/presscorner/detail/en/IP_22_2545.

104. European Commission, "Digital Services Act: Commission Designates First Set of Very Large Online Platforms and Search Engines" (press release), April 25, 2023, https://ec.europa .eu/commission/presscorner/detail/en/IP_23_2413.

105. European Commission, April 23, 2022.

106. The full list, including online platforms that are not primarily used for social networking, comprises Alibaba AliExpress, Amazon Store, Apple AppStore, Booking.com, Facebook, Google Play, Google Maps, Google Shopping, Instagram, LinkedIn, Pinterest, Snapchat, TikTok, Twitter, Wikipedia, YouTube, and Zalando. European Commission, April 25, 2023.

107. European Parliament, January 19, 2022.

108. European Commission, "Questions and Answers: Digital Services Act," February 23, 2024, https://ec.europa.eu/commission/presscorner/detail/en/QANDA_20_2348.

109. Freedom House, "Freedom on the Net 2023," https://freedomhouse.org/sites/default /files/2023-10/Freedom-on-the-net-2023-DigitalBooklet.pdf; Human Rights Watch, *World Report 2018*, https://www.hrw.org/world-report/2018; Human Rights Watch, *World Report 2019*, https://www.hrw.org/world-report/2019; Human Rights Watch, *World Report 2020*, https://www.hrw.org/world-report/2020; Human Rights Watch, *World Report 2021*, https:// www.hrw.org/world-report/2021; Human Rights Watch, *World Report 2022*, https://www.hrw .org/world-report/2022; Human Rights Watch, *World Report 2023*, https://www.hrw.org/world -report/2023; Tech Against Terrorism, "The Online Regulation Series: The Handbook," July 16, 2021, https://www.techagainstterrorism.org/2021/07/16/the-online-regulation-series-the -handbook/.

110. Michael Coppedge et al., "V-Dem [Country-Year/Country-Date] Dataset v13," 2023, https://doi.org/10.23696/vdemds23.

111. United Kingdom, "Online Safety Act 2023," legislation.gov.uk, October 26, 2023, https:// www.legislation.gov.uk/ukpga/2023/50/contents/enacted.

112. Ministry of Electronics and Information Technology, "Information Technology (Intermediary Guidelines and Digital Media Ethics Code) Rules," February 25, 2021, https://mib.gov
.in/sites/default/files/IT%28Intermediary%20Guidelines%20and%20Digital%20Media%20
Ethics%20Code%29%20Rules%2C%202021%20English.pdf; Ministry of Electronics and
Information Technology, "Mandatory Verification of Social Media Accounts," December 9,
2022, https://pib.gov.in/PressReleaseIframePage.aspx?PRID=1882060.

113. Adrian Shahbaz, "The Rise of Digital Authoritarianism," Freedom House, 2018, https://
freedomhouse.org/report/freedom-net/2018/rise-digital-authoritarianism.

114. For more details, see Coppedge, Michael et al., *Varieties of Democracy Codebook, v13*,
March 2023, Varieties of Democracy (V-Dem) Project, 288, https://v-dem.net/documents/24
/codebook_v13.pdf.

115. Federal Democratic Republic of Ethiopia, "Proclamation No. 1185/2020: Hate Speech
and Disinformation Prevention and Suppression Proclamation," March 23, 2020, https://www
.accessnow.org/wp-content/uploads/2020/05/Hate-Speech-and-Disinformation-Prevention
-and-Suppression-Proclamation.pdf.

116. Government of Pakistan, "Citizens Protection (Against Online Harm) Rules," January 21, 2020, https://tinyurl.com/3khbz3mu.

117. See Coppedge 2023, "Freedom of Expression Index Ordinal (D) (e_v2x_freexp)," in
Varieties of Democracy Codebook, 361.

4: Adapting to Moderation through Migration

1. Ryan Greer, "Weighing the Value and Risks of Deplatforming," Global Network on Extremism and Technology, May 11, 2020, https://gnet-research.org/2020/05/11/weighing-the
-value-and-risks-of-deplatforming/.

2. Justin Littman, "Islamic State Extremists Are Using the Internet Archive to Deliver Propaganda," Medium, January 22, 2018, https://medium.com/on-archivy/islamic-state-extremists
-are-using-the-internet-archive-to-deliver-propaganda-a132597dd16; Europol, "Jihadist Content Targeted on Internet Archive platform," July 16, 2021, https://www.europol.europa.eu
/media-press/newsroom/news/jihadist-content-targeted-internet-archive-platform.

3. Taylor Telford, "YouTube Removes 8,000 Channels Promoting False Election Claims,"
Washington Post, December 9, 2020, https://www.washingtonpost.com/business/2020/12/09
/youtube-false-2020-election-claims/; Stanford Internet Observatory, "Analyses of a Muslim
Brotherhood–Linked Information Operation and a Facebook Network That Originated in Iran
and Afghanistan," November 5, 2020, https://cyber.fsi.stanford.edu/news/november-2020
-takedowns.

4. The full list of platforms is Facebook, Instagram, LinkedIn, Parler, Pinterest, Reddit,
Telegram, TikTok, Twitter, YouTube, Discord, and Gab.

5. Stanford Center for International Security and Cooperation, "About the Mapping Militants Project," https://cisac.fsi.stanford.edu/mappingmilitants/about.

6. I used the 2020 version of the SPLC dataset at https://www.splcenter.org/hate-map?year
=2020.

7. For this purpose, I used the Yandex search engine, which allows for image-based searching.
For more information, see https://yandex.com/images/search?rpt=imageview.

8. I calculated this number by dividing the coefficient on *Size* in the first column of table 4.3 by the unconditional average of militant and hate groups' use of smaller platforms (0.14).

9. Bill Roggio, "US Targets al Qaeda's al Furqan Media Wing in Iraq," *FDD's Long War Journal*, October 28, 2007, https://www.longwarjournal.org/archives/2007/10/us_targets_al_qaedas.php.

10. Jessica Stern and J. M. Berger, *ISIS: The State of Terror* (New York: Ecco, 2015).

11. John M. Berger, "How ISIS Games Twitter," *Atlantic*, June 16, 2014, https://www.theatlantic.com/international/archive/2014/06/isis-iraq-twitter-social-media-strategy/372856/.

12. Stern and Berger 2015, 147.

13. Tamar Mitts, "From Isolation to Radicalization: Anti-Muslim Hostility and Support for ISIS in the West," *American Political Science Review* 113, no. 1 (2019): 173–94.

14. Efraim Benmelech and Esteban F. Klor, "What Explains the Flow of Foreign Fighters to ISIS?" *Terrorism and Political Violence* 32, no. 7 (2020): 1458–81.

15. Joseph A. Carter, Shiraz Maher, and Peter R. Neumann, "#Greenbirds: Measuring Importance and Influence in Syrian Foreign Fighter Networks," International Centre for the Study of Radicalisation and Political Violence, April 22, 2014, https://icsr.info/2014/04/22/icsr-report-inspires-syrian-foreign-fighters/; Lorenzo Vidino and Seamus Hughes, "ISIS in America: From Retweets to Raqqa," George Washington University Program on Extremism, December 2015, https://extremism.gwu.edu/sites/g/files/zaxdzs5746/files/downloads/ISIS%20in%20America%20-%20Full%20Report.pdf.

16. Karen J. Greenberg, "Case by Case ISIS Prosecutions in the United States, March 1, 2014–June 30, 2016," Center on National Security at Fordham Law, 2016, https://static1.squarespace.com/static/5b16a000e17ba39f6f3825ba/t/5d55bbda5e0ed8000152e7cb/1565899739918/CNS_case_by_case_ISIS_july2016.pdf.

17. United Kingdom Secretary of State for the Home Department, "Radicalization: The Counter-Narrative and Identifying the Tipping Point," December 2017, https://www.parliament.uk/globalassets/documents/commons-committees/home-affairs/Correspondence-17-19/Radicalisation-the-counter-narrative-and-identifying-the-tipping-point-government-response-Eighth-Report-26-17-Cm-9555.pdf.

18. Amar Toor, "France Wants Facebook and Twitter to Launch an 'Offensive' against ISIS Propaganda," *The Verge*, December 3, 2015, https://www.theverge.com/2015/12/3/9842258/paris-attacks-facebook-twitter-google-isis-propaganda.

19. Ellen Nakashima, "Obama's Top National Security Officials to Meet with Silicon Valley CEOs," *Washington Post*, January 7, 2016, https://www.washingtonpost.com/world/national-security/obamas-top-national-security-officials-to-meet-with-silicon-valley-ceos/2016/01/07/178d95ca-b586-11e5-a842-0feb51d1d124_story.html.

20. Natalie Andrews, "Facebook Steps up Efforts against Terrorism," *Wall Street Journal*, February 11, 2016, https://www.wsj.com/articles/facebook-steps-up-efforts-against-terrorism-1455237595.

21. Jigsaw, "Creating Future-Defining Technology: Violent Extremism," https://jigsaw.google.com/issues/.

22. Twitter, "Tweets Still Must Flow," January 26, 2012, https://blog.twitter.com/en_us/a/2012/tweets-still-must-flow.

23. CNN Transcripts, "Erin Burnett Outfront: ISIS Urges English Speakers to Join Cause," CNN, June 20, 2014, http://transcripts.cnn.com/TRANSCRIPTS/1406/20/ebo.01.html.

24. Jenna McLaughlin, "Twitter Is Not at War with ISIS. Here's Why," *Mother Jones*, November 18, 2014, http://www.motherjones.com/politics/2014/11/twitter-isis-war-ban-speech.

25. Ryan J. Reilly, "If You're Trying to Join ISIS through Twitter, the FBI Probably Knows about It," *HuffPost*, July 9, 2015, https://www.huffpost.com/entry/isis-twitter-fbi-islamic-state_n_7763992.

26. Twitter, "Combating Violent Extremism," February 5, 2016, https://blog.twitter.com/official/en_us/a/2016/combating-violent-extremism.html.

27. Twitter, "An Update on Our Efforts to Combat Violent Extremism," August 18, 2016, https://blog.twitter.com/official/en_us/a/2016/an-update-on-our-efforts-to-combat-violent-extremism.html.

28. Laura Huey, Rachel Inch, and Hillary Peladeau, "'@ Me if You Need Shoutout': Exploring Women's Roles in Islamic State Twitter Networks," *Studies in Conflict and Terrorism* 42, no. 5 (2019): 445–63.

29. Steven Stalinsky, *Germany-Based Encrypted Messaging App Telegram Emerges as Jihadis' Preferred Communications Platform* (Washington, DC: Middle East Media Research Institute Books, 2020).

30. For a description of Telegram's channels feature, see https://telegram.org/faq_channels.

31. Stalinsky 2020.

32. Ken Yeung, "Telegram Delivers 12B Messages a Day, CEO Pavel Durov Says WhatsApp Sucks," *VentureBeat*, September 21, 2015, https://venturebeat.com/social/telegram-delivers-12b-messages-a-day-ceo-pavel-durov-says-whatsapp-sucks/.

33. Nico Prucha, "IS and the Jihadist Information Highway—Projecting Influence and Religious Identity via Telegram," *Perspectives on Terrorism* 10, no. 6 (2016): 48–58.

34. Amarnath, Amarasingam, Shiraz Maher, and Charlie Winter, "How Telegram Disruption Impacts Jihadist Platform Migration," Centre for Research and Evidence on Security Threats, January 8, 2021, 27.

35. Prucha 2016.

36. Cole Bunzel, "'Come Back to Twitter': A Jihadi Warning against Telegram," *Jihadica*, July 18, 2016, https://www.jihadica.com/come-back-to-twitter/.

37. Europol, "Referral Action Day with Six EU Member States and Telegram," October 5, 2018, https://www.europol.europa.eu/media-press/newsroom/news/referral-action-day-six-eu-member-states-and-telegram.

38. Europol, "Europol and Telegram Take on Terrorist Propaganda Online," November 25, 2019, https://www.europol.europa.eu/media-press/newsroom/news/europol-and-telegram-take-terrorist-propaganda-online.

39. Europol 2019.

40. Data from Amarasingam, Maher, and Winter 2021.

41. Gavin McInnes, "Introducing: the Proud Boys," *Taki*, September 15, 2016, https://www.takimag.com/article/introducing_the_proud_boys_gavin_mcinnes/#axzz51jGjsfOa.

42. McInnes 2016.

43. McInnes 2016.

44. Proud Boys, "Save the West," https://archive.vn/b77lQ#selection-435.68–435.110.

45. Sharona Coutts, "How Hate Goes 'Mainstream': Gavin McInnes and the Proud Boys," *Rewire News Group*, August 28, 2017, https://rewirenewsgroup.com/2017/08/28/hate-goes -mainstream-gavin-mcinnes-proud-boys/.

46. Taylor Hatmaker, "Facebook Is the Recruiting Tool of Choice for Far-Right Group the Proud Boys," *TechCrunch*, August 10, 2018, https://techcrunch.com/2018/08/10/proud-boys -facebook-mcinnes/.

47. Gavin McInnes, "Some Clarification on the 4th Degree," *Proud Boys Magazine*, July 2017, https://archive.vn/o1ia1#selection-627.0–627.403.

48. Southern Poverty Law Center, "Facebook's Fight Club: How the Proud Boys Use the Social Media Platform to Vet Their Fighters," August 2, 2018, https://www.splcenter.org /hatewatch/2018/08/02/facebooks-fight-club-how-proud-boys-use-social-media-platform -vet-their-fighters.

49. Southern Poverty Law Center, "Proud Boys," https://www.splcenter.org/fighting-hate /extremist-files/group/proud-boys.

50. Julia Carrie Wong, "Twitter Suspends Proud Boys on Eve of Deadly Unite the Right Rally Anniversary," *Guardian*, August 10, 2018, https://www.theguardian.com/technology/2018 /aug/10/twitter-suspends-proud-boys-charlottesville.

51. Brianna Sacks, "Facebook Has Banned the Proud Boys and Gavin McInnes from Its Platforms," *Buzzfeed News*, October 30, 2018, https://www.buzzfeednews.com/article /briannasacks/facebook-bans-proud-boys.

52. Ryan Mac and Blake Montgomery, "Twitter Suspended Proud Boys' and Founder Gavin McInnes' Accounts Ahead of the "Unite the Right" Rally," *BuzzFeed News*, August 11, 2018, https://www.buzzfeednews.com/article/ryanmac/twitter-suspends-proud-boys-and-founder -gavin-mcinnes.

53. Hatmaker 2018.

54. Craig Timberg and Elizabeth Dwoskin, "Trump's Debate Comments Give an Online Boost to a Group Social Media Companies Have Long Struggled Against," *Washington Post*, September 30, 2020, https://www.washingtonpost.com/technology/2020/09/30/trump -debate-rightwing-celebration/.

55. Timberg and Dwoskin 2020.

56. Michael Schwirtz, "Telegram, Pro-Democracy Tool, Struggles over New Fans from Far Right," *New York Times*, January 26, 2021, https://www.nytimes.com/2021/01/26/world /europe/telegram-app-far-right.html.

5: Safe Havens for Mobilizing and Recruiting

1. Alvin Smallberg is a pseudonym.

2. I collected Gab and Twitter data on over ninety thousand users active on the platforms between 2019 and 2021.

3. Gab post from December 26, 2020.

4. Gab post from December 26, 2020.

5. Data reflect monthly active users as of 2021.

6. Cody Buntain, Martin Innes, Tamar Mitts, and Jacob Shapiro, "Cross-Platform Reactions to the Post-January 6 Deplatforming." *Journal of Quantitative Description: Digital Media* 3 (2023), https://doi.org/10.51685/jqd.2023.004.

7. Shagun Jhaver, Christian Boylston, Diyi Yang, and Amy Bruckman, "Evaluating the Effectiveness of Deplatforming as a Moderation Strategy on Twitter," *Proceedings of the ACM on Human-Computer Interaction* 5, no. CSCW2 (2021): 1–30; Amaury Trujillo and Stefano Cresci, "Make Reddit Great Again: Assessing Community Effects of Moderation Interventions on r/the_donald," *Proceedings of the ACM on Human-Computer Interaction* 6, no. CSCW2 (2022): 1–28.

8. Eshwar Chandrasekharan, Umashanthi Pavalanathan, Anirudh Srinivasan, Adam Glynn, Jacob Eisenstein, and Eric Gilbert, "You Can't Stay Here: The Efficacy of Reddit's 2015 Ban Examined through Hate Speech," *Proceedings of the ACM on Human-Computer Interaction* 1, no. CSCW (2017): 1–22.

9. Daniel Robert Thomas and Laila A. Wahedi, "Disrupting Hate: The Effect of Deplatforming Hate Organizations on Their Online Audience," *Proceedings of the National Academy of Sciences* 120, no. 24 (2023): e2214080120.

10. Nathan Cofnas, "Deplatforming Won't Work," *Quillette*, July 8, 2019, https://quillette.com/2019/07/08/deplatforming-wont-work/; Tom Bennett, "Gab Is the Alt-Right Social Network Racists Are Moving To," *Vice News*, April 15, 2018, https://www.vice.com/en/article/ywxb95/gab-is-the-alt-right-social-network-racists-are-moving-to.

11. Buntain et al. 2023.

12. Carolina Are and Pam Briggs, "The Emotional and Financial Impact of De-platforming on Creators at the Margins," *Social Media + Society* 9, no. 1 (2023): 20563051231155103; Jhaver et al. 2021.

13. Margaret E. Roberts, *Censored: Distraction and Diversion inside China's Great Firewall* (Princeton, NJ: Princeton University Press, 2018).

14. This point relates to the larger body of research on the repression-dissent nexus, especially the newer work on the impact of repression in the online sphere that has shown how repression can lead to backlash. Here I do not study repression by governments, but will note that the reaction to content moderation by private technology companies mimics the way individuals in more authoritarian settings react to censorship. Christian Davenport, "Repression and Mobilization: Insights from Political Science and Sociology," in *Repression and Mobilization*, edited by Christian Davenport, Hank Johnston, and Carol Mueller (Minneapolis: University of Minnesota Press, 2005), vii–xli; Mark Irving Lichbach, "Deterrence or Escalation? The Puzzle of Aggregate Studies of Repression and Dissent," *Journal of Conflict Resolution* 31, no. 2 (1987): 266–97; Will H. Moore, "Repression and Dissent: Substitution, Context, and Timing," *American Journal of Political Science* 42, no. 3 (1998): 851–73; Jennifer Pan and Alexandra A. Siegel, "How Saudi Crackdowns Fail to Silence Online Dissent," *American Political Science Review* 114, no. 1 (2020): 109–25; Anita R. Gohdes, "Repression Technology: Internet Accessibility and State Violence," *American Journal of Political Science* 64, no. 3 (2020): 488–503.

15. Hunt Allcott and Matthew Gentzkow, "Social Media and Fake News in the 2016 Election," *Journal of Economic Perspectives* 31, no. 2 (2017): 211–36; Nir Grinberg, Kenneth Joseph, Lisa Friedland, Briony Swire-Thompson, and David Lazer, "Fake News on Twitter during the 2016 US Presidential Election," *Science* 363, no. 6425 (2019): 374–78.

16. Guy Rosen et al., "Helping to Protect the 2020 US Election," Meta, October 21, 2019, https://about.fb.com/news/2019/10/update-on-election-integrity-efforts/.

17. Tony Romm, "Twitter to Ban All Political Ads amid 2020 Election Uproar," *Washington Post*, October 30, 2019, https://www.washingtonpost.com/technology/2019/10/30/twitter

-ban-all-political-ads-amid-election-uproar/; Sara Fischer, "Scoop: Google to Block Election Ads after Election Day," *Axios*, September 25, 2020, https://www.axios.com/2020/09/25/google-to-block-election-ads-after-election-day; Kate Conger, "Twitter Will Turn Off Some Features to Fight Election Misinformation," *New York Times*, October 9, 2020, https://www.nytimes.com/2020/10/09/technology/twitter-election-ban-features.html.

18. Gab, "About," https://gab.com/about.

19. Travis M. Andrews, "Gab, the Social Network That Has Welcomed Qanon and Extremist Figures, Explained," *Washington Post*, January 11, 2021, https://www.washingtonpost.com/technology/2021/01/11/gab-social-network/.

20. Using the API (application programming interface) of the Mastodon social network, on which Gab has been operating since July 2019, I collected information on all posts that were viewable on Gab's public timeline. Mastodon is a decentralized, open-source social network that allows smaller social media platforms to run their platforms on its servers. Gab's data are available through Mastodon's API. For more information, see https://docs.joinmastodon.org. In June 2020, Gab disabled the public timeline. To continue collecting data, I moved to a retrospective collection in which I obtained all historical posts by Gab users who were in my dataset by that point, that is, those who had made a public post prior to June 2020. After January 2021, I was again able to access Gab's public timeline, which allowed me to resume both prospective and retrospective data collection.

21. My approach was simple: I queried the Twitter API for screen names used by Gab users. Matching screen names is a popular approach to finding user linkages across platforms. There are other methods that one can use, some of which draw on the similarity in the content that users post across platforms, as well as similarity in user metadata (profile pictures, profile descriptions, and so on). See, for example, Kai Shu, Suhang Wang, Jiliang Tang, Reza Zafarani, and Huan Liu, "User Identity Linkage across Online Social Networks: A Review," *ACM SIGKDD Explorations Newsletter* 18, no. 2 (2017): 5–17; Asmelash Teka Hadgu and Jayanth Kumar Reddy Gundam, "User Identity Linking across Social Networks by Jointly Modeling Heterogeneous Data with Deep Learning," *Proceedings of the 30th ACM Conference on Hypertext and Social Media* (2019): 293–94. Although matching screen names is likely to undercount users who do not use the same name across platforms, this approach is less likely to include accounts of unrelated users.

22. Manual validation of the matched accounts confirmed that these accounts were owned by the same individuals.

23. Margaret E. Roberts, Brandon M. Stewart, Dustin Tingley, Christopher Lucas, Jetson Leder-Luis, Shana Kushner Gadarian, Bethany Albertson, and David G. Rand, "Structural Topic Models for Open-Ended Survey Responses," *American Journal of Political Science* 58, no. 4 (2014): 1064–82.

24. I estimated a model with twenty topics using the R package "stm," while setting the platform on which the post was posted (Twitter or Gab) as a parameter for topic prevalence. I preprocessed the raw text of the Twitter and Gab posts by removing punctuation, special characters, numbers, and stop words, lowercasing all letters, and stemming. To allow for more context when analyzing the posts, I generated two-word phrases ("bigrams") as the features to represent the text as data.

25. All coefficients are statistically significant at the 0.05 level or less.

26. Twitter post from November 4, 2020.

27. Twitter post from November 4, 2020.

28. Twitter post from November 4, 2020.

29. To ensure that the accounts I identified as suspended were indeed banned from the platform, I had research assistants manually validate the list of suspended accounts by checking their user status on Twitter on July 2021.

30. Igor Bonifacic, "Twitter Bans Far-Right Extremist Group the Oath Keepers," *Engadget*, September 10, 2020, https://www.engadget.com/twitter-the-oath-keepers-211426663.html; Tony Romm and Elizabeth Dwoskin, "Twitter Purged More than 70,000 Accounts Affiliated with QAnon Following Capitol Riot," *Washington Post*, January 11, 2021, https://www .washingtonpost.com/technology/2021/01/11/trump-twitter-ban/.

31. Specifically, I used nearest-neighbor matching by employing the MatchIt package in R. I matched users on the basis of the age of their accounts (in days), the numbers of their friends and followers, the number of tweets they posted on the platform, and the average daily level of hate speech they posted on Twitter.

32. Saif Mohammad and Peter Turney, "Emotions Evoked by Common Words and Phrases: Using Mechanical Turk to Create an Emotion Lexicon," *Proceedings of the NAACL HLT 2010 Workshop on Computational Approaches to Analysis and Generation of Emotion in Text* (2010): 26–34.

33. I used seven days to capture more context around the suspension. My findings are the same when I limit the analysis to one to six days before and after the suspensions.

34. The keywords I used were: censor*, suspend*, banned, delet*, de*platform*, speech, tech, and big tech*.

35. Gab post from November 9, 2020.

36. Gab post from January 11, 2021.

37. Gab post from January 9, 2021.

38. Gab post from January 9, 2021.

39. Gab post from January 9, 2021.

40. Gab post from January 10, 2021.

41. Gab post from November 25, 2020.

42. Gab post from December 30, 2020.

43. Gab post from December 10, 2020.

44. Gab post from January 9, 2021.

45. Gab post from January 9, 2021.

46. Gab post from January 9, 2021.

47. Lynda Lee Kaid and Christina Holtz-Bacha, eds., *Encyclopedia of Political Communication* (Thousand Oaks, CA: SAGE Publications, 2007).

48. Ashley Parker and Toluse Olorunnipa, "Trump 'White Power' Tweet Set Off a Scramble inside the White House—But No Clear Condemnation," *Washington Post*, June 29, 2020, https://www.washingtonpost.com/politics/trump-white-power-tweet-set-off-a-scramble -inside-the-white-house--but-no-clear-condemnation/2020/06/29/6fd88c2c-ba21-11ea-8cf5 -9c1b8d7f84c6_story.html; Michael D. Shear, "Trump Retweets Racist Video Showing Supporter Yelling 'White Power,'" *New York Times*, June 28, 2020, https://www.nytimes.com/2020 /06/28/us/politics/trump-white-power-video-racism.html.

49. Kaid and Holtz-Bacha 2007.

50. Danika Fears, "Twitter Bans Far-Right Militia Group the Oath Keepers for Violating Violent Extremism Policy," *The Daily Beast*, September 10, 2020, https://www.thedailybeast.com/twitter-bans-far-right-militia-group-the-oath-keepers; Shirin Ghaffary, "Does Banning Extremists Online Work? It Depends," *Vox*, February 3, 2022, https://www.vox.com/recode/22913046/deplatforming-extremists-ban-qanon-proud-boys-boogaloo-oathkeepers-three-percenters-trump.

51. Gab post from September 20, 2020.

52. Gab post from November 23, 2020.

53. Gab post from September 13, 2020.

54. Message posted on the Oath Keepers' website that was linked to Gab on November 9, 2020.

55. Gab post from December 24, 2020.

56. Gab post from November 6, 2020.

57. Gab post from December 5, 2020.

58. Message posted on the Oath Keepers website that was linked to Gab on November 10, 2020.

59. Message posted on the Oath Keepers website that was linked to Gab on November 11, 2020.

60. Matthew Kriner and Jon Lewis, "The Oath Keepers and Their Role in the January 6 Insurrection," *CTC Sentinel* 14, no. 10 (2021): 1–18.

61. Message posted on the Oath Keepers website that was linked to Gab on January 5, 2021.

62. The keywords I used were: oath keepers, oathkeeper, oathkeepers, oathkeep, oath, oathkeeper, oath-keep, join-oath.

6: Reaching the Masses by Changing Messaging

1. Of course, in recent years we have seen some political actors banned from social media platforms for violating platform rules. A notable example is the suspension of Donald Trump's Twitter and Facebook accounts after the January 6 storming of the US Capitol, along with similar actions targeting other political figures around the world.

2. Shirin Ghaffary, "How Facebook, Twitter, and YouTube Are Handling the Taliban," *Vox*, August 18, 2021, https://www.vox.com/recode/22630869/facebook-youtube-twitter-taliban-ban-social-media-afghanistan.

3. International Crisis Group, "Taliban Propaganda: Winning the War of Words?" July 24, 2008, https://www.justice.gov/sites/default/files/eoir/legacy/2014/09/29/icg_07242008.pdf.

4. Joshua Keating, "The Taliban's YouTube Channel," *Foreign Policy*, October 13, 2009, https://foreignpolicy.com/2009/10/13/the-talibans-youtube-channel/.

5. Emerson T. Brooking, "Before the Taliban Took Afghanistan, It Took the Internet," Atlantic Council, New Atlanticist (blog), August 26, 2021, https://www.atlanticcouncil.org/blogs/new-atlanticist/before-the-taliban-took-afghanistan-it-took-the-internet/.

6. Johnson, DuPee, and Shaaker 2018.

7. Johnson, DuPee, and Shaaker 2018.

8. Charlie Winter and Abdullah Alrhmoun, "Mapping the Extremist Narrative Landscape in Afghanistan," *Extrac*, November 2020, https://public-assets.extrac.io/reports/ExTrac_Afghanistan_1120.pdf.

9. Brooking 2021.

10. Brooking 2021.

11. Alyssa Kann, "As the Taliban Offensive Gained Momentum, so Did Its Twitter Propaganda Campaign," Atlantic Council Digital Forensic Research Lab, August 19, 2021, https://medium.com/dfrlab/as-the-taliban-offensive-gained-momentum-so-did-its-twitter-propaganda-campaign-75021ba3082.

12. David Zucchino, "Collapse and Conquest: The Taliban Strategy That Seized Afghanistan," *New York Times*, August 18, 2021, https://www.nytimes.com/2021/08/18/world/asia/taliban-victory-strategy-afghanistan.html.

13. Mark Mazzetti, Julian E. Barnes, and Adam Goldman, "Intelligence Warned of Afghan Military Collapse, Despite Biden's Assurances," *New York Times*, September 8, 2021, https://www.nytimes.com/2021/08/17/us/politics/afghanistan-biden-administration.html; *New York Times*, "Read the Full Transcript of President Biden's Remarks on Afghanistan," August 16, 2021, https://www.nytimes.com/2021/08/16/us/politics/biden-taliban-afghanistan-speech.html.

14. Meta, "Dangerous Individuals and Organizations," Transparency Center, https://transparency.fb.com/policies/community-standards/dangerous-individuals-organizations/.

15. Naomi Fix and Emily Chang, "Facebook 'Proactively' Removing Taliban Content, Executive Says," *Bloomberg*, August 16, 2021, https://www.bloomberg.com/news/articles/2021-08-16/facebook-proactively-removing-taliban-content-executive-says.

16. YouTube, "Violent Criminal Organizations Policy," https://support.google.com/youtube/answer/9229472.

17. Catherine Thorbecke, "How the Taliban Uses Social Media to Seek Legitimacy in the West, Sow Chaos at Home," *ABC News*, August 19, 2021, https://abcnews.go.com/Technology/taliban-social-media-seek-legitimacy-west-sow-chaos/story?id=79500632.

18. Twitter, "Our Policy on Glorification of Violence," March 2019, https://web.archive.org/web/20210109225338/https://help.twitter.com/en/rules-and-policies/glorification-of-violence.

19. I assembled the list with considerable help from research assistants who were closely familiar with the Taliban's use of social media. The full list of accounts is available upon request.

20. Winter and Alrhmoun 2020; Charlie Winter, Abdul Sayed, and Abdullah Alrhmoun, "A 'New' Islamic Emirate? The Taliban's Outreach Strategy in the Aftermath of Kabul," Resolve Network, January 2022, https://public-assets.extrac.io/reports/RESOLVE_ExTrac_New_Islamic_Emirate_January_2022_0.pdf.

21. Link to tweet: https://twitter.com/i/web/status/1391548906887122947.

22. Link to tweet: https://twitter.com/i/web/status/1392083191087910914.

23. Pedro L. Rodriguez and Arthur Spirling, "Word Embeddings: What Works, What Doesn't, and How to Tell the Difference for Applied Research," *Journal of Politics* 84, no. 1 (2022): 101–15.

24. The appendix shows the top words associated with "attack" in each language.

25. The results are similar if I expand the list to the top thirty, forty, or fifty words in each language.

26. Twitter post from July 30, 2021, translated from Pashto.

27. Twitter post from September 1, 2021, translated from Pashto.

28. Twitter post from August 15, 2021, translated from Pashto.

29. Twitter post from June 8, 2021, translated from Pashto.

30. Twitter post from June 8, 2021, translated from Pashto.

31. Twitter post from August 28, 2021, translated from Pashto.

32. Twitter post from July 3, 2021, translated from Pashto.

33. Winter, Sayed, and Alrhmoun 2022.

34. Sarah Atiq, "The Taliban Embrace Social Media: 'We Too Want to Change Perceptions,'" *BBC News*, September 6, 2021, https://www.bbc.com/news/world-asia-58466939.

35. To measure Taliban activists' discourse on governance-related issues, I employed the same methodology that I used to identify posts talking about violent attacks. In particular, I used keywords that were closely linked to the word "government" in the Taliban's Twitter posts, including "minister," "authority," "regime," "president," and "republic," among other terms.

36. The prevalence of governance-related tweets in Taliban discourse in the months before the Kabul takeover was about 8 percent; after the takeover, it rose to over 13 percent.

37. Mike Rothschild, *The Storm Is upon Us: How QAnon Became a Movement, Cult, and Conspiracy Theory of Everything* (Brooklyn, NY: Melville House, 2021).

38. Edward Tian, "The QAnon Timeline: Four Years, 5,000 Drops, and Countless Failed Prophecies," Bellingcat, January 29, 2021, https://www.bellingcat.com/news/americas/2021/01/29/the-qanon-timeline/.

39. Kevin Roose, "What Is QAnon, the Viral Pro-Trump Conspiracy Theory?" *New York Times*, September 3, 2021, https://www.nytimes.com/article/what-is-qanon.html.

40. Brandy Zadrozny and Ben Collins, "How Three Conspiracy Theorists Took 'Q' and Sparked Qanon," *NBC News*, August 14, 2018, https://www.nbcnews.com/tech/tech-news/how-three-conspiracy-theorists-took-q-sparked-qanon-n900531.

41. Julia Carrie Wong, "Down the Rabbit Hole: How QAnon Conspiracies Thrive on Facebook," *Guardian*, June 25, 2020, https://www.theguardian.com/technology/2020/jun/25/qanon-facebook-conspiracy-theories-algorithm.

42. Kevin Roose, "YouTube Cracks Down on QAnon Conspiracy Theory, Citing Offline Violence," *New York Times*, October 15, 2020, https://www.nytimes.com/2020/10/15/technology/youtube-bans-qanon-violence.html.

43. Ari Sen and Brandy Zadrozny, "QAnon Groups Have Millions of Members on Facebook, Documents Show," *NBC News*, August 10, 2020, https://www.nbcnews.com/tech/tech-news/qanon-groups-have-millions-members-facebook-documents-show-n1236317.

44. Melanie Smith, "Interpreting Social Qs: Implications of the Evolution of QAnon," *Graphika*, August 2020, https://public-assets.graphika.com/reports/graphika_report_interpreting_social_qs.pdf.

45. Ipsos, "More than 1 in 3 Americans Believe a 'Deep State' Is Working to Undermine Trump," December 30, 2020, https://www.ipsos.com/en-us/news-polls/npr-misinformation-123020.

46. Sam Jackson, Brandon Gorman, and Mayuko Nakatsuka, "QAnon on Twitter: An Overview," George Washington University, Institute for Data, Democracy & Politics, March 5, 2021, https://iddp.gwu.edu/qanon-twitter-overview.

47. Jackson, Gorman, and Nakatsuka 2021.

48. Chris Taylor, "QAnon Conspiracy Blew Up Because of a Bigger Internet Problem," *Mashable*, August 3, 2018, https://mashable.com/article/q-anon.

49. Ben Collins and Brandy Zadrozny, "Twitter Bans 7,000 QAnon Accounts, Limits 150,000 Others as Part of Broad Crackdown," *NBC News*, July 21, 2020, https://www.nbcnews.com/tech/tech-news/twitter-bans-7-000-qanon-accounts-limits-150-000-others-n1234541.

50. Brandy Zadrozny and Ben Collins, "Reddit Bans Qanon Subreddits after Months of Violent Threats," *NBC News*, September 12, 2018, https://www.nbcnews.com/tech/tech-news/reddit-bans-qanon-subreddits-after-months-violent-threats-n909061.

51. Brandy Zadrozny and Ben Collins, "Arizona Veterans Group Finds Homeless Camp—And Fuels a New 'Pizzagate'-Style Conspiracy," *NBC News*, June 7, 2018, https://www.nbcnews.com/tech/social-media/arizona-veterans-group-finds-homeless-camp-fuels-new-pizzagate-style-n880956; Elisha Fieldstadt, "Colorado Woman, Inspired by QAnon Conspiracy, Sought to Kidnap Her Own Child, Police Say," *NBC News*, January 7, 2020, https://www.nbcnews.com/news/crime-courts/colorado-mom-inspired-qanon-conspiracy-sought-kidnap-her-own-child-n1111711; Nolan D. McCaskill, "QAnon Believer Who Plotted to Kill Nancy Pelosi Came to DC Ready for War," *Politico*, January 13, 2021, https://www.politico.com/news/2021/01/13/qanon-nancy-pelosi-murder-plot-458981.

52. Ben Collins, "Local FBI Field Office Warns of 'Conspiracy Theory–Driven Domestic Extremists,'" *NBC News*, August 1, 2019, https://www.nbcnews.com/tech/tech-news/local-fbi-field-office-warns-conspiracy-theory-driven-domestic-extremists-n1038441.

53. Link to tweet: https://web.archive.org/web/20200722013455/https://twitter.com/TwitterSafety/status/1285726277719199746.

54. Meta, "An Update to How We Address Movements and Organizations Tied to Violence," October 17, 2022, https://about.fb.com/news/2020/08/addressing-movements-and-organizations-tied-to-violence/.

55. Sheera Frenkel, "Facebook Amps Up Its Crackdown on QAnon," *New York Times*, October 6, 2020, https://www.nytimes.com/2020/10/06/technology/facebook-qanon-crackdown.html.

56. Meta 2022.

57. YouTube Team, "Managing Harmful Conspiracy Theories on YouTube," YouTube Official Blog, October 15, 2020, https://blog.youtube/news-and-events/harmful-conspiracy-theories-youtube/.

58. Rachel E. Greenspan, "Pinterest Is the Latest Social Platform to Announce a Stance against the QAnon Conspiracy Theory," *Insider*, October 14, 2020, https://www.insider.com/pinterest-qanon-is-latest-platform-to-ban-conspiracy-theory-content-2020-10.

59. Sheera Frenkel, "Facebook Removes 790 QAnon Groups to Fight Conspiracy Theory," *New York Times*, August 19, 2020, https://www.nytimes.com/2020/08/19/technology/facebook-qanon-groups-takedown.html.

60. Andrew Torba, "A Discussion with Business Insider about QAnon," *Gab News*, November 30, 2020, https://news.gab.com/2020/11/30/a-discussion-with-business-insider-about-qanon/.

61. Rebecca Heilweil and Shirin Ghaffary, "How Trump's Internet Built and Broadcast the Capitol Insurrection," *Vox*, January 8, 2021, https://www.vox.com/recode/22221285/trump-online-capitol-riot-far-right-parler-twitter-facebook.

62. The full list of hashtags includes: #q, #adrenochrome, #blackhat, #cabal, #cbts, #deepstate, #drainttheswamp, #dreadcrumbs, #enjoytheshow, #followthewhiterabbit, #greatawakening, #normies, #pedogate, #pedophile, #qanon, #qdrop, #redpill, #saveourchildren, #savethechildren, #thegreatawakening, #theplan, #thestorm, #thestormishere, #thestormisuponus, #trumpknows, #trusttheplan, #whitehat, #whiterabbit, #wwg1wga, #wwg1wgaworldwide.

63. Since my data were collected prospectively, I am able to include in my observations QAnon content that was later removed.

64. I use difference-in-differences models with clean controls that regress the QAnon content variable on an interaction between a variable capturing whether the content was posted on Twitter or Gab and an indicator variable that captures whether it appeared before or after Twitter's policy change. In all regressions, I use user fixed effects and cluster the standard errors at the user level. Full tabular results are reported in the appendix.

65. Link to tweet: https://twitter.com/_MAArgentino/status/1308879250049695748.

66. Moustafa Ayad, "The Propaganda Pipeline: The ISIS Fuouaris Upload Network on Facebook," Institute for Strategic Dialogue, July 13, 2020, https://www.isdglobal.org/wp-content/uploads/2020/07/The-Propaganda-Pipeline-1.pdf.

67. https://web.archive.org/web/20220612171550/https://twitter.com/moustafaayad/status/1536033261318701058.

68. Tech Against Terrorism, "Tracking Violent Far-Right Behaviour Online," March 15, 2022, https://tech-against-terrorism-podcast.podcastpage.io/episode/tracking-violent-far-right-behaviour-online; link to tweet: https://web.archive.org/web/20220818134639/https://twitter.com/MoustafaAyad/status/1560261567026831360.

69. For an example of adding noise to text, see https://web.archive.org/web/20220825154530/https://twitter.com/MoustafaAyad/status/1562827848649297922.

70. https://web.archive.org/web/20220828005752/https://twitter.com/moustafaayad/status/1561302620672823296.

71. Moustafa Ayad, Anisa Harrasy, and Mohammed Abdullah A., "Under-moderated, Unhinged, and Ubiquitous: Al-Shabaab and the Islamic State Networks on Facebook," Institute for Strategic Dialogue, June 2022, https://www.isdglobal.org/wp-content/uploads/2022/06/Undermoderated-Unhinged-and-Ubiquitous-al-shabaab-and-islamic-state-networks-on-facebook.pdf.

72. Starting from the core list of Taliban-affiliated accounts, I identified the followers of each member and downloaded the messages that they posted on Twitter during the same time period. I collected the data prospectively, tracking each account every day beginning in March 2021. This yielded over eleven million posts generated by ninety-two thousand accounts that followed the Taliban on Twitter. To identify messages promoting violent attacks, I used the method described earlier in this chapter: identifying keywords used by Taliban accounts to promote violence on the platform.

73. Warning: this post shares graphic violence: https://twitter.com/i/web/status/1388120480532504576.

74. Warning: these posts share graphic violence: https://twitter.com/i/web/status/1421348015416254465; https://twitter.com/i/web/status/1441710583737458690.

7: Is Convergence in Moderation a Solution?

1. I focus on convergence on a more restrictive threshold—all platforms restricting more content on their sites. In theory, moderation policies can also be aligned at a higher level, when platforms become less restrictive in their moderation of harmful content. I focus on a lower threshold because of recent trends in social media regulation, which point to a desire for more, not less, moderation (see chapter 2).

2. Chris Sonderby, "Update on New Zealand," Meta, March 18, 2019, https://about.fb.com /news/2019/03/update-on-new-zealand/; Graham Macklin, "The Christchurch Attacks: Livestream Terror in the Viral Video Age," *CTC Sentinel* 12, no. 6 (2019): 18–29.

3. Macklin 2019.

4. Sonderby 2019.

5. Elizabeth Dwoskin and Craig Timberg, "Inside YouTube's Struggles to Shut Down Video of the New Zealand Shooting—And the Humans Who Outsmarted Its Systems," *Washington Post*, March 18, 2019, https://www.washingtonpost.com/technology/2019/03/18/inside -youtubes-struggles-shut-down-video-new-zealand-shooting-humans-who-outsmarted-its -systems/.

6. Dwoskin and Timberg 2019.

7. Evelyn Douek, "The Rise of Content Cartels," Columbia University, Knight First Amendment Institute, February 11, 2020, https://knightcolumbia.org/content/the-rise-of-content -cartels.

8. "The Christchurch Call to Action to Eliminate Terrorist and Violent Extremist Content Online," https://www.christchurchcall.com/assets/Documents/Christchurch-Call-full-text -English.pdf.

9. New Zealand Government, "NZ and France Seek to End Use of Social Media for Acts of Terrorism," April 24, 2019, https://www.beehive.govt.nz/release/nz-and-france-seek-end-use -social-media-acts-terrorism.

10. "The Christchurch Call to Action to Eliminate . . ."

11. "The Christchurch Call to Action to Eliminate . . ."

12. Global Internet Forum to Counter Terrorism, "About," https://gifct.org/about/.

13. In particular, GIFCT's mission relates to the debate in international relations regarding compliance with international agreements, which is framed around two possible solutions: enforcement (for example, through sanctions) or management (through transparency, dispute resolution, and financial assistance). The notion that cooperation between technology companies on content moderation can be achieved via "inter-platform organizations" such as GIFCT is deeply rooted in the principles advocated by the managerial school of thought. See Abram Chayes, Antonia Handler Chayes, and Ronald B. Mitchell, "Managing Compliance: A Comparative Perspective," in *Engaging Countries: Strengthening Compliance with International Environmental Accords*, edited by Edith Brown Weiss and Harold K. Jacobson (Cambridge, MA: MIT Press, 1998), 44–45; George W. Downs, David M. Rocke, and Peter N. Barsoom, "Is the Good News about Compliance Good News about Cooperation?" *International Organization* 50, no. 3 (1996): 379–406; Jonas Tallberg, "Paths to Compliance: Enforcement, Management, and the European Union," *International Organization* 56, no. 3 (2002): 609–43.

14. Global Internet Forum to Counter Terrorism, "GIFCT's Hash-Sharing Database," https://gifct.org/hsdb/.

15. Evelyn Douek, "Content Moderation as Systems Thinking," *Harvard Law Review* 136 (2022): 526; Ernst & Young LLP, "Understanding How Platforms with Video-Sharing Capabilities Protect Users from Harmful Content Online," August 2021, https://assets.publishing .service.gov.uk/government/uploads/system/uploads/attachment_data/file/1008128/EYUK -000140696_EY_Report_-_Web_Accessible_Publication_2.pdf.

16. For more details on Tech Against Terrorism's mentorship program, see Tech Against Terrorism, "The Tech Against Terrorism Mentorship, 2018–2020 Overview," May 18, 2021, https://www.techagainstterrorism.org/2021/05/18/the-tech-against-terrorism-mentorship -2018-2021/.

17. Carmen Fishwick, "How a Polish Student's Website Became an ISIS Propaganda Tool," *Guardian*, August 15, 2014, https://www.theguardian.com/world/2014/aug/15/-sp-polish-man -website-isis-propaganda-tool; Douek 2020.

18. Tech Against Terrorism, "Tech Policy Evolution and the Human Side of Moderating Terrorist Content (Part 2)," March 30, 2022, https://podcast.techagainstterrorism.org/1684819 /10338244. Part 2 of this podcast includes an interview with Jessica Mason, head of global policy and public affairs at Clubhouse.

19. Douek 2020.

20. The data include historical versions of sixty platforms, not sixty-seven as in chapter 4, for three reasons: First, I excluded Instagram, as the platform is governed by the same standards as Facebook. Second, Dtube, ZeroNet, Quitter, GoFile, and Threema did not have content moderation documentation online. Finally, Quora was excluded from the Internet Archive's Wayback Machine (https://archive.org), so I could not access a historical version of its content moderation rules. The Internet Archive says that sites may be excluded if they requested being excluded; if the archive's automated crawlers "were unaware of their existence at the time of the crawl"; or if they were "password protected, blocked by robots.txt, or otherwise inaccessible to our automated systems." For more information, see https://help.archive.org/help/using-the -wayback-machine/.

21. Almost all historical versions were in English. I translated those that were not—Top4top in Arabic, Dosya Upload in Turkish, and File Host PT in Portuguese—into English using Google Translate.

22. R = 0.67, significant at 0.001 level.

23. I created the convergence measure as follows. For each time period in the data, I calculated the cosine similarity between each pair of platforms along the nine categories of harmful content that made up the moderation threshold. Then, for each platform, I counted the number of other platforms with which its cosine similarity score was greater than the average for that time period. See the appendix for more details on the algorithm.

24. Converging platforms for which I had data on extremist activity included Discord, Facebook, Instagram, LinkedIn, Pinterest, TikTok, Twitter, and YouTube; the nonconverging platforms included Parler, Reddit, Telegram, and Gab.

25. Full regression results are reported in the appendix.

26. Danielle Keats Citron, "Extremist Speech, Compelled Conformity, and Censorship Creep," *Notre Dame Law Review* 93 (2017): 1035; Kate Klonick, "The Facebook Oversight Board: Creating an Independent Institution to Adjudicate Online Free Expression," *Yale Law Journal* 129 (2019): 2418.

27. Douek 2020.

28. Ángel Díaz and Laura Hecht-Felella, "Double Standards in Social Media Content Moderation," New York University, Brennan Center for Justice, August 4, 2021, https://www.brennancenter.org/sites/default/files/2021-08/Double_Standards_Content_Moderation.pdf.

29. Díaz and Hecht-Felella 2021.

30. In a recent study on the experiences of human rights activists in Syria, Erin Walk and her colleagues found that activists running afoul of moderation rules tried to adapt by posting nonvisual content on Facebook and Twitter but taking advantage of Telegram's lax policies to post various types of multimedia there. See Erin Walk, Kiran Garimella, Ahmet Akbiyik, and Fotini Christia, "Social Media Narratives on Conflict from Northern Syria," working paper, Massachusetts Institute of Technology, 2022.

31. Citron 2017.

32. Citron 2017.

33. Global Internet Forum to Counter Terrorism, "Broadening the GIFCT Hash-Sharing Database Taxonomy: An Assessment and Recommended Next Steps," July 2021, https://gifct.org/wp-content/uploads/2021/07/GIFCT-TaxonomyReport-2021.pdf.

34. Larry Diamond, "Liberation Technology," in Diamond, *In Search of Democracy* (New York: Routledge, 2015), 132–46; Tiberiu Dragu and Yonatan Lupu, "Digital Authoritarianism and the Future of Human Rights," *International Organization* 75, no. 4 (2021): 991–1017; Joshua A. Tucker, Yannis Theocharis, Margaret E. Roberts, and Pablo Barberá, "From Liberation to Turmoil: Social Media and Democracy," *Journal of Democracy* 28 (2017): 46.

35. Philip N. Howard, Sheetal D. Agarwal, and Muzammil M. Hussain, "The Dictators' Digital Dilemma: When Do States Disconnect Their Digital Networks?" Brookings, October 2011, https://www.brookings.edu/wp-content/uploads/2016/06/10_dictators_digital_network.pdf; Philipp M. Lutscher, Nils B. Weidmann, Margaret E. Roberts, Mattijs Jonker, Alistair King, and Alberto Dainotti, "At Home and Abroad: The Use of Denial-of-Service Attacks during Elections in Nondemocratic Regimes," *Journal of Conflict Resolution* 64, nos. 2/3 (2020): 373–401; Jennifer Earl, Thomas V. Maher, and Jennifer Pan, "The Digital Repression of Social Movements, Protest, and Activism: A Synthetic Review," *Science Advances* 8, no. 10 (2022): eabl8198; Anita R. Gohdes, "Pulling the Plug: Network Disruptions and Violence in Civil Conflict," *Journal of Peace Research* 52, no. 3 (2015): 352–67.

36. Gary King, Jennifer Pan, and Margaret E. Roberts, "How Censorship in China Allows Government Criticism but Silences Collective Expression," *American Political Science Review* 107, no. 2 (2013): 326–43; Jennifer Pan, "How Market Dynamics of Domestic and Foreign Social Media Firms Shape Strategies of Internet Censorship," *Problems of Post-Communism* 64, nos. 3/4 (2017): 167–88; William R. Hobbs and Margaret E. Roberts, "How Sudden Censorship Can Increase Access to Information," *American Political Science Review* 112, no. 3 (2018): 621–36; Jane Esberg, "Censorship as Reward: Evidence from Pop Culture Censorship in Chile," *American Political Science Review* 114, no. 3 (2020): 821–36; Xu Xu, "To Repress or to Co-opt? Authoritarian Control in the Age of Digital Surveillance," *American Journal of Political Science* 65, no. 2 (2021): 309–25.

37. Margaret Roberts, *Censored: Distraction and Diversion inside China's Great Firewall* (Princeton, NJ: Princeton University Press, 2018); Seva Gunitsky, "Corrupting the Cyber-Commons: Social Media as a Tool of Autocratic Stability," *Perspectives on Politics* 13, no. 1 (2015): 42–54.

38. Douek 2020.

39. Anti-Money Laundering Permanent Committee, Kingdom of Saudi Arabia, "Law on Combating the Financing of Terrorism," https://www.aml.gov.sa/en-us/RulesAndRegulations/Combating%20Terrorism%20and%20Financing%20of%20Terrorism%20Law.pdf.

40. Bolin Zhang and Joan Barata, "Provisions on the Governance of the Online Information Content Ecosystem: Order of the Cyberspace Administration of China," March 1, 2020, https://wilmap.stanford.edu/entries/provisions-governance-online-information-content-ecosystem.

41. Human Rights Watch, "Russia: Growing Internet Isolation, Control, Censorship," June 18, 2020, https://www.hrw.org/news/2020/06/18/russia-growing-internet-isolation-control-censorship.

42. Tech Against Terrorism. "Transparency Report: Terrorism Content Analytics Platform, Year One: 1 December 2020–30 November 2021," https://www.techagainstterrorism.org/wp-content/uploads/2022/03/Tech-Against-Terrorism-TCAP-Report-March-2022_v6.pdf.

43. Tech Against Terrorism, "The Threat of Terrorist and Violent Extremist–Operated Websites," January 2022, https://www.techagainstterrorism.org/hubfs/The-Threat-of-Terrorist-and-Violent-Extremist-Operated-Websites-Jan-2022-1.pdf.

8: Conclusion: The Future of Online Harms

1. It is still an open question whether alignment in social media platforms' content moderation policies can eventually lead to extremist groups' demise. Since my focus in this book has been on the online media activity of extremist organizations (as opposed to their "offline" operations), I did not examine the extent to which content moderation influences these actors' activity in other spaces. A fruitful direction for future research would be to examine the relationship between online content moderation and extremists' resilience in the physical world.

2. The fact that technology companies are responsible only for harmful content on their own platforms and do not pay the costs that their decisions incur for other platforms (or society as a whole) reflects a classic externalities problem. A fruitful area for future research would be to examine whether and how existing solutions to negative externalities can be applied to the context of content moderation on social media. For an introduction to externalities, see Richard Cornes and Todd Sandler, *The Theory of Externalities, Public Goods, and Club Goods* (Cambridge: Cambridge University Press, 1996).

3. Lauren Hirsch and Mike Isaac, "How Twitter's Board Went from Fighting Elon Musk to Accepting Him," *New York Times*, April 30, 2022, https://www.nytimes.com/2022/04/30/technology/twitter-board-elon-musk.html.

4. See Statista, "Number of X (Formerly Twitter) Users Worldwide from 2019 to 2024 (in Millions)," https://www.statista.com/statistics/303681/twitter-users-worldwide/; Elon Musk, tweet from October 27, 2022, https://twitter.com/elonmusk/status/1585619322239561728.

5. Elon Musk, tweet from October 27, 2022, https://twitter.com/elonmusk/status/1585619322239561728.

6. Elon Musk, tweet from April 26, 2022, https://twitter.com/elonmusk/status/1519036983137509376.

7. Most policies remained the same, but the company changed its policy on hateful conduct to remove protections for transgender users. Angela Yang, "Twitter Quietly Changes Its Hateful

Conduct Policy to Remove Standing Protections for Its Transgender Users," *NBC News*, April 18, 2023, https://www.nbcnews.com/tech/twitter-changes-hateful-conduct-policy-rcna80338.

8. Barbara Ortutay and Matt O'Brien, "Musk's Latest Twitter Cuts: Outsourced Content Moderators," *Associated Press*, November 13, 2022, https://apnews.com/article/elon-musk-twitter-inc-technology-misinformation-social-media-a469130efaebc8ed029a647a149c5049.

9. Matt O'Brien and Barbara Ortutay, "Musk's Twitter Disbands Its Trust and Safety Advisory Group," *Associated Press*, December 13, 2022, https://apnews.com/article/elon-musk-twitter-inc-technology-business-a9b795e8050de12319b82b5dd7118cd7?utm_source=homepage&utm_medium=TopNews&utm_campaign=position_03; *Associated Press*, "Elon Musk's X, Formerly Twitter, Sues California over Content Moderation Transparency Law," First Amendment Watch at New York University, September 12, 2023, https://firstamendmentwatch.org/elon-musks-x-formerly-twitter-sues-california-over-content-moderation-transparency-law/.

10. Clare Duffy, "The Mass Unbanning of Suspended Twitter Users Is Underway," *CNN Business*, December 8, 2022, https://www.cnn.com/2022/12/08/tech/twitter-unbanned-users-returning/index.html.

11. Lisa O'Carroll, "EU Warns Elon Musk after Twitter Found to Have Highest Rate of Disinformation," *Guardian*, September 26, 2023, https://www.theguardian.com/technology/2023/sep/26/eu-warns-elon-musk-that-twitter-x-must-comply-with-fake-news-laws; Byron Kaye, "Musk's X Disabled Feature for Reporting Electoral Misinformation—Researcher," *Reuters*, September 26, 2023, https://www.reuters.com/technology/musks-x-disabled-feature-reporting-electoral-misinformation-researcher-2023-09-27.

12. Limited enforcement of its rules is in fact partly intentional. On April 17, 2023, X announced a new policy: "Freedom of Speech, Not Reach." According to the new policy, content that violates the company's content moderation policies will be labeled but not removed, and its reach on the platform will be restricted. X Safety, "Freedom of Speech, Not Reach: An Update on Our Enforcement Philosophy," April 17, 2023, https://blog.twitter.com/en_us/topics/product/2023/freedom-of-speech-not-reach-an-update-on-our-enforcement-philosophy.

13. Center for Countering Digital Hate, "The Musk Bump: Quantifying the Rise in Hate Speech under Elon Musk," December 6, 2022, https://counterhate.com/blog/the-musk-bump-quantifying-the-rise-in-hate-speech-under-elon-musk/; see also American Defense League's tweet on its Center on Extremism report on antisemitic tweets: https://twitter.com/ADL/status/1593714819932332034.

14. Sheera Frenkel and Steven Lee Myers, "Antisemitic and Anti-Muslim Hate Speech Surges across the Internet," *New York Times*, November 15, 2023, https://www.nytimes.com/2023/11/15/technology/hate-speech-israel-gaza-internet.html.

15. O'Carroll 2023.

16. The Observers, "How Pro-Terrorism Accounts Are Circumventing Moderation on Social Media," *France 24*, November 25, 2022, https://observers.france24.com/en/middle-east/20221125-social-media-propaganda-islamic-state-terrorism.

17. Věra Jourová, vice president of the European Commission for Values and Transparency, quoted in O'Carroll 2023.

18. Steven Lee Myers and Nico Grant, "Combating Disinformation Wanes at Social Media Giants," *New York Times*, February 14, 2023, https://www.nytimes.com/2023/02/14/technology/disinformation-moderation-social-media.html.

19. Shannon Bond, "Meta Says Chinese, Russian Influence Operations Are among the Biggest It's Taken Down," *All Things Considered*, NPR, August 29, 2023, https://www.npr.org/2023/08/29/1196117574/meta-says-chinese-russian-influence-operations-are-among-the-biggest-its-taken-d.

20. Bond 2023.

21. Shannon Bond, "Facebook Takes Down Russian Network Impersonating European News Outlets." NPR, September 27, 2022, https://www.npr.org/2022/09/27/1125217316/facebook-takes-down-russian-network-impersonating-european-news-outlets.

22. Bond 2022.

23. International Centre for Missing and Exploited Children, "Child Sexual Abuse Material: Model Legislation and Global Review," 10th ed., 2023, https://cdn.icmec.org/wp-content/uploads/2023/10/CSAM-Model-Legislation_10th-Ed-Oct-2023.pdf.

24. International Centre for Missing and Exploited Children 2023.

25. Mar Negreiro, "Curbing the Surge in Online Child Abuse: The Dual Role of Digital Technology in Fighting and Facilitating Its Proliferation," European Parliamentary Research Service, November 2020, https://www.europarl.europa.eu/RegData/etudes/BRIE/2020/659360/EPRS_BRI(2020)659360_EN.pdf.

26. Meta, "Child Endangerment: Nudity and Physical Abuse and Sexual Exploitation," Transparency Center, https://transparency.fb.com/reports/community-standards-enforcement/child-nudity-and-sexual-exploitation/facebook/#content-actioned.

27. Paul Bischoff, "The Rising Tide of Child Abuse Content on Social Media," Comparitech, January 25, 2023, https://www.comparitech.com/blog/vpn-privacy/child-abuse-online-statistics/.

28. Paul Bleakley, Elena Martellozzo, Ruth Spence, and Jeffrey DeMarco, "Moderating Online Child Sexual Abuse Material (CSAM): Does Self-Regulation Work, or Is Greater State Regulation Needed?" *European Journal of Criminology* (2023): 14773708231181361.

29. David Thiel, Renée DiResta, and Alex Stamos, "Cross-Platform Dynamics of Self-Generated CSAM," Stanford University Internet Observatory, Cyber Policy Center, June 6, 2023, https://stacks.stanford.edu/file/druid:jd797tp7663/20230606-sio-sg-csam-report.pdf.

30. Thiel et al. 2023.

31. Thiel et al. 2023.

32. Larry Diamond, "Liberation Technology," in Diamond, *In Search of Democracy* (New York: Routledge, 2015); Joshua A. Tucker, Yannis Theocharis, Margaret E. Roberts, and Pablo Barberá, "From Liberation to Turmoil: Social Media and Democracy," *Journal of Democracy* 28, no. 4 (2017): 46–59.

33. Joshua Goldstein, "The Role of Digital Networked Technologies in the Ukrainian Orange Revolution," Berkman Center Research Publication 2007-14 (2007); Jeffrey Ghannam, "Social Media in the Arab World: Leading Up to the Uprisings of 2011," report for the Center for International Media Assistance, February 3, 2011, https://ciaotest.cc.columbia.edu/wps/ned/0021255/f_0021255_17663.pdf; Felix Tusa, "How Social Media Can Shape a Protest Movement: The Cases of Egypt in 2011 and Iran in 2009," *Arab Media and Society* 17, no. 2013 (2013): 1–14; Zachary C. Steinert-Threlkeld, "Spontaneous Collective Action: Peripheral Mobilization during the Arab Spring," *American Political Science Review* 111, no. 2 (2017): 379–403.

34. Jennifer Pan and Alexandra A. Siegel, "How Saudi Crackdowns Fail to Silence Online Dissent," *American Political Science Review* 114, no. 1 (2020): 109–25; Han Zhang and Jennifer Pan, "CASM: A Deep-Learning Approach for Identifying Collective Action Events with Text and Image Data from Social Media," *Sociological Methodology* 49, no. 1 (2019): 1–57; Margaret Roberts, *Censored: Distraction and Diversion inside China's Great Firewall* (Princeton, NJ: Princeton University Press, 2018).

35. Anita R. Gohdes, *Repression in the Digital Age: Surveillance, Censorship, and the Dynamics of State Violence* (Oxford: Oxford University Press, 2023).

36. Erin Walk, Kiran Garimella, Ahmet Akbiyik, and Fotini Christia, "Social Media Narratives on Conflict from Northern Syria," working paper, Massachusetts Institute of Technology, 2022.

37. Sheera Frenkel and Steven Lee Myers, "Hamas Seeds Violent Videos on Sites with Little Moderation," *New York Times*, October 10, 2023, https://www.nytimes.com/2023/10/10/technology/hamas-violent-videos-online.html.

38. Steven Lee Myers, "Fact or Fiction? In This War, It Is Hard to Tell," *New York Times*, October 13, 2023, https://www.nytimes.com/2023/10/13/business/israel-hamas-misinformation-social-media-x.html; Barbara Ortutay, "Social Media Is Awash in Misinformation about Israel-Gaza War, but Musk's X is the Most Egregious," *Associated Press*, October 11, 2023, https://apnews.com/article/social-media-gaza-israel-hamas-misinformation-cb5192215d0f89d8a413606d0ec73cf4; Will Oremus and Naomi Nix, "Graphic War Videos Go Viral, Testing Social Media's Rules," *Washington Post*, October 11, 2023, https://www.washingtonpost.com/technology/2023/10/11/tiktok-youtube-israel-hamas-content-moderation/.

39. Aisha Counts, "Israel-Hamas War Gives Parents a Reason to Delete Kids' Social Apps," *Bloomberg*, October 13, 2023, https://www.bloomberg.com/news/newsletters/2023-10-13/delete-instagram-and-tiktok-is-what-some-parents-do-during-israel-war.

40. Darrell M. West, "Posting Murder on Social Media Platforms," Brookings, October 12, 2023, https://www.brookings.edu/articles/posting-murder-on-social-media-platforms/.

41. Andrea Kane, "How to Protect Your Mental Health while Keeping Tabs on the Israel-Hamas War," CNN, October 17, 2023, https://www.cnn.com/2023/10/14/health/mental-health-israel-hamas-wellness/index.html.

42. For Breton's letter to Meta, see https://twitter.com/ThierryBreton/status/1712126600873931150.; for Breton's October 10, 2023, letter to Elon Musk at X, see https://twitter.com/ThierryBreton/status/1711808891757944866; for Breton's October 12, 2023, letter to Shou Zi Chew at TikTok, see https://twitter.com/ThierryBreton/status/1712472108222329056; for Breton's letter to Sundar Pichai at YouTube, see: https://twitter.com/ThierryBreton/status/1712866215591379259.

43. James Vincent, "Meta's Powerful AI Language Model Has Leaked Online—What Happens Now?" *The Verge*, March 8, 2023, https://www.theverge.com/2023/3/8/23629362/meta-ai-language-model-llama-leak-online-misuse.

44. Daniel Siegel, "'RedPilled AI': A New Weapon for Online Radicalisation on 4chan," Global Network on Extremism and Technology, June 7, 2023, https://gnet-research.org/2023/06/07/redpilled-ai-a-new-weapon-for-online-radicalisation-on-4chan/.

45. Daniel Siegel and Bilva Chandra, "'Deepfake Doomsday': The Role of Artificial Intelligence in Amplifying Apocalyptic Islamist Propaganda," Global Network on Extremism and Technology, August 29, 2023, https://gnet-research.org/2023/08/29/deepfake-doomsday-the-role-of-artificial-intelligence-in-amplifying-apocalyptic-islamist-propaganda/.

46. Of course, in some cases, "bot" accounts helped amplify messaging campaigns, but the information operations were controlled and operated by human actors.

47. OpenAI, "Product Safety Standards," https://openai.com/safety-standards; Microsoft, "The New Bing: Our Approach to Responsible AI," April 2023, https://blogs.microsoft.com/wp-content/uploads/prod/sites/5/2023/04/RAI-for-the-new-Bing-April-2023.pdf.

9: Appendix

1. Mastodon is a decentralized, open-source social network that allows smaller social media platforms to run their platforms on its servers. Gab's data are available through Mastodon's API. For more information, see https://docs. joinmastodon.org.

2. Kai Shu, Suhang Wang, Jiliang Tang, Reza Zafarani, and Huan Liu, "User Identity Linkage across Online Social Networks: A Review," *ACM SIGKDD Explorations Newsletter* 18, no. 2 (2017): 5–17; Asmelash Teka Hadgu and Jayanth Kumar Reddy Gundam, "User Identity Linking across Social Networks by Jointly Modeling Heterogeneous Data with Deep Learning," *Proceedings of the 30th ACM Conference on Hypertext and Social Media* (2019): 293–94.

3. Lynda Lee Kaid and Christina Holtz-Bacha, eds., *Encyclopedia of Political Communication* (Thousand Oaks, CA: SAGE publications, 2007).

WORKS CITED

Alava, Séraphin, Divina Frau-Meigs, and Ghayda Hassan. *Youth and Violent Extremism on Social Media: Mapping the Research.* Paris: UNESCO Publishing, 2017.

Aleksejeva, Nika, Lukas Andriukaitis, Luiza Bandeira, Donara Barojan, Graham Brookie, Eto Buziashvili, Andy Carvin, Kanishk Karan, Ben Nimmo, Iain Robertson, and Michael Sheldon. "Operation 'Secondary Infektion': A Suspected Russian Intelligence Operation Targeting Europe and the United States." Atlantic Council Digital Forensic Research Lab, August 2019. https://www.atlanticcouncil.org/wp-content/uploads/2019/08/Operation-Secondary-Infektion_English.pdf.

Allcott, Hunt, and Matthew Gentzkow. "Social Media and Fake News in the 2016 Election." *Journal of Economic Perspectives* 31, no. 2 (2017): 211–36.

Amarasingam, Amarnath, Shiraz Maher, and Charlie Winter. "How Telegram Disruption Impacts Jihadist Platform Migration." Centre for Research and Evidence on Security Threats, January 8, 2021, 27.

Amnesty International. "The Social Atrocity: Meta and the Right to Remedy for the Rohingya." Amnesty International, September 29, 2022. https://www.amnesty.org/en/documents/ASA16/5933/2022/en/.

Appel, Ruth E., Jennifer Pan, and Margaret E. Roberts. "Partisan Conflict over Content Moderation Is More than Disagreement about Facts." *Science Advances* 9, no. 44 (November 3, 2023). https://doi.org/10.1126/sciadv.adg6799.

Are, Carolina, and Pam Briggs. "The Emotional and Financial Impact of De-platforming on Creators at the Margins." *Social Media + Society* 9, no. 1 (2023): 20563051231155103.

Atwan, Abdel Bari. *Islamic State: The Digital Caliphate.* Berkeley: University of California Press, 2019.

Ayad, Moustafa. "The Propaganda Pipeline: The ISIS Fuouaris Upload Network on Facebook." Institute for Strategic Dialogue, July 13, 2020. https://www.isdglobal.org/wp-content/uploads/2020/07/The-Propaganda-Pipeline-1.pdf.

Ayad, Moustafa, Anisa Harrasy, and Mohammed Abdullah A. "Under-moderated, Unhinged, and Ubiquitous: Al-Shabaab and the Islamic State Networks on Facebook." Institute for Strategic Dialogue, June 2022. https://www.isdglobal.org/wp-content/uploads/2022/06/Undermoderated-Unhinged-and-Ubiquitous-al-shabaab-and-islamic-state-networks-on-facebook.pdf.

Baele, Stephane J., Katharine A. Boyd, and Travis G. Coan, eds. *ISIS Propaganda: A Full-Spectrum Extremist Message.* Oxford: Oxford University Press, 2019.

Bambauer, Derek E. "What Does the Day after Section 230 Reform Look Like?" Brookings, January 22, 2021. https://www.brookings.edu/articles/what-does-the-day-after-section-230 -reform-look-like/.

Barberá, Pablo. "Social Media, Echo Chambers, and Political Polarization." In *Social Media and Democracy: The State of the Field, Prospects for Reform*, edited by Joshua A. Tucker and Nathaniel Persily, 34–55. Cambridge: Cambridge University Press, 2020.

Bass, Loretta E. "What Motivates European Youth to Join ISIS?" *Syria Comment*, November 20, 2014. https://bit.ly/2AsjhFH.

Benkler, Yochai, Robert Faris, and Hal Roberts. *Network Propaganda: Manipulation, Disinformation, and Radicalization in American Politics*. Oxford: Oxford University Press, 2018.

Benmelech, Efraim, and Esteban F. Klor. "What Explains the Flow of Foreign Fighters to ISIS?" *Terrorism and Political Violence* 32, no. 7 (2020): 1458–81.

Berger, J. M. *Extremism*. Cambridge, MA: MIT Press, 2018.

Berger, J. M., and Heather Perez. "The Islamic State's Diminishing Returns on Twitter: How Suspensions Are Limiting the Social Networks of English-Speaking ISIS supporters." George Washington Program on Extremism, February 2016. https://extremism.gwu.edu /sites/g/files/zaxdzs5746/files/downloads/JMB%20Diminishing%20Returns.pdf.

Bischoff, Paul. "The Rising Tide of Child Abuse Content on Social Media." Comparitech, January 25, 2023. https://www.comparitech.com/blog/vpn-privacy/child-abuse-online-statistics/.

Bleakley, Paul, Elena Martellozzo, Ruth Spence, and Jeffrey DeMarco. "Moderating Online Child Sexual Abuse Material (CSAM): Does Self-Regulation Work, or Is Greater State Regulation Needed?" *European Journal of Criminology* (2023): 14773708231181361.

Bodó, Loránd. "Decentralised Terrorism: The Next Big Step for the So-Called Islamic State (IS)?" *Voxpol*, December 12, 2018. https://www.voxpol.eu/decentralised-terrorism-the-next -big-step-for-the-so-called-islamic-state-is/.

Bradford, Anu. *The Brussels Effect: How the European Union Rules the World*. Oxford: Oxford University Press, 2020.

Braley, Alia, Gabriel S. Lenz, Dhaval Adjodah, Hossein Rahnama, and Alex Pentland. May 22, in Democratic Backsliding." *Nature Human Behaviour* (2023): 1–12.

Brooking, Emerson T. "Before the Taliban Took Afghanistan, It Took the Internet." Atlantic Council, New Atlanticist (blog), August 26, 2021. https://www.atlanticcouncil.org/blogs /new-atlanticist/before-the-taliban-took-afghanistan-it-took-the-internet/.

Buntain, Cody, Martin Innes, Tamar Mitts, and Jacob Shapiro. "Cross-Platform Reactions to the Post–January 6 Deplatforming." *Journal of Quantitative Description: Digital Media* 3 (2023).

Busch, Ella, and Jacob Ware. "The Weaponisation of Deepfakes: Digital Deception by the Far-Right." International Centre for Counter-Terrorism, December 2023. https://www.icct.nl /sites/default/files/2023-12/The%20Weaponisation%20of%20Deepfakes.pdf.

Byman, Daniel. *Spreading Hate: The Global Rise of White Supremacist Terrorism*. Oxford: Oxford University Press, 2022.

Carter, Joseph A., Shiraz Maher, and Peter R. Neumann. "#Greenbirds: Measuring Importance and Influence in Syrian Foreign Fighter Networks." International Centre for the Study of Radicalisation and Political Violence, April 22, 2014. https://icsr.info/2014/04/22/icsr -report-inspires-syrian-foreign-fighters/.

Center for Countering Digital Hate. "Deadly by Design: TikTok Pushes Harmful Content Promoting Eating Disorders and Self-Harm into Young Users' Feeds." Center for Countering Digital Hate, December 15, 2022. https://counterhate.com/research/deadly-by-design/.

———. "The Musk Bump: Quantifying the Rise in Hate Speech Under Elon Musk." Center for Countering Digital Hate, December 6, 2022. https://counterhate.com/blog/the-musk-bump-quantifying-the-rise-in-hate-speech-under-elon-musk/.

Chandrasekharan, Eshwar, Umashanthi Pavalanathan, Anirudh Srinivasan, Adam Glynn, Jacob Eisenstein, and Eric Gilbert. "You Can't Stay Here: The Efficacy of Reddit's 2015 Ban Examined through Hate Speech." *Proceedings of the ACM on Human-Computer Interaction* 1, no. CSCW (2017): 1–22.

Chauchard, Simon, and Kiran Garimella. "What Circulates on Partisan WhatsApp in India? Insights from an Unusual Dataset." *Journal of Quantitative Description: Digital Media* 2 (2022).

Chayes, Abram, Antonia Handler Chayes, and Ronald B. Mitchell. "Managing Compliance: A Comparative Perspective." In *Engaging Countries: Strengthening Compliance with International Environmental Accords*, edited by Edith Brown Weiss and Harold K. Jacobson (Cambridge, MA: MIT Press, 1998), 44–45.

Cinelli, Matteo, Walter Quattrociocchi, Alessandro Galeazzi, Carlo Michele Valensise, Emanuele Brugnoli, Ana Lucia Schmidt, Paola Zola, Fabiana Zollo, and Antonio Scala. "The COVID-19 Social Media Infodemic." *Scientific Reports* 10, no. 1 (2020): 1–10.

Citron, Danielle Keats. "Extremist Speech, Compelled Conformity, and Censorship Creep." *Notre Dame Law Review* 93 (2017): 1035.

Clifford, Bennett. "Migration Moments: Extremist Adoption of Text-Based Instant Messaging Applications." Global Network on Extremism and Technology, November 9, 2020. https://gnet-research.org/2020/11/09/migration-moments-extremist-adoption-of-text-based-instant-messaging-applications/.

Clifford, Bennett, and Helen Christy Powell. "De-platforming and the Online Extremist's Dilemma." *Lawfare*, June 6, 2019. https://www.lawfaremedia.org/article/de-platforming-and-online-extremists-dilemma

Commission nationale consultative des droits de l'homme (CNCDH). "Avis relatif à la proposition de loi visant à lutter contre la haine sur internet." CNCDH, July 9, 2019. https://perma.cc/HR2L-GH9Q.

Cornes, Richard, and Todd Sandler. *The Theory of Externalities, Public Goods, and Club Goods.* Cambridge: Cambridge University Press, 1996.

Davenport, Christian. "Repression and Mobilization: Insights from Political Science and Sociology." In *Repression and Mobilization*, edited by Christian Davenport, Hank Johnston, and Carol Mueller, vii–xli. Minneapolis: University of Minnesota Press, 2005.

Diamond, Larry. "Liberation Technology." In Diamond, *In Search of Democracy*, 132–46. New York: Routledge, 2015.

Díaz, Ángel, and Laura Hecht-Felella. "Double Standards in Social Media Content Moderation." New York University, Brennan Center for Justice, August 4, 2021. https://www.brennancenter.org/sites/default/files/2021-08/Double_Standards_Content_Moderation.pdf

Douek, Evelyn. "Content Moderation as Systems Thinking." *Harvard Law Review* 136 (2022): 526.

Douek, Evelyn. "The Rise of Content Cartels." Columbia University, Knight First Amendment Institute, February 11, 2020. https://knightcolumbia.org/content/the-rise-of-content-cartels.

Downs, George W., David M. Rocke, and Peter N. Barsoom. "Is the Good News about Compliance Good News about Cooperation?" *International Organization* 50, no. 3 (1996): 379–406.

Dragu, Tiberiu, and Yonatan Lupu. "Digital Authoritarianism and the Future of Human Rights." *International Organization* 75, no. 4 (2021): 991–1017.

Drouhot, Lucas G., Karen Schönwälder, Sören Petermann, and Steve Vertovec. "Who Supports Refugees? Diversity Assent and Pro-Refugee Engagement in Germany." *Comparative Migration Studies* 11, no. 1 (2023): 4.

Dubé, Ève, Jeremy K. Ward, Pierre Verger, and Noni E. MacDonald. "Vaccine Hesitancy, Acceptance, and Anti-Vaccination: Trends and Future Prospects for Public Health." *Annual Review of Public Health* 42, no. 1 (2021): 175–91.

Earl, Jennifer, Thomas V. Maher, and Jennifer Pan. "The Digital Repression of Social Movements, Protest, and Activism: A Synthetic Review." *Science Advances* 8, no. 10 (2022): eabl8198.

Echikson, William, and Olivia Knodt. "Germany's NetzDG: A Key Test for Combatting Online Hate." CEPS Policy Insight, Centre for European Policy Studies, November 2018. http://wp.ceps.eu/wp-content/uploads/2018/11/RR%20No2018-09_Germany's%20NetzDG.pdf.

Ekman, Mattias. "Anti-Refugee Mobilization in Social Media: The Case of Soldiers of Odin." *Social Media + Society* 4, no. 1 (2018): 2056305118764431.

Epicenter Works. "First Analysis of the Austrian Anti-Hate Speech Law (NetDG/KoPlG)." EDRi, September 10, 2020. https://edri.org/our-work/first-analysis-of-the-austrian-anti-hate-speech-law-netdg-koplg/.

Esberg, Jane. "Censorship as Reward: Evidence from Pop Culture Censorship in Chile." *American Political Science Review* 114, no. 3 (2020): 821–36.

European Commission. "European Commission and IT Companies Announce Code of Conduct on Illegal Online Hate Speech" (press release). European Commission, May 31, 2016. https://ec.europa.eu/commission/presscorner/detail/en/IP_16_1937.

———. "Proposal for a Regulation of the European Parliament and of the Council on a Single Market for Digital Services (Digital Services Act) and Amending Directive 2000/31/EC." European Commission, December 15, 2020. https://eur-lex.europa.eu/legal-content/en/TXT/?uri=COM%3A2020%3A825%3AFIN.

———. "Digital Services Act: EU's Landmark Rules for Online Platforms Enter into Force." European Commission, November 16, 2022. https://ec.europa.eu/commission/presscorner/detail/%20en/ip_22_6906.

———. "Digital Services Act: Commission Welcomes Political Agreement on Rules Ensuring a Safe and Accountable Online Environment" (press release). European Commission, April 23, 2022. https://ec.europa.eu/commission/presscorner/detail/en/IP_22_2545.

———. "Digital Services Act: Commission Designates First Set of Very Large Online Platforms and Search Engines" (press release). European Commission, April 25, 2023. https://ec.europa.eu/commission/presscorner/detail/en/IP_23_2413.

———. "Shaping Europe's Digital Future: The Digital Services Act Package." European Commission, updated February 16, 2024. https://digital-strategy.ec.europa.eu/en/policies/digital-services-act-package.

———. "Questions and Answers: Digital Services Act." European Commission, February 23, 2024. https://ec.europa.eu/commission/presscorner/detail/en/QANDA_20_2348.

Fishman, Brian. "Dual-Use Regulation: Managing Hate and Terrorism Online before and after Section 230 Reform." Brookings, March 14, 2023. https://www.brookings.edu/articles/dual -use-regulation-managing-hate-and-terrorism-online-before-and-after-section-230 -reform.

Franks, Mary Anne. "Beyond the Public Square: Imagining Digital Democracy." *Yale Law Journal* 131 (2021): 427.

Friendly, Fred W. *The Good Guys, the Bad Guys, and the First Amendment: Free Speech vs. Fairness in Broadcasting.* New York: Random House, 2013.

Garimella, Kiran, and Dean Eckles. "Images and Misinformation in Political Groups: Evidence from WhatsApp in India." *Harvard Kennedy School Misinformation Review* 1, no. 5 (July 7, 2020). https://doi.org/10.37016/mr-2020-030.

Ghannam, Jeffrey. "Social Media in the Arab World: Leading Up to the Uprisings of 2011." Report for the Center for International Media Assistance, February 3, 2011, https://ciaotest.cc .columbia.edu/wps/ned/0021255/f_0021255_17663.pdf.

Gillespie, Tarleton. *Custodians of the Internet.* New Haven, CT: Yale University Press, 2018.

Gohdes, Anita R. "Pulling the Plug: Network Disruptions and Violence in Civil Conflict." *Journal of Peace Research* 52, no. 3 (2015): 352–67.

———. "Repression Technology: Internet Accessibility and State Violence." *American Journal of Political Science* 64, no. 3 (2020): 488–503.

———. *Repression in the Digital Age: Surveillance, Censorship, and the Dynamics of State Violence.* Oxford: Oxford University Press, 2023.

Goldstein, Joshua. "The Role of Digital Networked Technologies in the Ukrainian Orange Revolution." Berkman Center Research Publication 2007-14 (2007).

Gorwa, Robert. *The Politics of Platform Regulation.* Oxford: Oxford University Press, 2024.

Greenberg, Karen J. "Case by Case ISIS Prosecutions in the United States, March 1, 2014– June 30, 2016." Center on National Security at Fordham Law, 2016. https://www.jstor.org /stable/resrep14126.1.

Greer, Ryan. "Weighing the Value and Risks of Deplatforming." Global Network on Extremism and Technology, May 11, 2020. https://gnet-research.org/2020/05/11/weighing-the-value -and-risks-of-deplatforming/.

Grinberg, Nir, Kenneth Joseph, Lisa Friedland, Briony Swire-Thompson, and David Lazer. "Fake News on Twitter during the 2016 US Presidential Election." *Science* 363, no. 6425 (2019): 374–78.

Gunitsky, Seva. "Corrupting the Cyber-Commons: Social Media as a Tool of Autocratic Stability." *Perspectives on Politics* 13, no. 1 (2015): 42–54.

Gurr, Ted Robert. *Why Men Rebel.* New York: Routledge, 2015.

Hadgu, Asmelash Teka, and Jayanth Kumar Reddy Gundam. "User Identity Linking across Social Networks by Jointly Modeling Heterogeneous Data with Deep Learning." *Proceedings of the 30th ACM Conference on Hypertext and Social Media* (2019): 293–94.

Heldt, Amélie Pia. "Reading between the Lines and the Numbers: An Analysis of the First NetzDG Reports." *Internet Policy Review* 8, no. 2 (2019).

Hobbs, William R., and Margaret E. Roberts. "How Sudden Censorship Can Increase Access to Information." *American Political Science Review* 112, no. 3 (2018): 621–36.

Holt, Jared. "After the Insurrection: How Domestic Extremists Adapted and Evolved after the January 6 US Capitol Attack." Atlantic Council Digital Forensic Research Lab, January 2022. https://www.atlanticcouncil.org/wp-content/uploads/2022/01/After-the-Insurrection.pdf.

Holt, Jared, and Max Rizzuto. "QAnon's Hallmark Catchphrases Evaporating from the Mainstream Internet." Atlantic Council Digital Forensic Research Lab, May 26, 2021. https://medium.com/dfrlab/qanons-hallmark-catchphrases-evaporating-from-the-mainstream-internet-ce90b6dc2c55.

Howard, Philip N., Sheetal D. Agarwal, and Muzammil M. Hussain. "The Dictators' Digital Dilemma: When Do States Disconnect Their Digital Networks?" Brookings, October 2011. https://www.brookings.edu/wp-content/uploads/2016/06/10_dictators_digital_network.pdf.

Huey, Laura, Rachel Inch, and Hillary Peladeau. "@ Me if You Need Shoutout": Exploring Women's Roles in Islamic State Twitter Networks." *Studies in Conflict and Terrorism* 42, no. 5 (2019): 445–63.

Human Rights Watch. "Germany: Flawed Social Media Law." February 14, 2018. https://www.hrw.org/news/2018/02/14/germany-flawed-social-media-law.

———. "Russia: Growing Internet Isolation, Control, Censorship." June 18, 2020. https://www.hrw.org/news/2020/06/18/russia-growing-internet-isolation-control-censorship.

Husovec, Martin. "The DSA's Scope Briefly Explained." July 4, 2023. http://dx.doi.org/10.2139/ssrn.4365029.

Hutchinson, Jade, Amarnath Amarasingam, Ryan Scrivens, and Brian Ballsun-Stanton. "Mobilizing Extremism Online: Comparing Australian and Canadian Right-Wing Extremist Groups on Facebook." *Behavioral Sciences of Terrorism and Political Aggression* 15, no. 2 (2023): 215–45.

International Centre for Missing and Exploited Children. "Child Sexual Abuse Material: Model Legislation and Global Review," 10th ed., 2023. https://cdn.icmec.org/wp-content/uploads/2023/10/CSAM-Model-Legislation_10th-Ed-Oct-2023.pdf.

International Crisis Group. "Taliban Propaganda: Winning the War of Words?" July 24, 2008. https://www.justice.gov/sites/default/files/eoir/legacy/2014/09/29/icg_07242008.pdf.

Jackson, Sam, Brandon Gorman, and Mayuko Nakatsuka. "QAnon on Twitter: An Overview." George Washington University, Institute for Data, Democracy & Politics, March 5, 2021. https://iddp.gwu.edu/sites/g/files/zaxdzs3576/f/downloads/QAnon%20on%20Twitter%3B%20Jackson.pdf.

Jhaver, Shagun, Christian Boylston, Diyi Yang, and Amy Bruckman. "Evaluating the Effectiveness of Deplatforming as a Moderation Strategy on Twitter." *Proceedings of the ACM on Human-Computer Interaction* 5, no. CSCW2 (2021): 1–30.

Johnson, Thomas, Matthew DuPee, and Wali Shaaker. "The Taliban's Use of the Internet, Social Media Video, Radio Stations, and Graffiti." In Johnson, DuPee, and Shaaker, *Taliban Narratives: The Use and Power of Stories in the Afghanistan Conflict.* Oxford: Oxford University Press, 2018.

Jiménez-Durán, Rafael. "The Economics of Content Moderation: Theory and Experimental Evidence from Hate Speech on Twitter." George J. Stigler Center for the Study of the Economy & the State Working Paper 324 (2023).

Kaid, Lynda Lee, and Christina Holtz-Bacha, eds. *Encyclopedia of Political Communication*. Thousand Oaks, CA: SAGE publications, 2007.

Kann, Alyssa. "As the Taliban Offensive Gained Momentum, So Did Its Twitter Propaganda Campaign." Atlantic Council Digital Forensic Research Lab, August 19, 2021. https://medium.com/dfrlab/as-the-taliban-offensive-gained-momentum-so-did-its-twitter-propaganda-campaign-75021ba3082.

Keating, Joshua. "The Taliban's YouTube Channel." *Foreign Policy*, October 13, 2009. https://foreignpolicy.com/2009/10/13/the-talibans-youtube-channel/.

Keller, Daphne. "Lawful but Awful? Control over Legal Speech by Platforms, Governments, and Internet Users." *University of Chicago Law Review Online*, June 28, 2022. https://lawreviewblog.uchicago.edu/2022/06/28/keller-control-over-speech/.

King, Gary, Jennifer Pan, and Margaret E. Roberts. "How Censorship in China Allows Government Criticism but Silences Collective Expression." *American Political Science Review* 107, no. 2 (2013): 326–43.

Klonick, Kate. "The Facebook Oversight Board: Creating an Independent Institution to Adjudicate Online Free Expression." *Yale Law Journal* 129 (2019): 2418.

———. "The New Governors: The People, Rules, and Processes Governing Online Speech." *Harvard Law Review* 131 (2017): 1598.

Kosseff, Jeff. *The Twenty-Six Words That Created the Internet*. Ithaca, NY: Cornell University Press, 2019.

Kriner, Matthew, and Jon Lewis. "The Oath Keepers and Their Role in the January 6 Insurrection." *CTC Sentinel* 14, no. 10 (2021): 1–18.

Lake, David A. "Rational Extremism: Understanding Terrorism in the Twenty-First Century." *Dialogue IO* 1, no. 1 (2002): 15–28.

Lauer, David. "Facebook's Ethical Failures Are Not Accidental; They Are Part of the Business Model." *AI and Ethics* 1, no. 4 (2021): 395–403.

Lichbach, Mark Irving. "Deterrence or Escalation? The Puzzle of Aggregate Studies of Repression and Dissent." *Journal of Conflict Resolution* 31, no. 2 (1987): 266–97.

Lu, Yingdan, Jack Schaefer, Kunwoo Park, Jungseock Joo, and Jennifer Pan. "How Information Flows from the World to China." *International Journal of Press/Politics* (2022): 19401612221117470.

Lutscher, Philipp M., Nils B. Weidmann, Margaret E. Roberts, Mattijs Jonker, Alistair King, and Alberto Dainotti. "At Home and Abroad: The Use of Denial-of-Service Attacks during Elections in Nondemocratic Regimes." *Journal of Conflict Resolution* 64, nos. 2/3 (2020): 373–401.

Lyons-Padilla, Sarah, Michele J. Gelfand, Hedieh Mirahmadi, Mehreen Farooq, and Marieke Van Egmond. "Belonging Nowhere: Marginalization and Radicalization Risk among Muslim Immigrants." *Behavioral Science and Policy* 1, no. 2 (2015): 1–12.

Macklin, Graham. "The Christchurch Attacks: Livestream Terror in the Viral Video Age." *CTC Sentinel* 12, no. 6 (2019): 18–29.

Mathew, Binny, Anurag Illendula, Punyajoy Saha, Soumya Sarkar, Pawan Goyal, and Animesh Mukherjee. "Hate Begets Hate: A Temporal Study of Hate Speech." *Proceedings of the ACM on Human-Computer Interaction* 4, no. CSCW2 (2020): 1–24.

McDonald, Brody. "Extremists Are Seeping Back into the Mainstream: Algorithmic Detection and Evasion Tactics on Social Media Platforms." Global Network on Extremism and

Technology, October 31, 2022. https://gnet-research.org/2022/10/31/extremists-are-seeping-back-into-the-mainstream-algorithmic-detection-and-evasion-tactics-on-social-media-platforms.

Miles Joyce, Renanah, and V. Page Fortna. "Extremism and Terrorism: Rebel Goals and Tactics in Civil Wars." *Perspectives on Politics*, forthcoming.

Miller-Idriss, Cynthia. *Hate in the Homeland: The New Global Far Right*. Princeton, NJ: Princeton University Press, 2020.

Mitts, Tamar. "From Isolation to Radicalization: Anti-Muslim Hostility and Support for ISIS in the West." *American Political Science Review* 113, no. 1 (2019): 173–94.

———. "Countering Violent Extremism and Radical Rhetoric." *International Organization* 76, no. 1 (2022): 251–72.

Mitts, Tamar, Gregoire Phillips, and Barbara F. Walter. "Studying the Impact of ISIS Propaganda Campaigns." *Journal of Politics* 84, no. 2 (2022): 1220–25.

Mitts, Tamar, and Kylan Rutherford. "The PIC Framework: Understanding the New Information Environment." Working paper. Columbia University, n.d.

Mohammad, Saif, and Peter Turney. "Emotions Evoked by Common Words and Phrases: Using Mechanical Turk to Create an Emotion Lexicon." *Proceedings of the NAACL HLT 2010 Workshop on Computational Approaches to Analysis and Generation of Emotion in Text* (2010): 26–34.

Moore, Will H. "Repression and Dissent: Substitution, Context, and Timing." *American Journal of Political Science* 42, no. 3 (1998): 851–73.

Müller, Karsten, and Carlo Schwarz. "Fanning the Flames of Hate: Social Media and Hate Crime." *Journal of the European Economic Association* 19, no. 4 (2021): 2131–67.

Nasser-Eddine, Minerva, Bridget Garnham, Katerina Agostino, and Gilbert Caluya. "Countering Violent Extremism (CVE) Literature Review." Defense Technical Information Center, March 1, 2011. https://apps.dtic.mil/sti/citations/ADA543686.

Nielsen, Richard A. *Deadly Clerics: Blocked Ambition and the Paths to Jihad*. Cambridge: Cambridge University Press, 2017.

Negreiro, Mar. "Curbing the Surge in Online Child Abuse: The Dual Role of Digital Technology in Fighting and Facilitating Its Proliferation." European Parliamentary Research Service, November 2020. https://www.europarl.europa.eu/RegData/etudes/BRIE/2020/659360/EPRS_BRI(2020)659360_EN.pdf.

Nouri, Lella, Nuria Lorenzo-Dus, and Amy-Louise Watkin. "Following the Whack-a-Mole: Britain First's Visual Strategy from Facebook to Gab." Global Network on Extremism and Technology, January 7, 2020. https://gnet-research.org/2020/01/07/following-the-whack-a-mole-britain-firsts-visual-strategy-from-facebook-to-gab/.

Pan, Jennifer. "How Market Dynamics of Domestic and Foreign Social Media Firms Shape Strategies of Internet Censorship." *Problems of Post-Communism* 64, nos. 3/4 (2017): 167–88.

Pan, Jennifer, and Alexandra A. Siegel. "How Saudi Crackdowns Fail to Silence Online Dissent." *American Political Science Review* 114, no. 1 (2020): 109–25.

Persily, Nathaniel, and Joshua A. Tucker. *Social Media and Democracy: The State of the Field, Prospects for Reform*. Cambridge: Cambridge University Press, 2020.

Ponce de León, Esteban, and Daniel Suárez Pérez. "Multi-Platform Troll Farm Linked to Nicaraguan Government." Atlantic Council Digital Forensic Research Lab, November 5, 2021.

https://medium.com/dfrlab/multi-platform-troll-farm-linked-to-nicaraguan-government-be79121d55b4.

Prucha, Nico. "IS and the Jihadist Information Highway—Projecting Influence and Religious Identity via Telegram," *Perspectives on Terrorism* 10, no. 6 (2016): 48–58.

Roberts, Margaret E. *Censored: Distraction and Diversion inside China's Great Firewall.* Princeton, NJ: Princeton University Press, 2018.

———. "Resilience to Online Censorship." *Annual Review of Political Science* 23 (2020): 401–19.

Roberts, Margaret E., Brandon M. Stewart, Dustin Tingley, Christopher Lucas, Jetson Leder-Luis, Shana Kushner Gadarian, Bethany Albertson, and David G. Rand. "Structural Topic Models for Open-Ended Survey Responses." *American Journal of Political Science* 58, no. 4 (2014): 1064–82.

Roberts, Sarah T. "Content Moderation." In *Encyclopedia of Big Data*, edited by Laurie A. Schintler and Connie L. McNeely, 1–4. Cham: Springer, 2017.

Rodriguez, Pedro L., and Arthur Spirling. "Word Embeddings: What Works, What Doesn't, and How to Tell the Difference for Applied Research." *Journal of Politics* 84, no. 1 (2022): 101–15.

Roggio, Bill. "US Targets al Qaeda's al Furqan Media Wing in Iraq." *FDD's Long War Journal*, October 28, 2007. https://www.longwarjournal.org/archives/2007/10/us_targets_al_qaedas.php.

Rothschild, Mike. *The Storm Is upon Us: How QAnon Became a Movement, Cult, and Conspiracy Theory of Everything.* Brooklyn, NY: Melville House, 2021.

Severson, Daniel. "France's Extended State of Emergency: What New Powers Did the Government Get?" *Lawfare*, November 22, 2015. https://www.lawfareblog.com/frances-extended-state-emergency-what-new-powers-did-government-get.

Schulz, Jacob. "What's Going On with France's Online Hate Speech Law?" *Lawfare*, June 23, 2020. https://www.lawfareblog.com/whats-going-frances-online-hate-speech-law.

Shahbaz, Adrian. "The Rise of Digital Authoritarianism." Freedom House, 2018. https://freedomhouse.org/report/freedom-net/2018/rise-digital-authoritarianism.

Shapiro, Jacob N. *The Terrorist's Dilemma.* Princeton, NJ: Princeton University Press, 2013.

Shu, Kai, Suhang Wang, Jiliang Tang, Reza Zafarani, and Huan Liu. "User Identity Linkage across Online Social Networks: A Review." *ACM SIGKDD Explorations Newsletter* 18, no. 2 (2017): 5–17.

Sipka, Andrea, Aniko Hannak, and Aleksandra Urman. "Comparing the Language of QAnon-Related Content on Parler, Gab, and Twitter." *Proceedings of the 14th ACM Web Science Conference 2022* (2022): 411–21.

Siripurapu, Anshu. "Trump and Section 230: What to Know." Council on Foreign Relations, December 2, 2020. https://www.cfr.org/in-brief/trump-and-section-230-what-know.

SITE Intelligence Group. "A SITE Study on the ICT Platforms Used to Spread ISIS and AQ Media." *Technology and Terrorism*, October 1, 2018. https://ent.siteintelgroup.com/inSITE-Report-on-Technology-and-Terrorism/insite-report-on-technology-and-terrorism-october-2018.html.

Smith, Aaron. "Public Attitudes toward Technology Companies." Pew Research Center, June 28, 2018. https://www.pewresearch.org/internet/2018/06/28/public-attitudes-toward-technology-companies/.

Smith, Melanie. "Interpreting Social Qs: Implications of the Evolution of QAnon." *Graphika*, August 2020. https://public-assets.graphika.com/reports/graphika_report_interpreting _social_qs.pdf.

Snyder, Jack. *Human Rights for Pragmatists: Social Power in Modern Times*. Princeton, NJ: Princeton University Press, 2022.

Southern Poverty Law Center (SPLC). "Proud Boys." https://www.splcenter.org/fighting-hate /extremist-files/group/proud-boys.

———. "Facebook's Fight Club: How the Proud Boys Use the Social Media Platform to Vet Their Fighters." SPLC, August 2, 2018. https://www.splcenter.org/hatewatch/2018/08/02 /facebooks-fight-club-how-proud-boys-use-social-media-platform-vet-their-fighters

St. Aubin, Christopher, and Jacob Liedke. "Most Americans Favor Restrictions on False Information, Violent Content Online." Pew Research Center, July 20, 2023. https://www .pewresearch.org/short-reads/2023/07/20/most-americans-favor-restrictions-on-false -information-violent-content-online/.

Stalinsky, Steven. *Germany-Based Encrypted Messaging App Telegram Emerges as Jihadis' Preferred Communications Platform*. Washington, DC: Middle East Media Research Institute Books, 2020.

Stanford Center for International Security and Cooperation. "About the Mapping Militants Project." https://cisac.fsi.stanford.edu/mappingmilitants/about.

Starbird, Kate, Renée DiResta, and Matt DeButts. "Influence and Improvisation: Participatory Disinformation during the 2020 US Election." *Social Media + Society* 9, no. 2 (2023): 20563051231177943.

Steinert-Threlkeld, Zachary C. "Spontaneous Collective Action: Peripheral Mobilization during the Arab Spring." *American Political Science Review* 111, no. 2 (2017): 379–403.

Stephens, William, Stijn Sieckelinck, and Hans Boutellier. "Preventing Violent Extremism: A Review of the Literature." *Studies in Conflict and Terrorism* 44, no. 4 (2021): 346–61.

Stern, Jessica, and J. M. Berger. *ISIS: The State of Terror*. New York: Ecco, 2015..

Tallberg, Jonas. "Paths to Compliance: Enforcement, Management, and the European Union." *International Organization* 56, no. 3 (2002): 609–43.

Tech Against Terrorism. "The Online Regulation Series: The Handbook." July 16, 2021. https:// www.techagainstterrorism.org/2021/07/16/the-online-regulation-series-the-handbook/.

———. "The Threat of Terrorist and Violent Extremist–Operated Websites." January 2022. https://www.techagainstterrorism.org/hubfs/The-Threat-of-Terrorist-and-Violent-Extremist -Operated-Websites-Jan-2022-1.pdf.

———. "Tracking Violent Far-Right Behavior Online," March 15, 2022. https://tech-against -terrorism-podcast.podcastpage.io/episode/tracking-violent-far-right-behaviour-online.

Thiel, David, Renée DiResta and Alex Stamos. "Cross-Platform Dynamics of Self-Generated CSAM." Stanford Internet Observatory, Cyber Policy Center, June 6, 2023. https://fsi .stanford.edu/publication/cross-platform-dynamics-self-generated-csam.

Thomas, Daniel Robert, and Laila A. Wahedi. "Disrupting Hate: The Effect of Deplatforming Hate Organizations on Their Online Audience." *Proceedings of the National Academy of Sciences* 120, no. 24 (2023): e2214080120.

Tian, Edward. "The QAnon Timeline: Four Years, 5,000 Drops, and Countless Failed Prophecies." Bellingcat, January 29, 2021. https://www.bellingcat.com/news/americas/2021/01 /29/the-qanon-timeline/.

Trujillo, Amaury, and Stefano Cresci. "Make Reddit Great Again: Assessing Community Effects of Moderation Interventions on r/the_donald," *Proceedings of the ACM on Human-Computer Interaction 6*, no. CSCW2 (2022): 1–28.

Tucker, Joshua A., Andrew Guess, Pablo Barberá, Cristian Vaccari, Alexandra Siegel, Sergey Sanovich, Denis Stukal, and Brendan Nyhan. "Social Media, Political Polarization, and Political Disinformation: A Review of the Scientific Literature." Prepared for the Hewlett Foundation, March 2018. https://hewlett.org/wp-content/uploads/2018/03/Social-Media -Political-Polarization-and-Political-Disinformation-Literature-Review.pdf.

Tucker, Joshua A., Yannis Theocharis, Margaret E. Roberts, and Pablo Barberá. "From Liberation to Turmoil: Social Media and Democracy." *Journal of Democracy 28*, no. 4 (2017): 46–59.

Tusa, Felix. "How Social Media Can Shape a Protest Movement: The Cases of Egypt in 2011 and Iran in 2009." *Arab Media and Society 17*, no. 2013 (2013): 1–14.

US Senate Committee on Interstate Commerce. "Study of Communications by an Interdepartmental Committee: Letter from the President of the United States to the Chairman of the Committee on Interstate Commerce." Washington: US Government Printing Office, 1934. https://docs.fcc.gov/public/attachments/DOC-328553A1.pdf.

Vidino, Lorenzo, and Seamus Hughes, "ISIS in America: From Retweets to Raqqa." George Washington University Program on Extremism, December 2015, https://extremism.gwu .edu/sites/g/files/zaxdzs5746/files/downloads/ISIS%20in%20America%20-%20Full%20 Report.pdf.

Walk, Erin, Kiran Garimella, Ahmet Akbiyik, and Fotini Christia. "Social Media Narratives on Conflict from Northern Syria." Working paper, Massachusetts Institute of Technology, 2022.

Walter, Barbara F. "The Extremist's Advantage in Civil Wars." *International Security 42*, no. 2 (2017): 7–39.

Whitten-Woodring, Jenifer, Mona S. Kleinberg, Ardeth Thawnghmung, and Myat The Thitsar. "Poison if You Don't Know How to Use It: Facebook, Democracy, and Human Rights in Myanmar." *International Journal of Press/Politics 25*, no. 3 (2020): 407–25.

Winter, Charlie, and Abdullah Alrhmoun. "Mapping the Extremist Narrative Landscape in Afghanistan." *Extrac*, November 2020. https://public-assets.extrac.io/reports/ExTrac _Afghanistan_1120.pdf.

Winter, Charlie, Abdul Sayed, and Abdullah Alrhmoun. "A 'New' Islamic Emirate? The Taliban's Outreach Strategy in the Aftermath of Kabul." Resolve Network, January 2022. https:// public-assets.extrac.io/reports/RESOLVE_ExTrac_New_Islamic_Emirate_January_2022 _0.pdf.

Xu, Xu. "To Repress or to Co-opt? Authoritarian Control in the Age of Digital Surveillance." *American Journal of Political Science 65*, no. 2 (2021): 309–25.

Zeitzoff, Thomas. "How Social Media Is Changing Conflict." *Journal of Conflict Resolution 61*, no. 9 (2017): 1970–91.

Zeng, Eric, Miranda Wei, Theo Gregersen, Tadayoshi Kohno, and Franziska Roesner. "Polls, Clickbait, and Commemorative $2 Bills: Problematic Political Advertising on News and Media Websites around the 2020 US Elections." *Proceedings of the 21st ACM Internet Measurement Conference* (2021): 507–25.

Zhang, Bolin and Joan Barata. "Provisions on the Governance of the Online Information Content Ecosystem: Order of the Cyberspace Administration of China." March 1, 2020.

https://wilmap.stanford.edu/entries/provisions-governance-online-information-content
-ecosystem.

Zhang, Han, and Jennifer Pan. "CASM: A Deep-Learning Approach for Identifying Collective
Action Events with Text and Image Data from Social Media." *Sociological Methodology* 49,
no. 1 (2019): 1–57.

Zurth, Patrick. "The German NetzDG as Role Model or Cautionary Tale? Implications for the
Debate on Social Media Liability." *Fordham Intellectual Property, Media, and Entertainment
Law Journal* 31, no. 4 (2021): 1101. https://ir.lawnet.fordham.edu/cgi/viewcontent.cgi?article
=1782&context=iplj.

INDEX

Italic pages refer to figures and tables

A NOTE ON THE TYPE

This book has been composed in Arno, an Old-style serif typeface in the
classic Venetian tradition, designed by Robert Slimbach at Adobe.